We Are Poor but So Many

South Asia Series
Edited by Balmiki Prasad Singh

We Are Poor but So Many: The Story of Self-Employed Women in India
Ela R. Bhatt

We Are Poor but So Many

The Story of Self-Employed

Women in India

Ela R. Bhatt

OXFORD
UNIVERSITY PRESS
2006

OXFORD
UNIVERSITY PRESS

Oxford University Press, Inc., publishes works that further
Oxford University's objective of excellence
in research, scholarship, and education.

Oxford   New York
Auckland   Cape Town   Dar es Salaam   Hong Kong   Karachi
Kuala Lumpur   Madrid   Melbourne   Mexico City   Nairobi
New Delhi   Shanghai   Taipei   Toronto

With offices in
Argentina   Austria   Brazil   Chile   Czech Republic   France   Greece
Guatemala   Hungary   Italy   Japan   Poland   Portugal   Singapore
South Korea   Switzerland   Thailand   Turkey   Ukraine   Vietnam

Published by Oxford University Press, Inc.
198 Madison Avenue, New York, New York 10016

www.oup.com

Oxford is a registered trademark of Oxford University Press

The depiction of a banyan tree shown on the title page of this book was created
by Mark W. Potter Jr.

Library of Congress Cataloging-in-Publication Data
Bhatt, Ela R.
We are poor but so many : the story of self-employed
women in India / Ela R. Bhatt.
p.   cm.
Includes bibliographical references and index.
ISBN-13 978-0-19-516984-3
ISBN 0-19-516984-0
1. Self-employed women—India.   2. Working poor—India.
3. Self-Employed Women's Association (Ahmedabad, India)   I. Title.
HD6072.6.I4B43 2005
338.7'2'0820954—dc22   2004025883

5700380S

1 3 5 7 9 8 6 4 2

Printed in the United States of America
on acid-free paper

For my husband, Ramesh Bhatt

Acknowledgments

Writing does not come easily to me; writing about SEWA is particularly difficult. How do I find words potent and pithy enough to describe our collective thoughts and actions that span more than thirty years? What do I say, and what do I leave out? I am never sure.

Howard Spodek, a historian of the city of Ahmedabad, had for many years encouraged me to reflect on my experiences among the self-employed and write about them. This book may not have been written without his initial encouragement.

I also thank my daughter, Ami, who encouraged me to write and re-write every chapter until the women and their work came alive. "Ma, you are writing a book, not a report," she kept reminding me. I could not have written this book without her by my side.

Renana Jhabvala read the entire draft carefully and showed me the gaps that needed to be filled. We have worked side by side through thick and thin.

My dear sisters and colleagues Namrata Bali, Mirai Chatterjee, Reema Nanavaty, Rahima Sheikh, Jyoti Macwan, Lalita Krishnaswamy, Jayashree Vyas, Manali Shah, and their large and powerful teams cannot be thanked enough for all their hard work, dedication, and love for the women of SEWA. I am grateful to them for sharing their experiences with me over the years. I have treasured their love and warmth. I shall always remain indebted to them.

Thank you, my son, Mihir, for reminding me there is a world beyond SEWA. You have helped me at many critical times.

Ravi and Mala Dayal, Tushar Bhatt, and Dr. Anandlaxmi read the manuscript at various stages and gave me many invaluable suggestions. I am grateful for their encouragement.

Most of this book was written at home in the company of two special women. Laxmi Iyer typed and retyped the manuscript for nearly two years, during which time she married and gave birth to a lovely son. We have been busy together. Jetunben Ahmedbhai cooked daily meals for me and insisted it was time to eat whenever she saw my energy fading. I am grateful for their loving kindness.

I can never thank my SEWA sisters enough. I owe them everything.

Contents

We Are Poor but So Many

Introduction

In writing about the lives and struggles of poor, self-employed women, I have been presumptuous. I have written about women who are unlikely to read what I have written about them. Moreover, my perception is unavoidably limited by the economic and social environment to which I belong. So in all honesty, I cannot claim to speak for the women I am writing about; I can only speak for myself.

And yet I have written this book because I have shared a good part of my life with these women. I have written about what I have seen and what I have learned about their struggles against poverty and prejudice. I want to talk about our interwoven lives, about how and why we join hands and what we have done, and still do, together—our hopes, actions, struggles, successes, and failures. The women have changed my life; they have inhabited it, enriched it, and shown me why life is worth living. In every possible sense, I am in their debt.

The Gujarati custom of addressing all women as *ben*, meaning sister, is, of course, not without consequences. It seems to instill a latent sense of sisterhood in relationships. SEWA, the Self-Employed Women's Association, owes much to this common sense of sisterhood in bringing together women of all castes, classes, trades, tribes, and faiths.

I begin this book with an account of myself and of the process by which I began to see the world of poor, working women. I have then attempted to take the reader into the world of these women, to provide an up-close look at their daily lives, the forces that overpower them, the conditions that perpetuate their poverty, the battles they fight, the attitudes they face, and the working and living conditions of both rural and urban working sisters. Although there are as many trades among the self-employed as there are opportunities, I have focused on only a few. I have tried to reveal the process that has led to the birth of a trade union of self-employed women, the basic philosophy of the organization, and the battles we face. I have also tried to highlight the role that trade cooperatives play in economic development and to show the impact of the larger economy on the lives of the women.

SEWA was born among the urban poor, so that is where I have begun; with the lowliest of workers—the rag pickers—and their attempts to change their working conditions. Following their account is the story of home-based workers—the women who stitch rags into quilts, or take piece-rate sewing jobs for small and large traders. The process is union building, but it is also a fight to forge an identity for self-employed women as workers.

Although this is a local account, their troubles are no different than those of home-based working women the world over. Equally universal are the problems of vendors and their constant fight to claim their space on the streets, in the markets, and on the planning blueprints of municipal authorities. I see vendors as small entrepreneurs who grow ever so organically; they are a true and direct expression of a lively economy. Their need for credit and other banking services leads us into SEWA's experiences making micro-loans to the urban poor and to examine the role of the SEWA Bank. The broader needs of the poor, especially in the area of health care, leads us into the issue of the living and working conditions of poor women and SEWA's efforts to provide them with access to medical services and life insurance.

As the numbers of the urban poor began to grow, SEWA extended its activities into rural areas from where the urban poor came. Today, rural members far outnumber their urban sisters. In the rural women, I have found the heart of India. The dry deserts of Gujarat are home to some of the most resilient women: the embroidery workers who labor in their homes, the agricultural workers—marginal farmers, gum pickers, and salt farmers to name but a few. SEWA has helped them to form producers' groups in order to build and own assets, enhanced their capacity to stand firm in the competitive market, and enabled them to gain access to health care, child care, shelter, insurance, and credit. The struggles of tribals displaced from their forestland and forced to come to terms with a new economy reveal how governments can also perpetuate poverty and vulnerability.

In the end, I hope my argument for placing women at the center of economic reform will be self-evident. There is ample proof to demonstrate that women can and do build strong, vital organizations around issues that are relevant to them, find viable solutions out of their own experiences, and in the process change our society and environment in a healthy, respectful, nonviolent, and sustainable way.

Ramesh opened my eyes to the world. It was 1949, and I was a shy and studious university student, who admired Ramesh from a distance. He was a fearless, handsome, student leader and an active member of the Youth Congress. He was collecting primary data on slum families for independent India's first census of 1951. When he invited me to accompany him on his rounds, I timidly agreed. I knew my parents would disapprove of their daughter "wandering in dirty neighborhoods with a young man whose family one knew nothing about."

My father was a successful lawyer with a thriving practice and a prominent position in society. My mother was more progressive; her father was a freedom fighter who had gone with Mahatma Gandhi on the Salt March. However, when it came to her daughters—my younger sister Rupa and me—my mother was protective and conservative.

The Maynafalia slum of Surat was not far from where I lived, but it could just as well have been worlds away. The air smelled of fish and fecal matter. The one-room houses common to the area had mud floors, no windows, and an appliqué of tin strips for roofs; flimsy jute sacks served as room partitions. Tiny backyards functioned as the common bathing, washing, and defecating grounds. The dirty water irrigated papaya trees and red canna lilies; both were sold in the market for income. Mosquitoes and flies settled on every object in sight.

The men and boys fished in the river; the women sold the fish. In the morning, they ate millet bread with chillies and garlic, and in the evening, they made a meal of boiled vegetables and any unsold fish. Their children, who cried a lot, were named after biblical movie characters—Delilah, Rebecca, Samson. The women invariably wore fresh flowers in their hair.

Ramesh was completely at ease in this environment, listening and laughing and teasing and gathering data from the slum dwellers like a nosy new neighbor. I, however, had never seen anything like this at such close quarters, and I was uncomfortable. I was paralyzed and passive, frustrated with my inability to step out of my shell. All the same, learning about "how the other half lives" was a liberating experience, and it made a deep impression on me.

India was a newly independent country at the time. Mahatma Gandhi's spirit encouraged the youth to live and work with the poor, to build "village republics" as basic units of a foundation on which Indian democracy could prosper. Politics was idealistic; it had the power to inspire and stimulate action. Ramesh gave me the writings of Gandhiji and J. C. Kumarappa on the economics of self-reliance and we read and discussed them avidly.

The son of an impoverished village Brahmin who had become an industrial mill worker, and of a young mother who died when he was only five, Ramesh experienced deep loss and deprivation early in life. His father put great emphasis on learning and educated him well. He studied economics and law, and soon began teaching economics at B.D. Arts College in Ahmedabad. The academic environment suited him well—he was a perpetual student and a compulsive teacher.

Ramesh was hardly ever on the scene with me later in my public life— he was a private man—but we were partners in life. He was my best friend. At SEWA, we were charting new territory all the time. His insight and analysis were critical in helping me come up with unconventional solutions to age-old problems. This is not to say that I always agreed with him. His approach was more defiant than mine. However, even in disagreement, Ramesh supported me every step of the way; that generosity of spirit allowed me to gain self-confidence and trust in my self.

In 1955, when I had completed my studies with a degree in law, I was offered a position as a junior lawyer in the legal department of the Textile Labour Association (TLA). Known as Majoor Mahajan in Ahmedabad, the trade union became my real alma mater. Founded in 1920 by Anasuyaben Sarabhai and Mahatma Gandhi, it was known for its unique approach in settling labor disputes. It put great emphasis on forging a partnership between labor and capital and solving disputes through mediation and negotiation. Strikes were considered less effective because their coerced solutions do not last. When I joined the TLA, it was one of the strongest

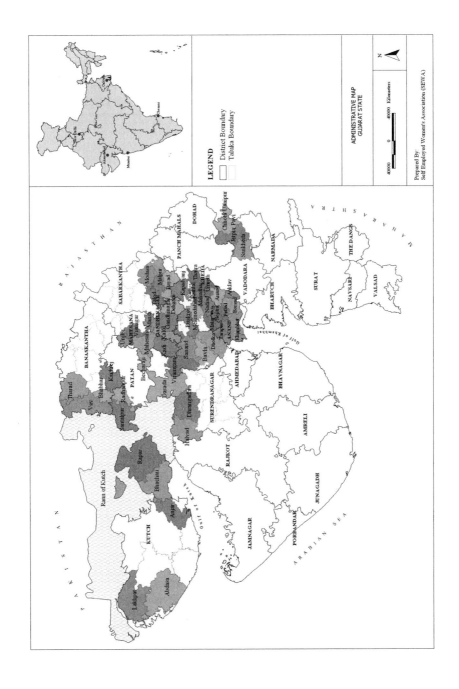

trade unions in India. It also had active political connections with the Congress Party and its government.

My early days in labor court were tense. The slightest comment about my clothes or my short height would upset me, and I would begin to stammer. There were hardly any women in court at the time, so I was self-conscious and alone. However, I was gaining some experience as a lawyer, arguing small cases on matters like inadequate leave compensation, lack of staff in the mill canteen, or denied requests for shift changes. At the union office, I helped in the preparation of the Gratuity Bill, which was soon to be presented in Parliament. On a personal front, my parents finally gave their consent for me to marry Ramesh. We were married in April 1956; I was twenty-three.

Gandhiji's ideas on work and economics made a deep impression on my young mind. I was drawn to his emphasis on simplicity—the idea that adding complexity is not progress; on nonviolence—that violence in any form cannot lead to lasting peace or reconstruction; on the dignity, or even the sanctity, of labor; on the importance of human values—that nothing that compromises a person's humanity is acceptable; that poverty is wrong because it is violent; it does not respect human labor, strips a person of his or her humanity, and takes away their freedom.

By the 1960s, the TLA had become a strong and large presence in the nation. TLA's philosophy of trusteeship, its methods of peaceful negotiations, and its large member base gave it enormous credibility. Members contested elections from labor constituencies for city municipal councils, state legislature, and the Parliament. But the textile industry in the country had begun showing symptoms of ill health late in the decade. A gradual decline in the textile industry of Ahmedabad had begun.

The event that brought me to this realization was the closure of two major textile mills in 1968 that rendered thousands of workers jobless. I was assigned to take a survey of the families affected by the closures. When I visited the homes of the laid-off workers, I saw that the burden of running the family had fallen to the women. While the men were busy agitating to reopen the mills, at the end of the day, it was the women who were earning money and feeding the family. They sold fruits and vegetables in the streets; stitched in their homes at piece-rate for middlemen; worked as laborers in wholesale commodity markets, loading and unloading merchandise; or collected recyclable refuse from city streets.

A great many children had stopped going to school so they could help their mothers make ends meet. These were informal, home-based jobs operated outside of any labor laws or regulations. They were jobs without definitions. I learned for the first time what it meant to be self-employed. None of the labor laws applied to them; my legal training was of no use in their case. Ironically, I first glimpsed the vastness of the informal sector while working for the formal sector. One was unprotected, the other protected—although both contributed to the national economy.

Looking at the women, invisible and isolated, working hard for earnings that barely supported their families, left me restless to do something. I began to think of what role the TLA could play in these women's lives. The union saw them as enterprising housewives stepping in to work at a time of crisis, but they did not really see them as workers. Other than provide more training on the use of sewing machines, the TLA felt it could do little for the women.

In 1968, the TLA hosted the Indian National Trade Union Congress (INTUC)—then the biggest central labor union in the country—in Ahmedabad. At the annual conference, I was appointed the first Convenor of INTUC's Women's Wing, a position that reflected a newly growing awareness of the issues of women workers. Soon after, I was sent to Israel to take a course in Labor and Cooperatives.

I arrived in Tel Aviv in 1969. Israel was immersed in integrating its people and building the nation's economy through labor unions and cooperatives. The country was putting great energy into developing the desert regions, and I had an opportunity to work in a desert kibbutz. I was excited by everything! But what interested me the most was the idea that unions and cooperatives could work so well together.

I returned to the TLA armed with a diploma and a head full of ideas. My heart was set on doing something for the women working in the homes who were once supported by the now unemployed mill workers. I wanted to organize the women workers in a union so that they could enjoy the same benefits that organized labor received. In the process, I came to a simple realization—a union is about coming together. Women did not need to come together *against anyone*, they just needed to come together *for themselves*. By forming a union—a bond—they affirmed their status as workers, and as a result of coming together, they had a voice. This time, I had the support of the TLA leaders, particularly A. N. Buch, who saw my efforts at unionizing self-employed women as something worth trying. I am not sure they—or, for that matter, I—realized the scope and significance of such a trade union, and a *women's* union in particular.

To lump such a vast workforce into categories viewed as "marginal," "informal," "unorganized," "peripheral," "atypical," or "the black economy" seemed absurd to me. Marginal and peripheral to what, I asked. The mainstream was shrinking and the margins were getting wider! In my eyes, they were simply "self-employed." The diverse occupations of the self-employed evolved out of traditional, inherited occupational skills adapted to the changing needs of the times. Such diversity and adaptability signified the strength of the women! What they needed was the support of society and their government. But all these realizations came later. When SEWA was established in April 1972, I had only a vague idea of these definitions.

Soopa Goba was my very first comrade-in-arms. Dark, voluptuous, and invariably dressed in a worn purple sari, Soopa was a migrant from Khandesh, a poor district in Maharashtra. She slept on the sidewalk by night and during the day carried bales of cloth on her head—transporting goods from wholesalers to retailers, from the railway yard to a warehouse, or from shop to shop in the Dhanlaxmi cloth market. She was paid two rupees per trip, and she made an average of twenty trips a day. I noticed that half of her income went directly from her employer to the contractor who had brought her from her village to work in the city. There were more than a hundred Soopas working in the cloth market, and their pay was appalling.

Soopa and the women headloaders taught me my first lessons in collective bargaining. I began to see the myriad forms of exploitation and how bravely the women faced and coped with all the humiliations and injustices done to them. I was surprised to see how willing they were to risk everything. They had so much to lose if we failed in our efforts for better wages, and yet it was *they* who showed faith and gave *me* the courage to fight on. It was my first real effort at organizing, and call it hard work or dumb luck, the women's piece rate went up by 30 percent. It was a good beginning.

There were other trades that made up a large portion of the informal job sector in Ahmedabad. Their existence was fundamental to the city's economy, and yet the city did not care about the rampant exploitation of these workers. In fact, there was no recognition of the existence of these poor citizens.

The telephone operator at the TLA office, Kacharabhai Jagaria, watched my efforts to organize the headloaders from the cloth market closely. Then, one day, he introduced me to his sister-in-law Chanda Papu, or Chandaben, a fair-faced woman who worked in Poori Bazar—the recycled clothes market. Chandaben would set out for the wealthier neighborhoods with a basket of brand new stainless steel utensils and fancy plastics on her head, where she would barter them for the hand-me-down clothes of the rich. She bought the steel pots on credit from a shopkeeper who was also her banker. She handed him her earnings, out of which he deducted whatever was owed to him and retained the rest for "safekeeping."

Chandaben's home was her workplace; it housed seven family members and two sewing machines; all nine bustling almost all hours of the day. She repaired the old, bartered clothes—in fact, the whole family patched, darned, cut, cleaned, ironed, and changed the face and the value of the clothing; even a worn towel was given a second life. Men too helped with the recycling work. The family hardly had time for housework; most of the time, they bought ready cooked food from the market and ate it at home.

The sellers in the market were all women; the men were mostly helpers. The women called themselves traders—they were good at determining value and better at negotiating the best price from customers. Sitting under makeshift awnings to shield themselves from the midday sun, the women drank innumerable cups of sweet, strong tea during the day and listened to popular film music on their loud transistor radios. Every Sunday, the Poori Bazar merged with the *gujari*—the flea market that has gathered on the riverbank for many centuries. It is a large recycled goods market where both the producers and the consumers are the laboring poor.

Week after week, Chandaben took me to the market on Sundays to meet other women who were producer-vendors like herself—carpenters, tinsmiths, quilt makers, idol makers, painters, cigarette rollers, incense-stick makers, and the like. Before Chandaben introduced me to a woman, she first primed me about her trade. I found that every woman I talked to was in debt—not for lack of enterprise or hard work, but because she did not have any working capital and because she did not own her tools of production. The interest the women paid on their borrowings were exorbitant! They ranged from 10 to 20 percent a day! No one could afford to pay such high interest and get out of poverty. The poor were on a treadmill, eternally struggling and never getting ahead. I began to explore ways in which SEWA could help the women get loans by mediating with local banks. In the end, this led us to establish our own cooperative bank.

Chandaben, Soopa, and Lakshmi Teta—a grand-looking vegetable vendor of Manekchowk market—became my closest allies, friends, and work sisters in shaping SEWA. We grew up together, learning, helping, guiding and caring about each other. Chandaben and Laxmiben were natural leaders—fearless, accessible, and good communicators. Chandaben and I were born on the same date so we felt a special kinship. She was my sounding board—immensely practical but never tied down by practicalities. A great orator, she had a large following among the vendors. Later on, she represented SEWA and the self-employed workers of India at several global conferences. She attended the United Nations Population Conference in Cairo as a SEWA delegate, as a panelist in the Micro Credit Summit in Washington, and as a keynote speaker at the inauguration of the Women's World Banking Global Conference in New Delhi. Everywhere she went, people were impressed by her quick mind, her articulateness, and her passion. When she died in 2003 of a heart attack, I lost my guide. Soopa died in the early days of SEWA from pulmonary tuberculosis. Lakshmi Teta suffers from severe asthma; her daughter-in-law has taken her place in the market, but no one can take her place in leadership.

In 1974, a bright, vivacious, Oxford-educated economist named Devaki Jain came to SEWA from Delhi. She visited the women's markets and homes and left excited—this was economics on a different scale. She invited me to Delhi to meet her family and some of her friends, who were government officials, journalists, and researchers. In Devaki and her husband, L. C. Jain, I found my first allies outside the TLA. I was excited to meet people who shared my interest in self-employed women and their work. I also met Dr. Kamla Chowdhry, a social scientist and an expert on the textile industry, who, in our very first meeting, impressed on me that if we could reach out to large numbers of poor women in India, SEWA could make a real difference. In Delhi, I also had the good fortune of meeting Dr. Vina Majumdar, from whom I learned my first lessons in Indian women's history.

In 1975, much to my surprise, I was invited to attend the International Women's Conference in Mexico City as part of India's nongovernmental delegation. In the heady atmosphere of the conference, my mind started opening up to women's issues that I had never known before—Bolivian mine workers resisting the violent techniques of its unions; Malaysian plantation workers insisting on housing; the practice of female circumcision in African countries. My eyes opened to the fact that white women in western countries could also be poor. Although I sympathized, it was years before I understood the significance of why black women lamented their missing voice in the recorded history of the United States. Women's demands for equal pay for equal work I could understand, but here were women from the United Kingdom demanding wages for housework. I found it unbelievable! In my country, housework was just another name for womanhood. It was all so new and so thought provoking. All these similarities, and yet so many differences among the women of the world. I was growing a new feminist consciousness.

I talked about our on-the-ground activities of unionizing and banking with poor women. On the last day of the conference, three of us, among others, spoke about women's need for access to credit. Esther Ocloo (a business woman from Ghana), Michaela Walsh (a Wall Street banker from New York), and I (founder and chair of SEWA Bank) conceived the idea of Women's World Banking—a network to provide credit access to women. Michaela turned that dream into reality. Today, Women's World Banking is a large and vital force in the arena of women's banking.

In SEWA, I now had a new colleague. Renana Jhabvala arrived from Delhi dressed in a clumsily tied *khadi* sari and equipped with recent degrees from both Harvard and Yale universities. She was a careful observer and a fast learner; within no time, she was an invaluable and integral part of SEWA. Renana also turned out to be a powerful organizer. She helped us think about issues more analytically—how to weigh risk and consequences and how to value experience. She came to conduct field research for one year; she never left.

I was young when I had my children. I had plenty of time to enjoy my daughter, Ami, and my son, Mihir, while they were growing up. By the time I became busy with SEWA, my children were ready to leave home—Ami was studying Chinese at the Jawaharlal Nehru University in Delhi, and Mihir was getting ready to follow her to Delhi at the School of Architecture and Planning.

In my enthusiasm to develop SEWA, I had failed to notice a growing crack in the foundation of SEWA's relationship with the TLA. SEWA's growing numbers and its uniqueness as an organization were drawing a lot of attention. The TLA considered SEWA its offspring, but found it difficult to control the pace and direction in which it was going. I did not realize that the TLA's attitude toward SEWA, too, was changing.

What I did notice was that the TLA had very little room for new ideas and a dwindling ability to face new challenges. It had become a top-down organization where the leaders had stopped listening to each other and, more important, to the members. Despite the looming changes in the textile industry, there was no real attempt to equip the workers to adapt to changing economic conditions. It was sad to watch the growing rift between the laid-off workers and the shrinking union. SEWA, however, was preoccupied with learning about the various ways in which families of the textile workers were coping and adapting and was trying its best to help them in their efforts.

Tensions came to a head in early 1981 during a period of bitter caste-class violence. The furor started when the Chief Minister of Gujarat proposed reserving two seats in the medical post-graduate course for scheduled caste and scheduled tribe students, commonly known as *dalit* (the oppressed) and *adivasi* (indigenous people), who have for generations formed the poorest of the poor. India's constitution provides for reserving a certain quota of seats in formal education institutions, government jobs, and elected bodies for them. The Gujarat government wanted to increase this quota at the state level.

Competition for medical school entry is fierce, and upper-caste students and their allies vehemently opposed the plan. The issue flared up and took on a broader political dimension. Incidents of violence broke out between the upper castes and the dalits. Most of the dalits, poor slum dwellers, became the victims of violence, losing both lives and property. The police clamped a curfew over the entire city.

SEWA could not remain silent while our dalit members were being attacked in their homes and on the streets. Because of the violence and the curfew, the daily wage earners and the self-employed in the city had no work, and therefore no income; consequently, they were starving. From SEWA's perspective, discrimination against dalits was rampant in all walks of life; those who had overcome so much adversity to become medical students certainly deserved support. Despite pressure from their dalit members in the mills, the TLA leaders thought it wise, for political reasons, to take no sides. Despite the curfew, all the mills in Ahmedabad continued to operate under government protection, while workers in the informal economy starved.

I called a meeting of the SEWA leaders. First, we prayed for peace, and then we passed a resolution to appeal to the citizens of Ahmedabad to restore peace. Communal harmony was a union issue and a feminist issue. It was fundamental to our existence.

Many upper-caste medical students felt that as a Brahmin, my sympathies should have been with them, not the dalits. They directed their anger toward me in the darkness of night. A band of young rioters gathered outside my home, pelting it with stones, breaking windows, and threatening to set it on fire. It was the most traumatic experience that Ramesh and I had ever faced; but there was more to follow.

On May 1, 1981, the TLA leadership asked me to leave and move SEWA's offices away from their headquarters. I had expected strained relations with the TLA leadership, but I never imagined for a second that they cared so little for SEWA and me. I felt hurt and betrayed. Never had I conceived of SEWA operating outside of the TLA, and I didn't think we could survive without their support. "Well, consider this a blessing," Ramesh said very quietly. He had long seen a break with the TLA as inevitable, but he had kept these thoughts to himself. I was not so sure.

After I had calmed down, a different picture began to emerge in my mind. I began to realize that women workers would always be of marginal importance to the TLA—their numbers in the textile mills had declined to 4 percent in fifty years.[1] In the process of modernizing the textile mills, union and industry had both agreed that women were dispensable; the mills found women to be "expensive," whereas the TLA's attitude was that it was better for women to be homemakers and for men to earn the higher wages. There was an unspoken boundary beyond which women were not allowed to step or speak.

Certainly, the TLA would never have allowed SEWA to move in the direction we have since taken. They would never have approved of us setting up large numbers of production cooperatives, or building women's networks that crossed geographical, political, and ideological boundaries. They would never have put modern technology in the hands of the women, nor would they have believed that poor women could manage an annual turnover of crores of rupees and enter the global market.

At the time of the break from the TLA, SEWA had 4,900 members, a small cooperative bank, an office building, a rural center, one vehicle, and

1. Renana Jhabvala. *Closing Doors*. Ahmedabad, India: Setu, 1985.

a few typewriters. But we also had a ten-year history of organizing. International unions promised us their support; national unions invited us to join them. But we wanted to stand on our own. We gathered all our strength and did not look back.

We began to recruit excellent new field organizers like Kamlaben, a second-generation *bidi* worker; Ramilaben, a contract factory worker; Rahimaben, a *chindi* stitcher; as well as many others who were young, strong, and determined to do something for their trade communities. We needed educated professionals who could speak on behalf of the women when they themselves could not, and in response we were joined by university graduates like Manali and Mina—both studied law and came from the middle class, but they managed to make workers' issues their own.

We have come a long way since. SEWA's membership climbed steadily from 6,000 in 1982 to 23,000 in 1984. Now, in 2004, we are the largest primary union in the country, with a membership of over 700,000. There are ten SEWAs spread over seven states in India, and together we form SEWA Bharat. Each SEWA is an independent and autonomous sister organization.

SEWA straddles the realms of both union and cooperatives. The union mobilizes and organizes the women to come together around their work issues. The women then form trade cooperatives in an effort to become owners of their labor. In villages, the producers groups, the savings groups, and their district associations and federations are, in broad terms, cooperative enterprises. Trade cooperatives give the women greater bargaining power; access to credit, training, and markets; and help to build assets. SEWA has nearly ninety different cooperatives—rural and urban—some built around products; others around services. There are vendors' cooperatives as well as midwives' cooperatives; rag pickers' cooperatives as well as weavers' cooperatives. There are as many trades as there are facets to a country's economy, and self-employed women can be found in every one of them.

The Registrar of Cooperatives would not initially register SEWA Bank because its members were illiterate women. Of course, these women could earn an income, run their own businesses, save, borrow, and repay, but they could not form their own banking cooperative because they could not sign their names. Literacy was more important to the registrar than the women's dynamic economic productivity. I've often felt that the real illiterates are on the other side of the table.

Similarly, we had trouble registering labor cooperatives. Our rag pickers' cooperative was suspect because they did not manufacture any products; the midwives' cooperative was asked why delivering babies should be considered an economic activity; the video producers' cooperative was denied registration because the directors, the producers, and the sound and camera technicians were illiterate—the officials had no concept of how much more powerful a visual medium is in the hands of those not enslaved by the written word. When vegetable vendors and producers wanted to form a joint cooperative, they were told that despite the fact that both belong to one common industry, they fell under separate category lists and therefore could not formally collaborate.

Other problems result from such classification and categorizing. Since the income of poor women from any one type of work is usually not enough to make ends meet, they must have several income-earning occupations. In fact, 80 percent of SEWA members are engaged in multiple types of work. Vegetable sellers also make kites at home. Should they qualify as home-based workers or are they street vendors? The following example is a common one.

A small farmer works on her own farm. In tough times, she also works on other farms as a laborer. When the agriculture season is over, she goes to the forest to collect gum and other forest produce. Year round, she produces embroidered items either at a piece rate for a contractor or for sale to a trader who comes to her village to buy goods. Now, how should her trade be categorized? Does she belong to the agricultural sector, the factory sector, or the home-based work sector? Should she be categorized as a farmer or a farm worker? Is she self-employed or is she a piece-rate worker? Because her situation cannot be defined and contained neatly in a box, she has no work status and her right to representation in a union is unrealized. She is denied access to financial services or training to upgrade her skills. The tyranny of having to belong to a well-defined "category" has condemned her to having no "identity."

When someone asks me what the most difficult part of SEWA's journey has been, I can answer without hesitation: removing conceptual blocks. Some of our biggest battles have been over contesting preset ideas and attitudes of officials, bureaucrats, experts, and academics. Definitions are part of that battle. The Registrar of Trade Unions would not consider us "workers"; hence, we could not register as a "trade union." The hardworking chindi workers, embroiderers, cart pullers, rag pickers, midwives, and forest-produce gatherers can contribute to the nation's gross domestic product, but heaven forbid that they be acknowledged as workers! Without an employer, you cannot be classified as a worker, and since you are not a worker, you cannot form a trade union. Our struggle to be recognized as a national trade union continues.

Because they fall through this web of terminology, the livelihoods of millions of people are not perceived as work and therefore remain uncounted, unrecorded, unprotected, and unaddressed by the nation. They remain conveniently "invisible" to policy makers, statisticians, and theoreticians. Dividing the economy into formal and informal sectors is artificial—it may make analysis easier, or facilitate administration, but it ultimately perpetuates poverty. Until the International Labor Organisation (ILO) was forced to acknowledge the growing numbers of home-based workers, even international trade unions did not wish to recognize them as workers; instead, they considered them a threat to the organized labor movement.

Today, SEWA is a family of organizations, similar in structure to a banyan tree that spreads its branches. Over time, the branches grow vines that reach for the ground and take root, becoming trunks themselves; in this way, they become a sprawling forest within the same, ever-expanding tree. Each one is independent and autonomous, both financially and in the decision-making process. At the same time, new growth draws strength from the old.

SEWA's organizational structure is fairly simple. The general body membership is made up of many trades like vendors, bidi makers, or gum collectors; they are from both rural and urban areas. Each trade elects their trade representative. The number of representatives depends on how large their membership is. The trade representatives form the Representative Council, whose job it is to represent different trade issues. The council elects the Executive Committee, which is made up of twenty-five members. They are the ultimate decision-making body. The Executive Committee elects the office bearers who must answer to them. Elections are held every three years; the Representative Council meets every three months and the Executive Committee meets monthly.

The elected representatives are quite powerful in their community and are in daily contact with the members. Union organizers, who are also from the same community, are young women with some education; their power comes in the form of access to information. Sometimes tensions arise between the two kinds of leaders. While the elected leaders have the decision-making power and are in constant contact with the Executive Committee, union organizers have wider contacts across the organization and sometimes possess a better perspective on issues that span different trades. The members humorously refer to this power play as "mother-in-law/daughter-in-law problems."

Periodically, SEWA has come under pressure from men who want to join the organization, since in many cases they work alongside the women in the same occupations and face similar problems. Initially, I was open to the idea of men joining our union struggles, because I felt that they would lend more strength to SEWA; however, the women emphatically refused. They said they would feel inhibited with men around, and they believed men would dominate and create tensions. In addition, they felt that the issues that were important to women were different from those important to men. Another major but unspoken reason was that the women wanted to keep their earnings and savings private—if not secret—from the men. The decision not to accept men in SEWA has been a good one; it has allowed us as women to explore unfamiliar territories, take on new roles, and expand our horizons with growing self-confidence.

SEWA is constantly changing. It has deep roots in some areas, while in others we are spread thin. The issues we face vary with our changing membership; each new member brings with her a new set of problems, a new set of solutions, and a full set of expectations. We are better equipped to face some challenges while we struggle with others. The process itself is our teacher. Most of the time we are venturing into uncharted territory—whether it is life insurance for the poor or setting up international marketing networks for marginal farmers. We do not always win; in fact, we fail in our efforts quite frequently. But maybe because we are all women who are not always rewarded for our efforts, we have learned to persevere. Our strength is in our ability to find solutions by staying flexible. Unfortunately our perseverance has been tested, time and again.

Calamities like floods, communal riots, consecutive droughts, and a major earthquake have affected our members on a large scale, year after year. Just when a woman has just paid off a long-term loan for her new house, an earthquake razes it to the ground; or a mad crowd of religious zealots burns to cinders the brand new sewing machine that a woman bought with her hard-earned savings. Time and again we are caught unawares, and the development work turns into relief and rehabilitation work. By keeping work and income generation in constant focus, SEWA has taken on the challenge of turning calamities into opportunities. By helping ourselves, we choose the kind of help we need and in what form. To rebuild a life after a disaster, people need work, not charity.

In 1969, during my TLA days, I witnessed my first Hindu-Muslim riot among the textile workers. I was assigned to a team bringing the injured from the streets and homes to the Civil Hospital. Many of the victims were dead when we arrived, so we loaded the bodies onto trucks and took them to the hospital where relatives claimed them. The riots were violent but mercifully short-lived. With its political weight and strong industrial base in the city, the TLA was able to intervene effectively in peacemaking and work along with other civic organizations, political parties, and the government.

Today, the situation is different. Daily life for the working class is harsher, costlier, and debilitating. In the 1990s, the impact of globalization began to affect the poor citizenry. The rate of rural migration was growing, and the urban informal sector was expanding. The social fabric of the city too began to change. Since the 1980s and 1990s, the frequency and intensity of communal outbreaks has increased. In early 1993, the city reacted violently to the destruction of the Babri Masjid in Ayodhya. In 1999, communal riots broke out in certain areas of the city. The poor suffered doubly from violence and hunger—weeks of curfew left them no opportunity to earn any money for food.

SEWA is a microcosm of what is happening in the rest of the country. The poisonous atmosphere of hatred threatens the unity of our members. SEWA has had to test its inner strength and rely on the bonds of working sisters to provide succor and strength to each other across religious boundaries. Large-scale disasters have struck in the space of two years—first, a massive earthquake in Kutch in 2001 that left close to 60,000 of our members homeless, and then the Hindu-Muslim riots in 2002. When the government failed in its primary duty to maintain law and order in the city, hundreds were left dead and approximately 40,000 of our urban members—some Hindu, the majority Muslim—were left homeless and huddled in relief camps.

A third of SEWA's urban members are Muslim, and they had became the primary targets of a systematic and vicious attack—rape, assault, murder, arson, and plunder. Wave after wave of violence left hundreds of innocents dead; men and women who had just days before shared the

Some of SEWA's movers and shakers. (Amit Dave)

same concerns of finding work and getting their children educated were now at each other's throats.

Their communities were pulling our Rahimas and Ramilas, Jetuns and Jayas, Sharadas and Salmas—who all worked and laughed and sang together—in different directions. As soon as they could, the women were the first to venture out to each other's neighborhoods to make sure their work sisters were safe. Under the leadership of our chief union organizer, Ramilaben, and the secretary of SEWA, Rahimaben, the members and organizers acted bravely and united to restore peace. They worked in relief camps under constant threats and at considerable risk to their personal safety. Moreover, they had to deal with their own families and their prejudices. It took almost eight to ten months for the city to regain some vestiges of normalcy. But the scars left within the hearts of the wounded are deep. It will take a generation to forget or forgive the dark happenings in their lives, and the shadows linger on.

Work is a great leveler. After the madness, no matter what one's religion, there is still the need to make a living, to pay off debts, and to find a new shelter. About 20,000 houses needed to be rebuilt or repaired. The widows needed to be cared for—their mental and financial health was far too vulnerable. SEWA's efforts at rehabilitation have been geared toward rebuilding the women's lives—providing housing, credit, training, medical help, and the comfort and company of other working women. We all firmly feel that our actions need to speak louder than words. Both Hindu and Muslim women at SEWA continue to work, laugh, and care for each other. That is the magic of being work sisters.

But what about tomorrow? Such man-made disasters have become so frequent and overwhelming that it seems SEWA is forced to work primarily in relief operations rather than continue its developmental work. The broader issues of unemployment, lack of adequate infrastructure for the working poor, lack of governmental commitment to alleviate poverty, and the continued division of people by caste or religious ideologies are all major reasons why we have such volatile crowds in our population. Poverty is a political as well as social issue, a humanitarian issue, a legal issue, and an economic issue. No matter how one looks at it, poverty affects us all. In India, our secular democracy is our strength; our hard-working people are our strength. This I have learned from my SEWA sisters.

1

Being Poor, a Woman, and Self-Employed

In 1986, while I was visiting a small village in Bankura district in Bengal, a tiny shrunken woman said to me, "*Kaaj naahi, kaaj kori maroo,*" meaning, "I have no work, but the grind of work is killing me." These words cut right through me, because they spoke of the life of every working poor man and woman in India—a lifetime of hard labor, but with earnings so meager that an end to poverty is nowhere in sight. Among the poor, every woman works. Although she toils from dawn to dusk, she feels that she has no work, and she is ever searching for work. All her life she waits for this elusive work, which can provide her with a steady income to feed her family, step out of poverty, and build a secure life.

To be poor is to be vulnerable. The condition of being poor, of being self-employed, and of being a woman are all distinct yet interrelated states of vulnerability. Poverty makes one become a chronic victim of forces beyond one's control. With every misfortune, problems compound, leaving one increasingly powerless and setting in motion a spiral descent into starker poverty. Only work, a steady source of income, and asset ownership can break one's fall.

For the working poor, most work is seasonal, irregular, or intermittent. Land-based occupations like agriculture—the main source of income for the rural poor—are seasonal. During periods of planting and harvesting, workers are busy from dawn to dusk but then go without work for the rest of the year. Traditionally, crafts supplement their agricultural incomes in such months, but as plastic replaces clay and bamboo; as cheap factory-made synthetic fabrics replace local hand-woven cloth; and as rubber flip-flops take the place of the local cobbler's hand-sewn leather footwear, there is less and less work for the home-based crafts worker. In rural areas, payment in kind once supplemented the need for cash, but today the poor are increasingly facing a cash-based economy. Cash income is hard to come by in rural areas, yet it is crucial to the survival of any poor family.

Because work is so intermittent and income is insufficient, the poor are constantly in need of the services of local moneylenders. Such private borrowing is usually the only source of financial support for the poor trying to tide over in lean times. Although the law prohibits uncertified moneylenders, informal lending is a thriving business that eventually leaves the poor poorer. The moneylender extracts an exorbitant rate of interest, and the poor agree to pay it because they have no alternative. India's banking structure is beyond their reach. Indebtedness is an integral part of poverty. The debt burden closes the door to any chance for betterment, especially when the young inherit the debts incurred by their parents.

Every *paisa* earned is used first to meet basic needs like food and shelter and, second, toward the repayment of debt. With hardly any surplus from their income, the poor cannot build assets. Every time they go to the moneylender or the local landlord, they lose yet another piece of their meager assets. Land, of course, is generally the first to go. Eventually, when even their house, cattle, and the woman's silver jewelry are mortgaged, the poor trade in their work tools, such as looms and ploughs and hoes. In dire times, even government-issued ration cards or any kind of official license can be mortgaged for a cash loan. Assets have a habit of turning up in the hands of the village moneylender or the biggest landowner.

An asset that the poor are left with are their own bodies. As long as they have physical strength, they can dig, carry, haul, and cut to earn some money. Such manual labor requires a strong and healthy body, but their bodies are often weak and overtaxed from overwork, inadequate food, and poor nutrition. On days that they are able to work, they earn; in times of illness, they still work but their productivity declines, and consequently they earn a lot less money. So during illness—precisely the time when they need good nutrition the most—the family half starves.

Because their work is predominantly manual, they need more calories, but there is not enough food. Rice or *roti* made of coarse grains constitutes their main dish, sometimes eaten with a dash of salt and hot chilies. *Dal* and green vegetables begin to appear on their plates only as their income level rises.

Water, perhaps the most important need of all, is an elusive commodity in parts of the country. Safe and sufficient drinking water is not easily available to most poor. In regions where water is scarce or unsafe to drink, dehydration is common, as are water-borne diseases. Malnutrition, compounded by diarrhea and dehydration, is a routine illness among the poor. With no energy reserves in their bodies, ailments can be chronic and long, leaving them weak and listless.

The poor use the public health care system wherever it is available, because it is affordable. The state health infrastructure, however, is often inadequate—unable to meet even the basic medical needs of the people. In rural areas, health care centers are located too far apart, health functionaries are frequently absent from their posts as they commute from town, equipment is often out of order, and medicines are in short supply. Even though private doctors and hospitals are expensive, they offer certain advantages: they are local and the staff is able to cope with emergencies. As a result, the poor will often pay very high prices for their medical care.

Since medical practitioners are predominantly urban and middle-class, they are far removed from the cultural traditions of the population they serve. A social bias against the poor, who seem dirty and ignorant, can influence the quality of health care they receive. Except when targeting diseases like tuberculosis or HIV/AIDS, general health education in preventive and social medicine is almost nonexistent. One traditional health functionary who still holds considerable credibility today is the village midwife, or *dai*. However, her role is slowly being made redundant by the modern medical system.

Normally, the houses of the rural poor are located on the outskirts of a village. Different caste groups and religious communities live in distinct clusters even in poor neighborhoods—each following their own customs, but living relatively amicably together because they depend on each other's help in their day-to-day lives.

Since they build their homes on the outskirts of the village—what is often the village wasteland—living space is not at a premium. In Gujarat, houses are simple structures, consisting of mud and brick walls, thatched or tin roofs, and mud floors. There is space to shelter their cattle, goats, and poultry, and a place to house their trade tools, their raw materials, like yarn or wool, and all their seasonal stock of agricultural produce. When a son brings home a wife, the house just gets extended. Usually, the rural poor own their homes, however makeshift or *kachcha* they are.

The simply made houses are prone to heavy wear and tear. They need regular and timely maintenance, which requires the efforts of the entire family. Such houses are not always able to withstand the elements—damage during heavy rains, floods, or strong winds is common. Thatched roofs are vulnerable to cooking fires, and roofs fly off during cyclones. The margin between having a house and being homeless is very narrow. Entire stocks of grain and supplies can get washed away or damaged in heavy rains, cattle and children can succumb to illnesses, and the family has to rebuild from scratch. There is no getting ahead, just a return to bare minimum.

Under such unstable living conditions, amenities like electricity, running water, or toilets are hard to come by. Most villagers fetch water from a communal well or pond. But because of social taboos, members of scheduled castes and dalits in certain communities are excluded from using the communal water, forcing them to either use less than potable water or to walk a distance to find another source of drinking water. The water in village ponds is sometimes so saline that it is not fit for human or animal consumption. Fetching water is a strenuous and a time-consuming activity in rural life.

Houses of the poor seldom have electricity. In Gujarat, where almost all villages are guaranteed an approach road and electricity by the government, the Panchayat (village council) can seldom afford to use the electricity for anything other than street lighting and running water pumps. Electric light in individual homes of the poor, although possible, is difficult to attain. As a result, the number of hours a family can be productive is low—the children have less time for study, because they must use daylight hours to assist in household chores, and for adults, because their workday is shortened, income-earning opportunities are lost. However, general living conditions in villages are relatively healthy compared to those in city slums.

In rural families, children are generally welcome. The poor perceive children as assets and as a source of security. More children mean more working hands, which in turn means a better earning capacity for the family. But with another mouth to feed and the added demands on the family's

Pots by a dry well at a relief site, waiting for water tankers
to bring water to the well. (Amit Dave)

limited resources—which also includes the mother's diminished capacity
to work—parental love is mixed with anxiety.

Among the very poor in Gujarat, because every member of the family—male or female—works, the birth of a daughter is not a cause for concern. Since she is an active economic component of the family, when she
marries and moves away, her family suffers an economic loss. Therefore,
the custom of bride money has found a place among the poor. Among families with an upward mobility and aspirations to the middle-class status,
daughters cease to work. Her marriage will then require a dowry, which is,
in a way, money for her upkeep. Boys, however, do not move away, and
they are expected to support their family and parents to the end of their days.

Young mothers work all through their pregnancy and seldom get
supplemental nutrition for the fetus. Their main source of information and
support is the dai, who, although untrained in medical science, has the
advantage of experience. Even today, the dai delivers most babies born in
rural areas. Other than a very brief rest for the mother, there is no postnatal care. At every stage of the birth process, lack of information, nutrition,

and medical care all have direct consequences on the well-being of both mother and child.

In rural families, children start working and adding to the family's income as soon as they are able. Children perform hundreds of small and big chores that dominate rural life. If the village school is close by, both boys and girls begin their education together; but how long they continue with their studies depends on the family's needs. Girls drop out sooner than boys because, more often than not, their services are needed to baby sit younger siblings at home while the parents are at work. If the school is at a distance from the safety of the village, parents are reluctant to allow a growing girl to commute every day.

With formal education scuttled, the child is then fit for manual work only. Boys are put to work grazing cattle or sent to work on a farm or at a road construction site. In the case of a girl, she mothers her younger siblings, cooks, and fetches water and fuel. She also learns some skills from her mother in their family occupation, like weaving or food processing.

Childhood is thus quickly over for the child worker, paid or unpaid. By law, a child is defined as one who is less than fourteen years of age; by law, this child has to be in school and not in the labor force; in reality, the rural child has already joined the workforce.

Since rural agricultural life is lived so close to nature, there is great respect for both nature's generosity and its fury. The poor are particularly attuned to nature's moods; after all, they depend on the free gifts of nature like bamboo to build their homes, firewood for fuel, forest fruits for food; rivers and ponds for fresh water, and clay to mold into earthen pots and bricks. Economically, nature is their last resort, because only nature will provide without cash.

Yet even this is now changing. The enormous pressure on natural resources has upset the balance between man and nature beyond a sustainable level. As a result, the local ecology has degenerated in innumerable villages in India. The consequence of this imbalance is the beginning of scarcity and a widespread abuse of the country's natural resources. The groundwater level drops deeper; forests diminish; natural raw materials once free and accessible to the poor begin to vanish; strip mining ravages the land; industrial effluents pollute the air and rivers. Nature's gifts are sold in markets at a price the poor cannot afford. As resources deplete, life gradually becomes more difficult, more inhuman. Growing pollution, scarcity, salinity, denudation, and desertification all push the poor deeper into poverty.

The rural poor are indeed the first and worst victims of natural disasters, precisely because they live so close to nature and depend on it for survival. Their fragile homes are the first ones to be damaged by floods, fire, or cyclone. Their rain-fed crops grown on low lands are the first to be flooded. Whatever relief they get is to a large measure due to the goodwill of neighboring villagers. But such help is limited. State relief invariably arrives late. Relief, when it does arrive, is never adequate and is a fraction of the actual losses to the poor. Again, in caste-ridden villages, the lower-caste poor are the last to receive relief packs.

Since they have very few resources or savings to fall back on, the poor take much longer to move beyond the relief stage. They do not have sufficient economic buoyancy to take advantage of rehabilitation support from the government. Just consider what must be overcome—they have to reconstruct their homes, retrieve and prepare their land for re-cultivation, and identify the items still in their possession that will fetch quick money in the market. Because roads are blocked and public transportation is disrupted, they cannot commute to the city to sell their salvaged products. Moreover, with everyone rushing to market to sell in distress, the prices of farm produce and household items plummet.

Having damaged or lost their means of production—their cattle, their handloom, or other processing equipment—there is no income in the family. In such times, the family's first and foremost need is to recover its means of production so that work and income can resume. But government relief efforts seldom consider replacement of their means of production as part of relief work. And borrowing from banks or the government is impossible. Being penniless and homeless, with no collateral of any sort, none but the usurious village moneylender will loan them money to rebuild. And the downward spiral begins.

In Gujarat, a great number of the very poor live in dry areas where there are intermittent or consecutive years of drought. They cannot afford to irrigate their lands with scarce and expensive water, so their crops are rain-fed. Year after year, they pray for the monsoon to arrive—not too early and not too late, so that they might have a decent harvest. Without the rains, there is a scarcity of drinking water, and there is no green fodder for the cattle. For the rural poor, there is little difference between their love for their children and their love for their cattle—all are vital and integral members of the family whose suffering is equally unbearable.

Until the government declares an area as officially drought-stricken, no one can expect any outside assistance. Hence, there is extensive lobbying by local political parties to attract the government's attention to the area's plight. After much delay, special fodder depots are opened at relatively affordable prices so that cattle can be fed. But it is often too late for some families who, rather than watch their cows and buffaloes starve to death, are forced to sell good head of cattle at rock bottom prices to traders with an eye for advantage.

When the government finally launches an employment program, those who come to work are invariably the most desperate of the poor, and they are officially entitled to less than minimum wage. Exploitation of the vulnerable is sanctioned by the state! Government relief employment takes the form of "digging and filling holes." The intention is to build durable public assets like roads and bridges, but, in reality, large-scale construction of this kind is neither durable nor an asset to the public. With the first rainfall, the road and the job wash away. Workers return to their fields, and the pockmarked earth fills up with water and becomes a breeding ground for mosquitoes. It would be far more productive to help villages build water ponds, communal buildings, and work sheds so that they have a stake in seeing their efforts bear fruit. Environmental work, such as nursery raising, water harvesting, recycling and sanitation, should also be considered part of relief work. However, like Sisyphus, the fruitless digging continues, year after year, drought after drought.

Daytime temperatures in summer are so high the parched earth is baked hard and is difficult to walk on, let alone to dig. It is backbreaking labor. Just one look will show that the workers are predominantly women with little children by their side. More energy is expended than any calories acquired by the food that can be purchased from the meager wages. Often, even supervisors will not come to the site because of the heat; in such cases, digging occurs at night. But because payments are made in the middle of the day, during office hours, the women are forced to camp at the site, since there is not enough time to go home and return. When droughts are frequent, the poor get poorer. When droughts are ignored year after year, there is famine. But it is only after mass hunger and deaths finally catch the public eye that any real support arrives. How we can fail to see that consecutive years of drought cause chronic starvation and famine?

Family working at a relief site. (Amit Dave)

With such an extensive track record, India should have a lot of experience in facing disasters and providing relief to victims. A good deal of this process has been spearheaded by voluntary agencies who have been catalysts of change in the government's attitudes and actions about what kind of relief is called for and for whom. The voice of the real victims, however, has yet to join in the decision making.

Since India has a democratic political structure, time and again politicians at local and national levels are forced to reckon with the sheer numbers of the poor who they perceive as a major vote bank to be wooed with promises. When the poor have stuck together and shown some leadership, they have to a certain extent been able to take a bargaining position with the politicians, particularly during elections. But their bargaining power is short-lived; as soon as the elections are over, the poor are forgotten and relegated to the back seat.

In rural India, political clout depends heavily on caste dominance. The caste system is well entrenched in villages and permeates every part of life. The dominance of the higher castes over the lower ones is overpowering, oppressive, and exploitative. The upper castes enjoy wealth and power in some form or other—as landowners, as traders, or in the form of education. Needless to say, the lower castes comprising the large number of landless laborers, weavers, potters, leather workers, and other crafts people are economically weak.

Besides the caste hierarchy, a few families who own productive land and assets like water enjoy enhanced power in a village. The rest of the families depend on them for their livelihood—working their lands, helping at harvest time, performing all kinds of agricultural and even domestic chores. In adverse times, the poor borrow from the landlords, pledging their silver, their small piece of land, and sometimes even their children. The position of being both employer and moneylender is one of great power, affording ample opportunities for exploitation and suppression.

While it divides so mercilessly, the caste system also unites in fragments. Within the same caste, bonds between caste members are strong, providing unquestioned loyalty and a great sense of security. But when caste divisions run deep, tensions can run high and violence can flare up easily. Any sign of independence or defiance by the lower castes would upset the existing power structure and result in serious consequences. Physical intimidation, trumped-up police cases, and land grabbing are common manifestations of the conflict. The police force is not perceived as an impartial supporter of justice, and to a very large extent, they are not. Invariably, the poor are usually the losers. The village may resume normalcy afterward, but the bitter memory and need for vengeance lives on for generations.

To assume that poverty is a leveling force is to underestimate the power of deep-seated hierarchical tendencies, even within the castes. Among the dalits, the *vankar*, the *chamar*, the *koli*, and the *bhangi* live in separate communities, conscious of their own status relative to others. Tribals rate even lower in this hierarchy. Even relatively egalitarian Islam is not impervious to some degree of hierarchical subdivisions in India.

With so many distinct identities of caste, class, trade, religion, and ethnicity in society, it takes very little effort to breed intolerance and create rifts between relatively peaceful cohabiting communities. Time and again such rifts are used to subdue, divide, and exploit for economic, political, or religious ends.

When a family's resources are stretched, a woman suffers twice the impact of vulnerability and instability. Even within the family, a hierarchy emerges based on social convention and economic need. Unfortunately, from birth, a girl grows up with a sense that she is entitled to less. Whether it is food, play, or education, she must make do with less than her brother does. She has less access to her family's meager income and their few assets. She can expect a lifetime of hard work and heavy responsibilities. Poverty permeates every part of her existence, including her self-esteem.

A daughter is trained early in life to serve meekly. She fetches and follows, lending a helping hand to everyone in the family. When she is old enough, she looks after her younger siblings, showing special deference to her brothers, big and small. While boys can roam and play, she must learn housework; while her brothers go to school, she must stay home and learn survival skills. At a tender age, she learns that her role is to work and stay useful. Even the most doting parents would be considered negligent if they did not train their daughters in all basic domestic and agricultural chores. How well she marries depends to a large extent on her skills, her capacity to please, and her capacity for hard work.

A farmer's life is hard, no matter what part of the world one is in, but in rural India, the greatest load of manual work falls on the woman. Most manual work is monotonous, back breaking, and never-ending. Consider a young mother's day.

She nurses the baby, fetches water, cooks the food, cleans the house, feeds the cattle, milks the cow, attends to the sick and elderly, serves the guests, works in the field, maintains the mud floor, repairs the roof, makes cow dung cakes for fuel, sews clothes, patches quilts, processes grain, stores fodder, tends to the vegetable plot, husks the paddy, puffs the rice, shells the cotton pods in summer and groundnuts in winter. . . . She is the last one to sleep and the first one to wake up. Even illness or pregnancy does not excuse her from most of her duties, no matter how heavy they are. When the children are young, any work she cannot do is work left undone. Her only ally is her daughter, who—as she grows older—helps lighten her mother's load until it is time for her to marry and move away.

This folk song from Vagad, in the desert area of Gujarat, is the lament of a young bride complaining about her new life.

> Dada ho dikri Vagad ma na desho!
> Grandpa, don't send your little girl to Vagad!
> My mother-in-law is such a tyrant,

She makes me spin at night, and grind flour by lamplight;
And in the dark of dawn, she sends me to fetch water.
So the *indhoni* is my pillow, and the rope is at my feet all night;
although it is long as my street, my rope barely reaches the water in
    the well;
How my poor arms ache, all day, all night.
O flying bird, take a message to my brother
And tell my Grandpa that his little girl will jump in the well,
Or she will drink some poison.
Her life is so unbearable!
Be sure to tell this to no one but my grandpa;
Because my mother will faint, if she hears of my pain.
Wait! wait! dear girl, do not jump in the well!
Do not swallow *apheen*!
On the eighth moonlit night, your family will come to rescue you.
So on the eighth moonlit night,
My uncle drew water from the well,
My father put the pot on my head,
My dear brother broke that water pot
Right at the feet of my quarrelsome mother-in-law!

The young girl's fantasy that the men in her family will come and rescue her and take revenge on her behalf is touching. More touching is the fact that she wants to shield her mother from her unhappiness.

A direct correlation between an increase in poverty and the number of women-led households has often been noted. The most common reasons women become the main breadwinner in the family include migration, desertion, unemployment, illness, or widowhood. With poverty and unemployment rampant in rural areas, men leave their villages and migrate to the cities in search for work, leaving the women behind to take care of their rural households. Although a few are able to send some money home, most of the women are forced to subsist on their own income. Even in families where the men have been unemployed for long periods of time, they will not always seize an opportunity for work if they feel it is not worthy of them. Women are different; women are quick to step into almost any kind of economic activity to feed and clothe the family. In urban slums, the incidence of men abandoning their families is more common—when the situation gets too overwhelming, men find it easier to disappear in a large city, leaving the woman to fend for herself and the family. As a result, the hardest hit and most vulnerable of the poor is the woman in the family.

In rural Gujarat, women rarely own the land they work on. Even her husband's land is not quite hers to claim—legally she may be entitled to it, but in reality, her in-laws possess it. She can only hope that eventually her son will stake his claim on it. As de facto head of her family, she has more responsibilities than power.

Despite what the law says, the government officials normally do not recognize a woman as head of household. If the man of the family is absent, the household is simply overlooked. Families that most need assistance are deprived of any government schemes for poverty alleviation and rural development. So far, social security measures for widows or deserted women are few and far between.

In some areas, adverse forces are so powerful that despite great reluctance to leave their ancestral homelands, the rural poor pack up their belongings and head for the city in search of work. This kind of migration is painful and traumatic.

But greener pastures are nowhere to be found—certainly not in the cities where the migrating poor eventually arrive. Most bring with them the name of a contact—a relative or a member of their caste reputed to have made good in the city—in the hope that the familiar face will lead them to work and guide them through the maze of urban life. These contacts from the past are most often their only hope, and the desperation and dependence the new arrivals feel toward them are huge.

Of course, the first thing they need is a place to sleep—not an easy feat in cities where even sidewalks are spoken for. Public places like railway stations and bus depots are constantly patrolled by the police—less in the interest of public safety and more with an eye toward taking bribes to look the other way. In fact, both criminals and police are omnipresent, preying on newcomers. Rural migrants most often wind up sleeping on the far outskirts of the city, on the sidewalks of busy highways, along railway tracks, under bridges, or in those large, round cement water pipes left above ground by some road construction company. Even this humble accommodation is possible only with the help of a middleman who is sure to demand fees in cash or in kind. Whatever valuables were brought along from home vanish quickly. As they say, it is easier to find a job in a city than to find a few square feet to rest your head on.

Access to water is another daunting challenge. Sometimes it has to be fetched at night from some public institution after bribing the watchman; at other times, one might come upon a public tap. Public toilets are so vile and unpleasant, most people avoid them—instead, they use the cover of darkness to relieve themselves on sidewalks and in dusty alleys. Bathing has to be postponed for an opportune moment. Life is irregular and uncertain in such living conditions. Women and young girls have no privacy and are particularly vulnerable. Eventually, when the family is able to build a small shanty out of corrugated metal and recycled wood, it is on unattended private land or on public land—either way, they are encroaching and under constant threat of eviction.

Even in these humble circumstances, it is necessary for each family member to be tough and to be earning. For a fee, a tout—a contractor or subcontractor—can find them some work in an industry, at a shop or market, or at a construction site or godown, or in a private home. Women with young children or adolescent girls who need adult protection or supervision tend to be homebound. Most such women begin working in their own homes—rolling bidis or *agarbattis*—skills that can be picked up quickly, that even children can help with, and which will bring in daily cash. Some prepare foodstuff for vendors to sell; others sort garbage for waste dealers. Women and children can scour the streets together, rag picking. With a little daring, even the unskilled can find numerous ways in which to earn small amounts to feed themselves.

It takes time to build the confidence to walk into unfamiliar neighborhoods. Buses are expensive, so they tend to walk everywhere they go. Besides, one needs to be at least functionally literate in a city to follow bus routes and street signs. Traffic is daunting in the early days. The bustle, noise, pollution, aggression, and the constant need for vigilance are overwhelming after the silent monotony of rural life. However, at the end of the day, they must find work, and no matter what work they engage in, they must have cash income. Without cash in hand, survival in a city is almost impossible.

In the early days, their hard-earned income is not all theirs to keep. Others have claims to their earnings. To begin with, the first city contact that showed them the ropes must be given a cut. The tout who found them a job gets a cut. The grocer who sold them their daily necessities on credit must be repaid with interest. There is a cash value tied to every good deed, contact, and information, and those that can exploit it get ahead.

Repaying all these debts is a terribly slow process. Yet in a city, finding work is relatively easy. The temptation to turn to quicker ways of earning a living, like gambling, black-marketing, and prostitution is understandable. Even begging can be an income-earning opportunity, depending on the beat. Befriending policemen is particularly useful. After all, bribing a policeman to become your friend is cheaper in the long run than having to bribe him to leave you alone.

Within the family, men, women, and children take on new roles and tasks—a challenge for some members. Stresses on the family are huge, both internally and externally. Displaced from their traditional culture, living amidst a clash of castes, cultures, and religions, the migrant family is constantly adapting, asserting, succumbing, fighting, and reconciling to fit in. But whatever the differences, each member of the family must learn to put them aside because no one can afford to lose their daily earnings.

The city municipal systems hardly touch this vast working population; with its numbers growing, their issues are overwhelming. Besides, their instability and illegality are of some advantage to the city. The city wants to capitalize on this cheap, docile, and easily available rural labor. However, by keeping their homes and work unauthorized, the laborers are denied identity. Their children are everywhere, visible, working in streets, in homes, in the markets. Providing daycare, health care, water, sanitation, or a shelter couldn't be lower on the priority list. The town planners' map makes no mention of outreach to the overcrowded areas where the poor live. It is as if their very existence is denied.

To get grains and fuel at reasonable, subsidized prices, the migrants need government-issued ration cards. In India, a ration card takes the form of an identity card because it states the address and the number of family members living in that household. But new migrants do not get such cards for a very long time. This is done to discourage them from claiming permanent residency in the city. At the time of elections, the issuing of new ration cards is often the most common political demand. Success depends on the candidate's political clout and his commitment to his constituency after he wins the election.

Despite their daily cash earnings, banks do not consider the working poor creditworthy. Because the poor live in makeshift hovels and do not possess ration cards for identification, they are considered unreliable. The failure of the public system to invest in the basic needs of slum-dwellers is tragic. The constant feeling of being unwanted does not generate civic-mindedness or loyalty to a city where they live and work for long years.

The living conditions in urban slums are difficult. Boxed in her tiny one-room home, a woman is constantly surrounded by people—there are eyes everywhere you look. The constant roar of traffic, the squabbles of the neighbors, the blaring radios of street-sellers, and the whir of machinery invade her senses from dawn till late at night, until finally darkness falls and even the pariah dogs settle down in the cool of the night.

City mornings are frenzied. There is a rush to the municipal water taps to fetch the day's supply of water; in cities like Ahmedabad the two-hour supply is regular, but it is woefully inadequate. Municipal water taps are battlegrounds for women, where only the strong survive. This is not the village well; this is no place for slum women to bond. Even at six o'clock in the morning, tension fills the air. Waiting for her turn at the trickling tap, every woman is anxious to obtain the day's water supply for drinking and washing before rushing home to cook and fill the tiffin boxes for husbands on their way to work and children getting ready for school.

Around the municipal water taps, where every minute of water is fought over, the ground is slick and muddy with shallow puddles. These puddles are breeding grounds for mosquitoes. Public lavatories built and abandoned by the municipality are close by, unapproachable in their stink and filth. Instead, slum-dwelling women prefer to relieve themselves in the dark of the night or at the crack of dawn when there are few passersby. Bathing is done at midday when most men are out at work. At times, the unemployed young men loitering around the neighborhood become a problem, leaving the women little privacy. Finding privacy in a slum is essentially a woman's art.

Cooking in a one-room home is a challenge as well. Kerosene is the most commonly used fuel in slums, while cow dung cakes are more common in shanties. Kerosene is a rationed commodity, unless bought in the black market at a higher price. The smell of kerosene seeps into the cooked food and into every cup of tea. Kerosene is not a clean-burning fuel; the soot darkens the walls, and the pots need constant cleaning.

There is no space for storing food either. Groceries are bought in small quantities—just enough to last for a meal or two. Flour, oil, rice, dal, sugar, and tea are bought with cash, at prices far higher than if they'd been bought in bulk. Money constantly changes hands, in small amounts, several times

Laundry is always a challenge for a slum dweller.
(Menaben Harchandbhai, SEWA agricultural worker)

a day. If a child is crying, a few small coins can pacify her. The child then will rush to the vendor at the end of the alley to buy a sweet or a piece of overripe fruit. Children will also run quick errands for adults—fetching tea or a pack of *gutka* (chewing tobacco) several times a day. Tea and tobacco are the staple of slum life for men and women, at work and at home.

City life may be less prone to natural disasters, but floods are a recurring problem. Slums tend to be situated in low-lying areas, so a few days of heavy rains can wreak havoc. Since most city sewage and storm water disposal systems are inadequate, there is constant water logging, filling the streets and sidewalks with sewage and stagnant water. The municipality makes some attempt to clear the water, but mostly it stays there until the sun eventually dries it up. Public garbage floating into doorless homes is a common sight during monsoons. Residents come down with fever, diarrhea, and skin rashes; cholera and malaria epidemics are never far away. The death toll among children is the highest. Unlike the unavailability of emergency medicine in village populations, urban residents are fortunate because they can summon ambulances and get relatively prompt medical treatment. Unfortunately, because chronic anemia and malnutrition are common, their sick bodies are slow to respond to treatment. Besides, they live their lives from hand to mouth. A day without earnings is a day without food. Each passing day without work only puts them in debt.

Most slum children do go to school as long as the schools are within an accessible distance. Even girls get to attend regularly because their mothers begin to value school education. School hours afford mothers some time for quiet, productive work in the home. When a woman has to go out to work, neighbors will quite often keep an eye on the children.

The population of established city slums usually includes a relatively homogeneous group with a common background of origin, occupation, language, and caste. Other slums have a racial and religious mix that in times of crisis can either close ranks to form a strong community or turn on itself with great vengeance.

Elections are exciting events for everyone. Local political leaders in search of votes make their appearance and lend sympathetic ears. Others bring intimidation and criminal pressure. Gambling dens, liquor dens, and prostitution are facts of slum living that women deal with as best they can. With so much exposure to life, urban women are politically wiser than their rural sisters.

Living in crowded, tension-filled circumstances, migrant men and women find their own culture in transition. The rhythm of city life, its precarious lifestyle and promises, and their own hopes challenge every concept of work, gender roles, child rearing, housekeeping, and even the husband-wife relationship. The most significant change in the women's lives is the need and possibility for women to enter the urban informal economy and be self-employed.

An urban world is a literate world, where the written word reigns supreme. The illiterate are at a loss because entire systems pass them by. Public notices, street signs, newspapers, legal documents, bank accounts, and employment advertisements are all beyond their reach. They are forced to remain local, among things they know and people they trust, in order to survive. Often considered slow-witted and unskilled, they are thought fit for nothing more than manual labor. Such people are in the millions, and they form the backbone of India's informal economy.

Adult education is still a dream for most of India's illiterates. There are no schools teaching basic literacy skills to the working poor. Who can afford to spend day after day, year after year, in school when survival is at stake? The kind of education that is needed is one that looks to the needs of the working people. The working poor want to be able to read the text on a land title so that they are not cheated; they want to write letters to their loved ones; they want to read newspapers; they want to keep accounts and open bank accounts and take loans at low interest rates by signing their name on documents they understand, and so much more. There are no schools to teach these things.

The Indian Constitution provides every citizen with rights and duties, be they rich or poor, literate or illiterate. But when an overwhelming number of the population is poor, illiterate, and uncertain of its rights, they can neither exercise those rights nor benefit from them. Well-intended government policies, designed to help the poor, do not reach them. Political news reaches the poor through their local power structure so that they are never sure of the implications of the information they have received. Many rural households listen to the radio, but few broadcasts reflect their basic concerns. Television, which has the potential to play an important role in the lives of those who depend on the spoken word, offers plenty of entertainment, but very little of real value to a worker. The media are geared to the urban middle class; the rest are just onlookers.

Even government-controlled media makes no attempts to reach the working poor. Although banking with the poor has been an official government policy for the past two decades, there is no large-scale effort to broadcast and implement this policy. For the working poor who cannot sign their names, opening a bank account is nearly impossible. In the absence of literacy, the poor have to depend on memory. Even those that deal well with their own businesses and personal finances falter when they encounter the formal world of bureaucracy.

The government promotes economic and social self-help activities and provides for training and financial subsidies. But these inputs are far from adequate. If illiteracy is a factor in the ability of the poor to obtain help, other added input is needed by the government so that they reach the very people they want to help. Today, most subsidies land neatly in the laps of local vested interests. Several voluntary agencies have taken the initiative to point out and fill in the gaps that need to be closed in order to reach the poor.

The working poor use traditional skills and their manual labor to earn their livelihood. There are no formal jobs for them in the economy; they must create their own jobs and opportunities and employ themselves to participate in the economy.

Ironically, the self-employed sector is the backbone of the overall economy, in which formal jobs constitute just 7 percent of the total.[1] Among women, the numbers are even more revealing. Of all working women in India, 6 percent work in the formal sector, while 94 percent work in the informal or self-employed sector.[2] And since the nation's policy makers are only just beginning to recognize the existence of the informal sector, legal protection or access to credit is still not within their reach.

The self-employed are engaged in innumerable trades—in fact, since they look for niches in the economy, they are engaged in thousands of different occupations that rise and fall with the demands of the economy. They perform manual labor as agricultural workers, construction workers, movers, loaders, and cart pullers. They provide services as domestic workers engaged in cooking, and cleaning. They are home-based workers who have skills like garment stitching, bidi rolling, junksmithing, or basket making, and they are vendors and hawkers who sell fresh produce, recycled garments, or articles of everyday use.

The self-employed share certain characteristics. They are all economically active. They rarely own any capital or their own tools of production or trade. They have no access to credit. They are exploited by middlemen, who are an integral part of their work life. They are the unacknowledged, low-tech, labor-intensive, raw material–processing arm of industry. Even though they exist in such large numbers, they are scattered, isolated, and unaware of their position in the economy. They have very little bargaining power.

Certain trades tend to be dominated by specific castes and communities, while others absorb workers from all across India's religious spectrum. Labor laws provide for a minimum wage for some professions, as long as

1. *Women and Men in the Informal Economy: A Statistical Picture*. Geneva: International Labour Organization, 2002.

2. *Shramshakti: Report of the National Commission on Self-Employed Women and Women in the Informal Sector*. New Delhi: Government of India, Ministry of Women and Child Development, 1988.

Handcarts are an integral part of Ahmedabad's industrial goods
delivery system. (SEWA Academy)

the profession falls within their appointed list of recognized jobs. If the
trade falls outside of it, there is no legal recourse. The world is changing
too fast for governments to make trade lists—work has myriad faces. What
is needed is a national minimum wage. Unfortunately, even where a minimum wage is specified, there is almost no mechanism to enforce it.

Agricultural workers often take up construction labor during the off-
season. The entire family moves to the construction site and leaves when
the work is over. Since they are on the move and in unfamiliar surroundings,
these workers are easily exploited. The Inter State Migrant Workers Act is
rarely implemented for their protection. The worst kind of exploitation takes
place through the contract labor system. Since the contractor supplies the
labor, the employer takes no responsibility for the payment of wages or for
providing identity cards or social security benefits to his workers, according to the law. In this way, employers even evade accident compensation.

There are factory workers working within and outside the factory premises who are not registered on the employee roll because they are engaged through contractors. This arrangement has been going on for years.

As the workers advance in age, they are easily replaced by younger, more able-bodied labor under the same contract system. There is no legal obligation on the part of the employer toward these workers because, officially, they were never real employees. There is no proof on paper to establish the employer–employee relationship. All types of employers—even educational institutions, banks, and corporate companies—brazenly use the contract system. Since the workers are unrecognized, unrecorded, and unorganized, they remain invisible and voiceless.

Isolation is a bigger problem for the vast numbers of home-based workers. A majority of them are women confined within their homes for economic, social, or cultural reasons. They are invisible to the nation—in *"purdah,"* both literally and statistically. The piece-rate system is increasingly dominating most home-based production in the world today. Under this system, workers are paid a fixed sum for a specific amount of work. Although this sounds fair, the system favors the employer. First, when one calculates the wage on an hourly basis, it is lower than or close to minimum wage. Second, the work is farmed out under a series of contracts whereby each middleman gets a cut from the one under him. For the workers at the bottom, this implies that they often do not know who their principal employer is. One of the main reasons for this system is that employers can claim to not have employees, thus sidestepping all industrial labor laws.

Piece-rate workers are supplied raw material at home. When the finished goods are returned to the employer, workers receive payment as well as the next lot for production. Millions of women and men work on such terms; they roll bidis or incense sticks, make paper bags or garments, shell cotton pods or groundnuts, do embroidery, clean and winnow grains, do block printing, make matchsticks, assemble electrical and electronic goods, or package and label industrial goods. Innumerable production activities are done in the homes of the self-employed workers.

While home-based production has always existed, the trend toward piece rating has grown over the years. Earlier, workers rolled bidis in the employers' premises like factories, but at present around five million bidi rollers work in their homes. Those rolling bidis in factories were men, while those rolling in homes were women. Bidi workers are the only home-based workers protected by legislation, but the law is rarely enforced.

Similarly, there are *papad* rollers, agarbatti rollers, kite makers, fireworks makers, and millions of other trades without any legislative protection to ensure either minimum remuneration or social security measures. In some places, however, where the workers united to demand better returns, the contract process was converted to a sale-purchase system—meaning the employer sells the raw materials to workers and then purchases the finished goods back from them.

Because home-based workers are often unable to go out and negotiate on their own, they fall prey to agents and middlemen who become their sole source of work and income. Their tools of production are very often rented, and they must pay for some of the raw materials needed in production (for example, thread, needles, and accessories), which in reality subsidizes the middleman. And since production occurs at home, unpaid children and other family members help to fulfill quotas.

There are also numerous small, self-employed crafts producers who invest their own small capital to buy materials, process goods, and sell their products in the market. Their products range from clay pots to iron stoves and buckets, hand-loomed cloth to *zari* and other embroidery work, bamboo products to exquisite stone and wood carvings, and papier-mâché to bronze and metal work. Many fall under the purview of handicraft boards and other development corporations, so mercifully some reliable data on their work status are available. Men and women alike work in larger numbers in this sector.

Craftspeople like potters, weavers, and basket makers, who are experiencing a decline in the use of their crafts locally, are being employed under the piece-rate system by agents who have access to markets in cities and distant places. With the price of raw materials like bamboo, yarn, and scrap rising year after year, and the price of the product dictated by the middleman and his market, it is the craftspeople that absorb any loss. The craftspeople who were once genuinely self-employed can no longer stay afloat because they have no access to credit, no ability to buy raw materials in bulk and take advantage of better prices, no idea of who the end-user of their product is, and therefore no understanding of the market. Adequate space to store finished goods and raw materials is also a problem because their homes are small and cramped.

A small producer with traditional skills, like a basket weaver, uses age-old primitive tools. Her products sell at a low price locally, and she has limited access to markets where her products may fetch higher prices. Some of her traditional skills are becoming redundant because certain types of natural raw materials are becoming extinct, or their access is banned, or they are very expensive. The Forest Department prohibits forest dwellers from cutting bamboo even to build their own traditional homes. The timber merchants, however, may rob the forest by bribing the forest guards. Cane is vanishing from the forestland. Under official agreement, entire sections of the bamboo forest are sold to paper mills at a low price to turn into pulp. As a result, the basket weaver pays 15 rupees for a seven-foot bamboo in the open market, while the paper mill pays less than a single rupee.

The street vendors, ubiquitous in India, are also self-employed, and they face a different set of problems. Although they are, in effect, the country's prime market and distribution system for fresh produce, they are not considered workers either. There is a new national policy regarding vendors and hawkers, but much depends on if, and how, it is implemented. Even though the fresh produce market in every Indian city is made up of small vendors, their space in any market is constantly under dispute. There is a tendency to look down on traditional Indian markets. The reason may be that in a low-value goods market, both buyers and sellers are poor, and their needs do not factor into a grand vision of a modern city.

The ground reality of the self-employed is a sad reflection of the poverty and powerlessness experienced by the majority of the country's workforce. The questions that come to mind are unsettling. Why do we not revitalize traditional Indian economic structures instead of neglecting them? Why do we mindlessly imitate so-called modern systems and totally ignore the reality of Indian life? How can one have a vital banking system where large majorities of economically active people are unable to access its services? How do we build modern cities if we cannot plan for the businesses that actually make up the marketplace? How can one have a labor movement that does not even recognize more than three-fourths of the country's working population as workers? How can we say we have a women's movement if the multitude of poor, rural women has no voice? Because, as a nation, we have not yet made poverty removal a lodestar to guide the actions of all citizens and every government, and because our feeble attempts to help the poor are crumbs thrown to garner votes, we are still faced with these questions.

2

Rag Pickers

Since the late 1890s, two-thirds of the population of Ahmedabad was economically engaged around the textile industry. An entire subeconomy grew around the scrap thrown out by mills. Big traders purchased these discarded cut pieces and end strips of mill cloth and sent them through a chain of contractors to Muslim women in slums, who stitched them into garments and quilts in their homes. Iron and wood scraps were sold, also through subcontractors, to Marwari women junksmiths to turn into buckets, kitchen racks, cooking stoves, and small items of furniture. The main consumers of these recycled products were poor urban families. The lowest in the hierarchy of scraps went to the dalit women, who picked over the floor sweepings of mills, factories and shops, and salvaged any useable waste thrown out on the streets.

These waste pickers are like self-appointed recycling agents—visiting every worksite, roadside, and garbage dump in search for anything of value—newspapers and white paper, glass bottles, plastic bags, bottle tops, bits of broken machinery, iron nails and steel filings, discarded hair, and pieces of wood.

A rag picker's day begins at the crack of dawn. She picks up her large *thela* and sets off on her daily beat, her quick, trained eyes scouring the roads and sidewalks for marketable waste. She bends to pick it up with her right hand and drops it in the thela hanging over her left shoulder. She walks, she sees, she bends, she picks, she throws in her bag and walks on. She is home by nine o'clock in the morning, just as the morning rush begins. She quickly cooks lunch, feeds the family, and returns to the streets once again. At midday, she spreads the collection on the floor, sorts the various items into separate bags, and delivers the haul to a dealer. The dealer gives her cash—the price for each of the various categories she collects is different. There may be some rejects in her haul, but she can hardly argue with the dealer about their value. Back home, she lifts her thela and is off on her beat once again. She is home before dark. On the way home, she buys groceries for the evening meal from the cash she earned that day—flour, rice, salt, onions, and a few spoonfuls of oil. She cooks the supper, feeds her family the evening meal, and if she is not too tired, she will sort the waste collected in the afternoon. If there is some water left over in the bucket, she will take a bath and then go to sleep.

Scavenging is demeaning, backbreaking work, but it is available to anyone and everyone who needs to have work in a city. Even children, with their keen eyes, can be gainfully employed during the day, walking the streets with their mother or in small bands on their own. The hours are long, the health hazards numerous; much depends on luck, and a lot depends on the prices the dealer is willing to pay. The rag pickers themselves have no bargaining power.

In the late 1970s, a Gujarat University student Anjana Dave, who was interested in issues related to government-run labor welfare schemes, came to see me. I drew her attention to the rag pickers of Ahmedabad. All were poor working women, and yet no labor welfare schemes would ever reach them because they were self-employed. SEWA was just beginning to learn about their work and trade when this student expressed a desire to help us in our efforts. Under her direction, SEWA conducted a study of the rag pickers of Ahmedabad. It earned her a master's degree, and it gave SEWA a better understanding of the rag pickers' trade.

According to Anjana's survey,[1] the women's income from rag picking was very low—amounting to less than 200 rupees per month. Ninety

1. Anjana Dave. "A Socio-Economic Survey of Paper-Picking Ladies in Ahmedabad." Unpublished Master's thesis, Gujarat University, 1979.

Gleaning recyclables at a city dump. (Amit Dave)

percent lived in slums; their average family size was six members. More than half of their children were not enrolled in any school. In 18 percent of the families, women were the sole income earners. A majority of the women belonged to the landless rural artisan community who, until two generations ago, worked as weavers, cobblers, or leather-workers. Historically, they have been oppressed by the higher caste power structure—they are the dalits. They had left their village homes because of poverty and arrived in the thriving textile city of Ahmedabad, where they made their homes in city slums and searched for jobs.

The working conditions of rag pickers are hazardous. By constantly handling acid bottles, electrical wire, nails, glass, dirty paper, and cloth with their bare hands, they expose themselves to innumerable health risks. Skin diseases, eczema, and breathlessness are their complaints, as is chronic pain in their back, legs, neck, and shoulders. "I am exhausted before I start my work," is a rag picker's common complaint. Recently, a crude pipe bomb exploded in the hands of a rag picker and severed her arm. "Those who handle dust live a life worth dust," laments Dhooliben, whose very name means dust. Since most of the rag-picking community is dalit, caste prejudice, in addition to the lowly status of their work, increases their sense of worthlessness.

Prices of recyclable raw materials fluctuate from month to month and area to area, depending on the whim of the dealer and the supply of scrap imported from foreign countries. The women, however, accept whatever price their junk dealer offers.

Today, one kilo of waste paper sells at 3.50 rupees, carton boxes at 2.50 rupees, thick plastic bags at 5 rupees, plastic toys at 5 rupees, iron scrap at 4 rupees, and 1 kilo of hair sells at 100 rupees. The plastic from mineral water bottles sells at 2 rupees per kilo, while the bottle lids fetch anywhere from 5 to 35 rupees. This is because there is a thriving industry that refills these bottles with ordinary tap water and passes it off as mineral water. Unlike earlier decades, there is less paper in the garbage, and plenty of plastic. Today, in the first years of the new millennium, the women can earn approximately 500 rupees a month; in the late 1970s they made 200 rupees—inadequate income in both cases.

Two rag pickers—Dahiben from Girdharnagar and Chanchalben from Raikhad—took me to their communities on a summer day in 1980. We held meetings in the afternoons, when the women came home to sort their collection. I found the women to be open and surprisingly outspoken, their individual diffidence giving way to their collective eagerness to welcome change. Word spread in the communities so fast that, within a year, rag pickers formed a significant portion of SEWA's membership, led by Chanchalben. Also, by now, I had a new colleague—Ranjanben—to help with organizing rag pickers in other parts of the city.

Anjana was appointed to organize their union, a job she did with great dedication. She eventually left SEWA when she was appointed to the post of a government labor officer. Despite our loss, we were glad to have a voice in the labor bureaucracy.

With the help of TLA's contacts in the textile mills, one of the first things SEWA did was to convince the mills to allow our rag-picking members to pick paper and other waste directly from the factory floor and offices. While the managers in the mills had no problem with giving us access, in reality, the plan was tough to put into action. We found that an informal network for claiming garbage was already in place among some factory workers and their supervisors. They put up a brief but unexpected fight. Although SEWA women did finally get access, I was reminded never to underestimate the power of invisible vested interests.

Sorting garbage at a city dump. (Amit Dave)

Such an arrangement with the mills helped a few of the women, but what of the others? Demand from other women for "office work"—collecting waste from offices—was increasing. But by 1980, the mills were all facing hard times and their production was declining. As a result, scrap from mills declined considerably. According to the mill owners, the mills were dying out because of increased production costs; others felt the reasons were more complicated and perhaps lay in an unwillingness to invest and update their machinery. But by 1990, sixty mills had completely closed down, rendering more than 125,000 textile workers—almost all men—jobless.

With such fierce competition and few new jobs in sight, we found unemployed men of the family sitting and smoking at the doorsteps of our members' homes, nursing hopes of yet another industry job in the near future. In the meantime, though, the burden of supporting the family fell on the shoulders of the women. The poorest among them, having no capital and no marketable skills, were resorting to rag picking from roads to make a living. Chanchalben said, "Since rag picking is our lot in life, we accept it. But we cannot accept the low prices for the waste. That, we will fight for."

In order to get a better price for the waste, the women decided to side-step the middleman—the dealer. The demand was for "our own *pitha*" (godown). By setting up a cooperative that functioned like a dealership, the waste could be sorted and graded better, and the women would get better prices. The women needed a large enough space in the slums to sort and store, but none was readily available. Then one of the women leaders came to the front and offered her backyard for the purpose, at no cost to the members. These were rapid and exciting developments—the women's initiative and enthusiasm was gearing into action. Women bought shares and launched a new cooperative.

But SEWA's inexperience at starting an economic unit eventually led to dismal failure. The women's leader herself caused the most damage. With a thriving business in the backyard, it did not take long for her and her husband to set themselves up as middlemen—and corrupt ones at that. The other women had just substituted one dealer for another—a worse one. Quarrels and complaints began mounting, and our efforts at sorting the issues were complicated by the fact that the women were all from the same caste and most were related to each other in some way or another. Even a fair dissolution of the cooperative was difficult—the money from the group's bank account disappeared. Most of the members lost their share contribution and understandably turned bitter and hostile to the union. It also created rifts among the members and their families—even a wedding was called off. The experience cast dark shadows on the credibility of the union.

This failure was one of SEWA's major learning experiences. The planning, the checks and balances, the fair distribution, and proper implementation systems all require disciplined teamwork, and that important groundwork was crucial before any economic venture could be launched. I was also touched by the fact that despite the breach of trust, the women did not give up hope. It was time to explore other options.

For a long time, the women had an eye on the overflowing wastepaper bins in government offices. The white paper trash from a single office building could feed many families. So we turned our attention to the government offices, requesting permission to collect their trash. Our letters, however, did not receive any serious attention.

Meanwhile, SEWA's membership of rag pickers was increasing. We held a series of meetings in their neighborhoods to explore the women's options by learning about their latent skills, their inclination to learn new skills, and their level of motivation. What emerged at these exploratory meetings was quite interesting.

Those women who came from weaving communities in rural areas had an interest in reviving their weaving skills. Others preferred to get into domestic or institutional cleaning work. Some wanted to learn new skills, like making file folders and other office stationery from recycled paper. Yet the majority wanted to continue collecting waste from roads and public places; they just wanted a better price for their waste. They were afraid of any new uncertainty, as they were the poorest.

We noted that the women, who were all from the dalit community, still maintained a hierarchy within their own ranks—weavers considered themselves superior to cobblers, and they both felt superior to the *bhangi*—the cleaners. Despite great efforts to break down and commingle the various subcastes, in the end, the women preferred the company of their own community. In the early stages of organizing, this kind of insularity is fairly common, but eventually, as women become aware of the failures and successes of other cooperatives, barriers begin to break down and they begin to see other women as co-workers and sisters to sympathize and empathize with. This transformation cannot be forced; it has to undergo an internal process of realization—slow, but essential.

By enlisting the help of existing government training and support structures like the State Weaving Centre, the SEWA women received training to upgrade their weaving skills. They formed a cooperative—*mandali*—called *Vijay*, meaning victory, and began producing shirt fabrics for the open market. They could raise enough money to build their own shed in their slum neighborhood.

The younger lot of rag pickers and their daughters received training at a government polytechnic in making office stationery from new and recycled paper. The women made envelopes from scrap paper for office use, and for years now, they have been supplying government offices with files and stationery. They named their cooperative Gitanjali.

The cleaners named their cooperative Saundarya, which means beauty. The women received training in professional cleaning methods and proper product use. They were encouraged to use aprons and gloves, which they initially found amusing. Their cooperative gets contracted by large institutions to clean grounds and offices.

The majority of rag pickers who preferred rag picking formed a co-operative called Sujata, which, because of its size, later split into two. Unfortunately, one of them is defunct today.

Manekben Dhulabhai, an active member of the Saundarya cooperative, was a widow who worked hard to put her only son through high school and university. She was looking for an educated bride for her son, a girl who would be willing to make her home in a poor family, and she found her in Manjula, a young girl from her own cast who was studying in the first year of college. Manjula wanted a career in teaching.

Not long after the engagement, Manjula saw her future mother-in-law, Manekben, on the street, balancing a large rag picker's bag on her back. Manjula was taken aback. She had no idea that her mother-in-law was a rag picker. What worried her even more was that after marriage she too would be asked to go rag picking. Her dreams of becoming a teacher would come to nothing, despite her year of college. Her mother, however, had no sympathy for her feelings. She said, "All honest work is good work. Don't give yourself airs just because you've had some education." Despite her fears, Manjula got married.

Manekben set out for the streets every morning, but never asked Manjula to go with her. After about a month of marriage, Manekben brought Manjula to the SEWA office. The mandali had received a contract to clean the National Institute of Design (NID) and was conducting interviews to assign positions. Manjula was impressed by the beautiful grounds and buildings of NID but could not quite digest the idea of working as a cleaner there. Her husband had not found a job despite his education and had started selling steel cutlery and tableware from a pushcart in the market. So, setting aside her dreams of getting a "table-chair" job, she joined the new cleaning team with a good spirit.

Within a year, Manjula became pregnant and quit her work at NID. Her team members, however, wanted her back. A few months after delivery, Ratanben, the team supervisor, came to Manjula's house and offered her a supervisory assignment at another institution—the Physical Research Laboratory. Manjula hesitated, but the president of the cooperative, Hiraben, insisted. "We don't want to lose you, Manjula. You are smart and educated, and we all want you working with us." Touched by the women's faith in her abilities and education, Manjula returned to work. She put a lot of effort in organizing and maintaining efficiency at the work sites. Her leadership skills blossomed. Manjula was considered a good supervisor and an excellent spokesperson for her mandali.

In 1990, Manjula was chosen by her mandali to participate in a workshop in Germany. She was part of a larger group of SEWA women who were invited to share their experiences as self-employed workers. Unfortunately, her experience in Germany was cut short by the illness of two of her colleagues, whom she had to accompany home.

In 1991, the mandali appointed Manjula as manager of the Saundarya Cooperative. Within six years, Manjula earned her "table-chair" job. With that, she started intensive management training under Harshaben, a senior SEWA organizer. Her job was to keep accounts, make payments, buy and maintain all cleaning equipment, meet potential clients, present quotations, and run a 300-women strong mandali as efficiently as possible. She was up to the challenge.

The progress and problems of the Saundarya mandali are typical to any growing cooperative. New members receive training in cleaning services at a steady rate, but the cooperative has to work hard to place them. Under contract, the women clean several institutions, banks, and shopping complexes. Some teams work in apartment buildings, collecting garbage from individual homes and cleaning common spaces like the staircases and the compound.

Typically, the women work in teams of two or three, for two to three hours at a time. The women who clean offices are required to finish their work before the offices open for business. But that is easier said than done. Most of the women live in slums at the edge of town, far from the office buildings in wealthier neighborhoods across the river. Some walk ninety minutes each morning to get to work, while others rely on municipal buses that cost money and never run direct services between rich and poor neighborhoods. As a result, the women have trouble keeping to their schedules. They have been looking into operating a bus service of their own, a sort of "Saundarya Express" for commuting to work, but the cooperative needs more resources to make that a reality.

Initially, when the jobs included toilet cleaning and sweeping the grounds with a long broom, some women refused to do the work, calling it *"bhangi"* work. But when they saw that their toilet-cleaning, broom-wielding sisters were just as well paid for their work, it did not take long for them to step in when there was an empty slot. There are still Saundarya ladies and Toilet ladies, but increasingly, the distance between them is decreasing. The gloves and aprons help. "Just as the police has his uniform, and a nurse has hers, we too have our *olakh*. I have no problem with the uniform. It keeps my sari clean. Besides, earlier the officers would not drink a glass of water if we offered it because we were considered dirty, but these apron and gloves have somehow changed the *officewalla's* attitude toward us!"

Saundarya has diversified its activities, taking up small temporary jobs to meet the demands of the market. The wedding season keeps them busy—dressed in clean uniforms, the women clean and decorate the reception area with garlands, serve food and water to the wedding party, and help with the washing up. Saundarya also takes on the tasks of cleaning public swimming pools, baths, and toilets in public gardens. One team specializes in private house cleaning, another in hotel maid services. They are now constructing a website to market their diverse services.

After initial success, the nascent mandali received a major setback in the form of a lawsuit. How can a group of poor, self-employed women coming together to provide a simple service like cleaning be a threat to anyone? And yet, there has been a concerted effort by the employees' union at the institutes to keep the women from establishing a presence.

The legal argument made by the employees' union was that the members of the Saundarya cooperative have undertaken cleaning work in the institution on the basis of a contract, and that means the women are the "employees" of the cooperative, as well as the institution. While we want the court to recognize the cooperative as an entity, with a collective joint ownership as shareholders, who take joint responsibility in distributing the risks, both in profit or loss. The members of the cooperative are not on the payroll of the institution that they clean or of the cooperative itself. Only Saundarya as a cooperative is responsible to the institution and vice versa. So the question of proving any employer-employee relationship is out of question. The employees' union was afraid that union jobs in the institution would decrease.

This case has made the rounds of the Labor Court, the High Court, and the Supreme Court! If the courts do not accept the validity of the cooperative as an entity having the right to negotiate on behalf of its members, the future of all labor cooperatives will be seriously threatened. This is not an issue of wages—fair wage standards have already been met—this is a fight over fundamental concepts of labor.

Manjula's hands were full with trips to lawyers and courts. The number of institutional clients declined. No one wanted to be caught in the middle of a legal labor battle. The 1999 Government Resolution exempting women's cooperatives from the tender system was withdrawn, and the cooperative was forced to submit tenders for contracts to clean and to collect garbage.

In order to undermine SEWA's efforts to provide fair wages to its members, other contractors often quote very low rates for cleaning. "But we cannot," says Manjula. "Our cooperative secures at least the minimum wage, if not more, for our members."

For the Saundarya cooperative, the number of client institutions, members, and their income has been fluctuating since 1999. During the court cases, the demand for Saundarya's services decreased. It has since picked up, but increasingly, the institutions have been charging high fees for their tender form—ranging from 200 to 500 rupees—and asking for a deposit ranging from 10,000 to 50,000 rupees depending on the status of the client, which also includes the Government of India. "If we are asking for work, we need to fill up those forms and deposit the money, but when I apply to several clients, it means blocking off big amounts of money which our mandali cannot afford to do," says Manjula.

In the meantime, for old timers like Ratanben and Diviben, rag picking off the road is concurrent with such cooperative efforts. The women still collect and take in their recyclables to the dealer for cash. The dealer, however, is not as pleased with them, mostly because the women no longer borrow money from him or entrust their surplus with him for "safety." As members of the SEWA bank—which is also a cooperative—the women have savings accounts. Ratanben has about 10,000 rupees invested in a long-term fixed deposit scheme that pays higher interest, but Diviben finds it difficult to save or borrow much because she is old and supports her mentally retarded daughter. However, both earn a 15–percent dividend from their SEWA Bank shares every year.

I have often thought of taking over an empty factory building of one of Ahmedabad's closed mills and establishing a campus where the industries that engage the poor self-employed women can come together. It would house facilities for research, product design, storage, processing, financial services, and training in skill development; services related to building market infrastructure for every industry; and direct links to the mainstream markets of the country. The campus would have a library and childcare and health care centers for the women. The recycling industry would play a significant role on campus.

Recycling has an enormous capacity to generate income-earning opportunities. Here lies the opportunity to link the formal and informal sectors of the workforce in one industry. City plans need to recognize the enormous services provided by the rag pickers in keeping the city clean and integrate them into a fair, equitable system. Historically, every time an industry modernizes and formalizes, the women working in it as part of the informal sector get pushed out, and the formal sector, dominated by men, steps in to reap the benefits.

The rag picker picks recyclables from the garbage, sorts them into broad categories, and sells them to a dealer. The scrap dealer further sorts, cleans, packs, and sells the material to small-scale units and factories that process and prepare new raw material. This material is sold to manufacturing units, which are part of the formal sector. They in turn produce new products for the market from the recycled stuff. This is typical of most industries in India—more than half the production process, which is labor-intensive, is done by low-paid labor in the informal economy before it even reaches a factory. By recognizing every worker at every stage of the production process as integral to the industry and the economy, we can begin to build equitable, democratic, and participatory systems that are key to eliminating poverty.

3

Chindi and Garment Stitchers

Chindi Stitchers

In the late 1970s, Ahmedabad was the largest trade center for chindi, which are scrap strips of fabric two to eight inches in length—byproducts of the textile manufacturing process. Every year, some 3,500,000 kilos of chindi came out of the mills, while another 200,000 kilos were discarded by powerloom factories and processing houses that paid contractors to clear the waste from their premises.[1] Calcutta, the largest producer of children's clothes in India, bought the best quality chindi from the stock. About a fifth of the chindi was used as rags for cleaning machines, tools, and other factory equipment. The used, dirty, oily chindi, called *daghi chindi*, was also sold, but to small, local traders who in turn sold it by the kilo to the poor *khol* makers of Dariapur. A khol is a quilt cover made by joining pieces of chindi together.

Initially the mills paid contractors to remove the chindi from the mills, and then they started to give it away for free before the 1960s. By the 1960s, chindi was sold—its price ranged from 1 to 4 rupees per kilo. In the 1970s, it hovered for years at 4 rupees a kilo and then jumped to 11 rupees a kilo in the 1980s. According to the Ahmedabad Association of Chindi Traders,

---

1. Lalita Krishnaswamy. "Rags in a Revolution." Ahmedabad, India: Self-Employed Women's Association. Unpublished paper.

khols were in big demand during the 1980s. An average middle-level trader kept about a million khols in stock, supplying traders from Gujarat, as well as neighboring Rajasthan and Madhya Pradesh. It was a thriving, profitable business with very little risk. As the chindi industry grew, and with it the demand for chindi, prices began to rise.

The daghi chindi khols were in greater demand than ever because they were very cheap. At 7 to 10 rupees a khol, even the poor could afford them. Although a khol is a quilt cover, its users are generally too poor to stuff any cotton or cloth between the layers to turn it into an actual quilt. In the hilly areas of the Panchmahals and Dungarpur, the poor stuff their khols with old newspapers to keep warm. In Ahmedabad, a khol is an all-purpose article, used as a bedspread, a sleeping bag, a floor covering, a storage sack, or even a shawl.

The khol producers are just as poor as the khol purchasers. In the 1970s, about 3,000 women, mostly Muslim, living in the inner-city area of Dariapur, stitched these khols. The traders supplied the chindi by weight to the women to take home. The women would wash the oily strips in boiling water mixed with soda powder and kerosene, dry them, iron them, sort them according to size, and then finally stitch the chindi into a khol on a sewing machine in their one-room homes. One khol would contain anywhere from sixty to ninety rag pieces. It took two days to make a dozen khols. In the evenings, the women would carry the stitched khols to the trader, where on average four people processed the finished khols: one weighed them, noting the deficit from the previously sold raw material; a second checked the quality; a third calculated the amount of payment due and handed over the cash to a fourth person, who would then pay the women. The going rate was 60 paise per khol. Of course, after weighing the khols, any deficit in weight due to trimming was subtracted from this payment. A woman returned home with 7.20 rupees for a dozen khols. On the way home, she had plenty of opportunity to think about how much she had subsidized her trader in the cost of production. By using her own workplace and providing for her own sewing machine, electricity, vessels for washing, fuel for boiling the water, cleaning products, and even the thread for sewing—all of which she paid with her own money—she was, in fact, subsidizing the trader. In reality, her actual income was minuscule. No wonder the khol business was so profitable for the traders. However, because the women stitchers produced items from waste for the use of the poor—that is, the producers, the consumers, and the waste material were

Mother and daughter stitching chindi into khols on old machines.
(SEWA Academy)

all part of the informal economy—the chindi industry remained invisible
to the mainstream labor movement.

Dariapur was named after Daria Khan, a favorite noble of Ahmedshah
Badshah, the founder and ruler of Ahmedabad some six centuries ago.
Dariapur has a mixed population of Hindus and Muslims, rich and poor.
Many of the Muslims living in Dariapur were related. This was the center
of the chindi business, crowded with chindi godowns, khol shops, and the
homes of both the traders and the workers. While the men in Dariapur
worked in textile mills or drove auto rickshaws, their women stitched khols
at home. Almost every home had at least one sewing machine. Khol shops
lined the main road, called Jordan Road; the godowns were at the back of
the shops, and the traders lived with their families upstairs above their
khol shops. During the day, the traders conducted business in their shops
and received the deliveries of stitched khols and chindi after the evening
supper.

Zaidaben was brought to Dariapur as a bride, from Karnataka. Although she spoke some Urdu, she had trouble understanding the people

in Dariapur. Everyone spoke Gujarati, and their Urdu had a peculiar local flavor. But she liked her new home and the neighborhood because compared to where she came from, there were fewer restrictions on women's movements here. The Muslim women in Dariapur walked about without a *burkha*, talked loudly, shopped on their own, went to movies with their husbands, and worked on sewing machines at home.

Zaidaben did not know sewing, nor had she worked for an income before, but she was now keen to learn. Her mother-in-law stitched clothes for the entire family. Every few days, she would go to a textile mill with a group of neighborhood women to pick up a bundle of chindi for 5 rupees. She would wash and stitch these by hand into clothes for herself and the family. It was said that there was a time in Dariapur when everyone wore clothing made of chindi, hand stitched by the women. Although her husband often told her such stories about the neighborhood, Zaidaben sensed that her husband would not encourage her working in the chindi business.

But during the day, she often helped her friend and neighbor Hussainaben with cleaning and sorting the chindi. Next, she learned to use a sewing machine. Slowly, and rather surreptitiously, she began making khols on her own. Sensing her inexperience, the trader determined her rate at 30 paise per khol. She was glad to be bringing in some money, little though it was. Now she was all set to work, except that she did not have her own machine. She went to her neighbor's and took turns using her rented machine.

The day she delivered twenty dozen khols to her trader and received payment in hand, the injustice of it all hit her. "Only this much money for my days of labor! I worked so hard and here I do not have enough to take a sick child to the doctor!" Then she wondered why she was surprised at her wage rate, when she should be glad to earn just about anything at all. Moreover, a good portion of her earnings would have to be handed over to her neighbor, on whose machine she had stitched the khols.

Like Zaidaben, a majority of the stitchers worked on rented machines. The cut it took from their small, hard-earned income was painful but unavoidable. She turned to her friend Hussainaben for sympathy, and the two women gave each other courage. Both decided to muster up the courage and ask the trader for a raise. The following day, when they went to pick up their bundle of dirty chindi from the trader, they asked for a raise. Sensing the women's determination, the trader decided to give in, and the women succeeded in getting a ten paisa rate increase. However, as they were leaving, the trader turned to Hussainaben and said, "Next time, don't bring such Solapuri women to my shop." He was implying that non-Gujarati women were outsiders and should not have high expectations. Earning less pay for her labor, having no machine of her own, and being treated as an outsider in her home was too much for Zaidaben to bear. She talked to her husband that evening and received plenty of sympathy. He offered to use some of their savings to buy her a secondhand sewing machine. Zaidaben felt terribly lucky that she now owned her means of production, though she still had to rely on a wage rate arbitrarily decided by the trader.

Hussainaben's brother Shekhubhai, an elected representative in TLA, came to my office in 1977 and talked sympathetically about the chindi stitchers' plight. I went with him to meet the women in Dariapur. He showed me the chindi godowns and the shops. The first woman to greet me in the neighborhood was Karimaben, a short, dark, bespectacled widow of middle age who invited me to meet with a large group of women stitchers. Karimaben was a good spokesperson for the chindi workers—she knew them well, and she could talk clearly about the issues they all faced.

In order to better understand the problems of the chindi workers, we decided to conduct a survey in the seven *poles*, or streets, where most of the khols were stitched. Karimaben had no patience for a survey. She complained, "We all know exactly what the problem is. Let me tell you that I spend more on a khol than I earn from making it. That is the problem." It was obvious that an increase in the wage rate was the main issue. Fortunately, Renana Jhabvala came to SEWA at this critical juncture. She immediately began working on chindi workers' issues, and we discovered that Karimaben, Renana, and I worked well as a team.

We insisted on proceeding methodically and conducting a survey with the help of Karimaben and Hussainaben. Surveys are invaluable and have served SEWA well over the years. They help us gain a thorough understanding of the issues before taking any action, and the process helps us identify potential leaders in the community.

The survey findings were reported to the chindi workers at a large meeting. Then the women met in several small groups in one *pole* after the other, mustering courage to speak frankly and openly about the wages they received and the problems they faced. These meetings did not go unnoticed, and there were attempts to break them up with a few well-aimed stones. Undeterred, the women had heard enough from each other to know that their demand for a rate increase was justified and overdue.

Finally, as members of SEWA, the women sent a letter to the President of the Association of Chindi Traders listing their demands. A copy was also sent to the Labor Commissioner's office. Six hundred women members demanded that their wage rate be increased from Rs. 0.60 to 1.25 rupees per khol. If the women were surprised by their own bravado, one can imagine how stunned the traders were. An action committee was formed to meet with the different traders every day to discuss our demands. The traders listened to the delegates and gave them hope. Encouraged, the women waited for weeks for a positive outcome, but none came. Instead, one evening, we learned that the general body of the chindi traders' association had resolved to stop giving any work to SEWA members.

We pursued our meetings with the traders more vigorously but they did not budge. Instead, they accused SEWA of creating unrest among the poor in Dariapur. "The children on streets ran after us calling names. I could not complain to any one, not even in my own home," said Zaidaben. The family members supported the women's demands but did not approve of them attending meetings, going to SEWA's office, or moving about in the streets to talk to traders. "As soon as our husbands went to work, we would lock the house and run to attend meetings. Those meetings were like food to us during our days of unemployment. Our men would say, 'You have no work, just meetings to fill your belly with.' But we swallowed all such criticism," said Zaidaben.

One Friday, after the evening *namaz*, we met in an open space behind a mosque, pouring out our frustrations. After some debate, we made two decisions: we would start a production unit for the most needy, and we would be louder in our demands. The first action had to wait. For the second, we decided to hold a rally on the streets of Dariapur. At noon the following Sunday, when people were resting after lunch, the women of Dariapur would gather on the street and shout into megaphones: "*Hamari maange poori karo!*," "*Sava rupia leke rahenge!*" "Meet our demands!" and "No rest till we get our rupee and a quarter!" But on that Sunday, Karimaben found herself standing on the street with only a handful of women. Most of the women stayed at home, and even Zaidaben did not come. However, the event did not remain a secret in Dariapur.

On Monday, the president of the association called me to say that they were "never" against the demands of poor women! "We are ready to pay

1 rupee per khol." That evening, an agreement was signed between SEWA and the traders' association. The women went back to work, but the agreement was never honored. The traders did not pay the agreed rate of one rupee to any of the women.

The issue of piece-rate work is extremely important and has not been adequately addressed by policy makers. The employer determines the piece rate in such a way that he gets maximum profit at minimum cost. As long as the workers do not have collective strength to speak up for fair rates, employers have the advantage. Another advantage is that labor laws do not cover economic activities of piece-rate workers.

In India, the government lists various trades that fall under the Minimum Wages Act. But in a country where there are as many trades as there are people, such lists make little sense. Stitching, for example, is absent from the official list and so is not covered under the Schedule of the Minimum Wages Act. Even in trades where the act does apply, enforcement is lacking. Nor does India have an omnibus kind of national minimum wage that can be applied to workers, whether listed in the schedule or not. Labor laws are implemented through the government machinery of the Labor Department, whose understanding of the unorganized sector labor is very limited. The department's time is mostly consumed by industrial disputes in the state. In spite of the overwhelming numbers of self-employed workers, their issues remain invisible and unheard. Under such conditions, it is not unfair to question the relevance of a Labor Department and its labor laws.

Despite our reservations, we decided to file a formal complaint to the Labor Department. We felt that as citizens, we must be willing to make government departments answerable to the people, however slow, tedious, and frustrating the process may be. The women elected a five-person committee to accelerate the action. The committee prepared a complete list of which stitchers worked for which traders and the rates each one was paid.

The Labor Department called innumerable meetings with the workers' representatives and the traders, but the traders remained absent from key meetings in order to stymie progress. Negotiations continued for months without result, while in the meantime, one by one, the traders stopped giving work to the women, especially those for whom khol stitching was their only source of livelihood. The traders also singled out those active in the movement. SEWA, as a union, did not have any victims' fund to support the suffering women, so it started a small khol production unit as a means of support. The initial capital of 3,000 rupees came from the TLA. Such an arrangement provided a temporary breather. However, it posed a problem for us during negotiations. The traders repeatedly argued that SEWA itself was a trader just like them.

A compromise agreement to pay 1 rupee per khol was finally reached between the traders and SEWA in the presence of the Labor Commissioner. However, in practice, the rate varied between Rs. 0.80 to 1.00 rupee and even this small victory was short-lived. Just as the wage rate increased, the price of thread went up, making the rate increase redundant. Since the women paid for the thread with their own money, this was a major setback. The price of thread continued to rise, so the women felt that another wage rate increase was called for. The khol trade was thriving, and the families of the traders were doing well. Many were building additions onto their houses. On Jordan Road, two new fancy restaurants serving western dishes were opened. Weddings were celebrated more lavishly than before in Dariapur. There was money to be made in the chindi business.

In 1980, the state government levied a sales tax on chindi. The chindi traders were very agitated and lobbied with the authorities in the finance department to remove the tax. Their argument was that the new tax will bring the chindi production to a standstill and thousands of poor women will starve without work!

We were wide awake to this opportunity to assert our demands before the finance ministry. We pleaded that until the traders fulfilled the workers' demand for a rate increase, the tax should not be removed. Rarely does it happen, but to our good luck, Sanat Mehta, the finance minister, also happened to be a very senior labor leader. He tactfully put his weight on the side of labor. The traders finally agreed and started paying 1.25 rupees per khol to all the workers.

The word of our triumph spread to other parts of the city where the women stitched garments from chindi. A SEWA survey revealed that in the inner-city area of Shahpur, women stitched children's garments from chindi and in areas like Bapunagar, Amraiwadi, and Saraspur, women stitched petticoats from cut pieces—yet another type of textile scrap. Two leading chindi stitchers from Dariapur entered the lanes of Shahpur to organize the women garment workers.

The khol-making unit of SEWA served the victimized workers well to a certain extent. These khols were sold in a shop SEWA rented in the khol market. Selling them was not a problem, but procuring the raw chindi material from the mills was very difficult. The traders were hand in glove with the mills' sales departments. Although the TLA supported us and contacted the mills on our behalf, the vested interests among lower management proved to be more cunning. The price our unit was charged for the chindi was higher, the quality lower, and the quantity always in question. Pieces of bricks and dirty blankets would be found in the chindi bag. Zaidaben once found a rusty dagger in it! The opposition our small production unit faced in the chindi market in the 1980s was certainly fierce.

Yet the volume of business at the khol production unit was growing. Since it is SEWA's policy to not encourage any kind of commercial activities by the union, the khol unit was registered as the Sabina Cooperative in July 1982. The Sabina Co-op not only served the needs of the victimized members who were playing a leading role in the union movement, but it generated full-time work at higher stitching rates even during the monsoon months. As an outstanding, financially viable economic venture, Sabina received the first prize for excellence from the Gujarat State Cooperative Department. Many stitchers wanted to join the co-op and leave the traders, which was the surest way to pressure them to pay their workers well. The Sabina Co-op was made a member of the Chindi Price Committee in the Textile Corporation by the government. This was the heyday of the chindi trade and the highest visibility enjoyed by the chindi workers.

An old woman called Bismillah, whom everyone called Khala, was a regular but quick visitor at the Sabina shop. In the afternoon, while her husband was taking a nap, Khala would buy good-quality chindi from the shop and then go from house to house, selling it for a small profit. Before long, someone informed her husband about Khala's ventures. Her husband scolded her severely and told her to stay at home where she belonged. But the following day, Khala was back, making her rounds of business. When she returned home, she found her husband waiting with a stick in his hand. He was so furious that he hit her several times until the neighbors intervened on her behalf. After a few days, when she had recovered from her injuries, Khala was back at the Sabina shop. Thereafter, the Sabina sisters accompanied her back home, although nobody knew whether her husband had stopped beating her. A few days later, the women at the Sabina Co-op offered Khala a job at the weighing machine for a monthly salary of 500 rupees. No one knew if Khala convinced her husband to let her go to work, but she arrived every day, her face full of smiles and fear.

After a few months, the women saw a strange sight. Khala's husband began coming to the shop at noon every day, carrying a hot tiffin lunch for his wife!

Like Khala, other women going out to work faced similar reactions from their husbands and family, to varying degrees of disapproval. While SEWA does not intervene directly in the domestic matters of its members, we encourage the women to provide steady support to other sisters in the trade, particularly by strengthening their work security. Having economic security generates a gradual inner strength in the woman, which allows her to face and sort out her domestic problems with confidence.

With Zaidaben managing the Sabina Co-op and Karimaben serving as the vice president of SEWA, the economic interests of the chindi workers were well represented at various places. The women gained the respect of their community, the chindi traders' association, and their own men. For SEWA, this was one of the first attempts at a joint action of union and cooperatives as a way of bringing about change.

But as the years passed, the textile mills began closing down one by one, and without the mills, there was no chindi. By the 1990s, only ten mills had survived, and those were no longer producing cotton textiles. Synthetic-fiber chindi is tough to stitch and is of limited use. The Chindi Traders' Association was disbanded and both the traders and the khol stitchers lost their livelihoods. The Mukhtiar brothers—the traders with whom we had constantly negotiated for wage increases—closed down their khol shop and opened a long-distance telephone booth in a cold drink parlor.

Despite these changes across the city, the membership of SEWA in Dariapur remained unchanged. The SEWA Bank activities were thriving, and the Sabina shop became the hub for financial services including savings, credit, insurance, and housing. Young Dariapur girls came to SEWA for training in patchwork and cutting readymade garments. The Sabina shop still survives, but on a no-profit/no-loss basis. Zaidaben bought a small flat with her savings and a loan from SEWA Bank. But her leadership did not blossom further over the years; she stopped at being a good accountant and an amiable manager. Renana was elected the Secretary of SEWA.

As garments replaced khols, gradually, the sons of old traders with enough capital shifted their businesses to the various processes of the modern hosiery and garment industry like cutting, stitching, interlocking, pressing, and packing. They set up small factories serving big companies,

Stitching garments in her new home. (Shreya Shah)

mostly employing men and some girls from Dariapur. Electric machinery has replaced the half-wheel treadle machines. The garment industry has spread widely in the slums of the working-class areas of the city. SEWA's membership is now composed of garment workers as well.

As I see it, injustice has three faces. First, there is the face of injustice that the women see for themselves—that of the direct exploiter. That face may be of a hard-hitting policeman, a cold-hearted employer, or a vicious contractor. The system that supports the direct exploiter is the second level of injustice, which includes government agencies and the legal structure. The women do not see it as readily until they gain awareness. The Labor Department is designed to protect workers' interests, but it gets corrupted by the employers and traders and often ends up helping them circumvent the law. The municipality treats the poor vendors as criminals. The courts take years to give judgments, and more often than not, they are not supportive of the economic activities of the poor, especially those in the informal economy. All this exploitation is made possible by injustice at the third and highest level—that of policy and law making. Narrow minds, vested interests, and a complete disconnect with the realities of the poor are responsible for policies that are outdated, irrelevant, impractical, unenforceable, and at times out and out exploitative. SEWA takes on the struggle against all three levels of injustice. Besides direct negotiations with employers, contractors, and the police, we also hold rallies, go on strike, and file court cases. Such actions are taken at every level, either simultaneously or sequentially to draw attention to the issue. Campaigns, workshops, studies, lobbying, advocacy, preparing for court cases, and making alliances are all part of the struggle. But fundamental to all these struggles is organizing itself. All actions—whether direct, legal, or at policy level—are useful only if the women themselves stand united as one.

The Garment Stitchers

Garment making is considered more respectable work than stitching chindi. Over the past three decades, we have found an increasing trend toward garment production in women's homes. During the chindi workers' struggles, we witnessed that the traders maintained their competitiveness in the market by lowering their labor cost, especially in labor-intensive industries like garment making. The employers push for home-based production so they can exploit the women's preference for working from home to their advantage.

The women of the Shahpur neighborhood in Ahmedabad who stitched children's garments from printed chindi were carefully following the Dariapur chindi workers' struggle for a wage increase. Zaidaben and Karimaben both had relatives in Shahpur who stitched baby clothes from chindi, so in 1986, with the help of their contacts, a survey of the lives and livelihoods of the self-employed garment stitchers was conducted. During the survey, we were heartened to discover middle-aged women, already restless with the existing situation and quite ready to get organized to bring change.

The survey findings were not surprising.[2] As many as 84 percent of the women earned less than 500 rupees a month. The production cost was borne by the workers. Wage rates ranged from 1.50 rupees per dozen

2. Paula Kantor. "Estimating Numbers in Household Industry: The Case of Home-Based Garment Makers in Ahmedabad." Ahmedabad, India. Unpublished manuscript, 1986.

for small garments to 10 rupees per dozen for bigger garments. After excluding the expenses incurred for the sewing machine, thread, electricity, home space, and commuting to the trader's shop, the women's earnings were an average of 300 rupees per month. Ninety percent of the women complained of pain in their feet, swollen legs, stiff backs, and sleeplessness. Most women had medical expenses for the ailments related to their occupation. Meanwhile, the manufacturers enjoyed a profitable business. Sixty-two percent of the women changed employers because of low wages and irregular work. Twenty-two percent owned their sewing machines after taking a loan from SEWA Bank, and 51 percent had their name listed in the employer's register. All the workers recognized the value of having an identity card or an attendance register. Forty-two percent were members of the SEWA union, and 48 percent had a bank account in SEWA Bank.

When SEWA was asked to set up several workers' education classes under a government labor department scheme, we saw a perfect opportunity to organize the garment workers and identify potential field leaders. By 1983, we had organized 3,906 frock and petticoat stitchers. While the chindi workers were more fearful, these women were ready to take up the struggle as soon as they joined SEWA.

SEWA put the demands of the women to increase wage rates before the employers, but got no response. We urged the Labor Commissioner's office to intervene. Labor inspectors visited the homes of the workers and took evidence from them regarding the wage rates being paid by their employers. The employers' work sites were also visited—some were even raided—but the government inspection yielded no results.

The employers were agitated in those days because the Gujarat government had increased the sales tax on ready-made garments. Like the Chindi Traders' Association, the garment employers also approached SEWA to lend support to them for a reduction in the tax increase, but SEWA kept silent. The employers, in protest against the government, closed down all their production units. The workers were without work for three months.

Then came the riots.

In 1985, many of the workers faced communal riots, and the Muslim areas were the worst hit. The women's homes were looted and burned. The SEWA Bank provided additional loans for sewing machines, while the SEWA union contributed relief and subsidy to rehabilitate their stitching work. Even still, SEWA went through very difficult times.

During the riots of 1985, our SEWA office was under threat. Different parts of our building were named after some of our deceased leaders—Soopa, Zora, Kapila. Our Hindu neighbors took objection to the name "Zora," a Muslim name. Historically, the present site of the SEWA office was the Diwan Wada—the residential quarters of the ministers during the Maratha rule in Ahmedabad. Our present-day neighbors are their descendants, and they are very proud of their heritage. Even before the riots, they had frequently raised objection to the Zora nameplate. Now, during the riots, a direct message came to us: "Take down your signboard, or face the consequences."

When the office opened at 10:00 A.M., I called a meeting and put the facts before the council. The Hindus, who were in the majority, said, "We should not succumb to such threats, otherwise tomorrow they will stop our Muslim members from entering SEWA." But the Muslim women disagreed. Rahmatben, a block printer and master craftswoman, who is fondly called Mami, said, "We have to be practical in such critical times. We must choose. Are we here to defend signboards or to defend people? Who cares about a signboard?" The other women said, "If we take down Zora, then Soopa and Kapila must also be taken down."

After the meeting, I was sitting in my office when Mami and Manjula brought the three boards in, prickly with nails and hooks. I felt defeated. Suddenly, from the window behind my chair, the women saw big black flames going up in the sky. Raikhad was burning! Jamalpur was bound to be next, I quickly thought, and Mami and some others lived there. Before the entire city was put under curfew, they had to be taken home safely. The police were no help. Who could help us? No one, other than our neighbors, could get the women past the rioting crowds. I requested help from the very youths next door who had wanted the Zora board taken down. They were taken aback. Despite the posturing, Mami and her Muslim sisters were people they knew and cared about. They promptly put our women into their jeeps and delivered them to their doorsteps in the heart of the Muslim neighborhood. In return, the women escorted the young Hindu men out of their angry mohalla to the main road.

The women do not have much respect for politicians, because they know that riots are essentially political. "Why is it that no sooner do we have a new government in place, we have riots?" Karimaben asked. "I think the riots are engineered by politicians to discredit and bring down the government of their opposition party." Nor do the women have much faith in the police.

To stop riots, the police impose curfews, but the curfew is an age-old enemy of poor women. They live in crowded localities, in one-room homes, where they have to be shut in with their elders, in-laws, children, infants, visitors, and even goats twenty-four hours a day, for days on end, under curfew orders. After midnight, the lights have to be turned off. The tension, the congestion, the heat, and fear build up under such pressure. "Curfew is worse than riots," the women all agree.

Dariapur remained under curfew for more than two months during the 1985 riots. One hot day, it became so unbearable under the prolonged curfew that Karimaben, then SEWA's vice president, stepped out of her home, gathered SEWA women living in her neighborhood, marched to the army officer on duty, and "asked" him to lift the curfew from Dariapur. Amazed at her audacity, the officer took her to speak to his chief. Whether her account of the people's suffering affected his decision or because he felt law and order had been satisfactorily restored, the curfew was indeed lifted from Dariapur that evening.

The city slowly started regaining normalcy, but it took more time to recover from the destruction of life and livelihoods. The garment employers slowly revived their business and started giving work to the women, but at a lesser rate.

India exports garments worldwide, and the garment industry engages a large number of workers in factories and an even larger number who work in their homes. Yet garment stitching is not listed in the Schedule of the Minimum Wages Act. It was high time for SEWA to demand an official minimum wage for garment workers from the Gujarat government. In SEWA, 1986 was entirely devoted to the minimum wage campaign. Members in other trades, particularly the bidi workers, lent their full support to the garment workers' struggle. Women in other trades know that their struggles are similar, if not the same, and they are quick to offer mutual support.

After constant meetings with employers, contractors, traders, and the labor department we gained strength and confidence in our abilities. Our negotiations with frock traders proved fruitful. The wage rate for a dozen frocks shot up from 2.50 to 7.50 rupees. The workers were so happy that they sent a thank you note to the employers! In high spirits, some women gave television interviews explaining the reality of their lives—the hard work and low income, and how just their demand was in asking for a wage increase. Everyone felt that receiving favorable support from the general public was essential to winning justly.

While our negotiations with local employers met with some success, we were also pursuing the minimum wage issue at the government level. A campaign for the inclusion of garment stitching in the Schedule of Minimum Wages Act was building up. A rally of about 3,000 women garment workers started in their own neighborhood. Karimaben led a rally of chindi workers from Dariapur, and the scene was worth watching. Here were Muslim women, dressed in their black burkhas, perched on a pedal rickshaw, with a megaphone in hand, calling their sisters to join the rally. Zaidaben commented later on all their high spirits: "It was the first time in my life that I raised my arm up, all the way up, in public! But once I did it, I lost my shyness. In fact, I enjoyed impressing upon the general public that we are so many!"

The rally ended at the Labor Commissioner's office. A member of the delegation submitted a memorandum asking for the following: minimum wage, identity cards, welfare schemes for childcare, health care, and school scholarships. Some women, like Karimaben, were so excited that they began to get loud and argumentative with the Labor Commissioner, and I had a hard time restraining them. Other workers lobbied vigorously, going in groups to meet the ministers in their offices. A group of 200 workers gathered outside the office where the Minimum Wages Advisory Committee was being held. Our efforts were successful. In December 1987, the Gujarat government finally announced minimum wages for garment workers. The women were surprised by the prompt response, and without wasting a minute, they showered the Labor Minister with flowers at his office in Gandhinagar. Unfortunately, the very next day, he withdrew his own announcement. So strong was the employers' pressure on him that he felt compelled to turn his back on labor. We were stabbed in the back.

"Insha Allah, in God's name, we'll try again!" the women said, and like that proverbial spider climbing the wall only to slip again and again, we picked ourselves up. We released the story of our betrayal to the press. Other trade unions also joined in our protests. For months, we met and lobbied, in groups, with members of the legislature, and with party leaders, and we handed out leaflets outside the State Legislative Assembly. A delegation of 2,000 SEWA members approached the Gujarat Chamber of Commerce and presented our case for establishing a minimum wage, and they did us the courtesy of listening attentively. By now, we were ready with a full-length survey of the readymade garments industry in Gujarat, conducted by a competent authority like the International Labor Organisation.

Eventually, in 1988, the Gujarat government issued a fresh notification for the garment stitchers reinstating the promised minimum wage of 15.50 rupees for a dozen petticoats, *baba* suits, and midi-frocks. It was good news indeed, but bad news soon followed in its wake. Employers began dismissing their workers. This is the other side of the coin in any labor struggle, when you succeed in your demand. Whenever the workers ask for a higher wage, they are victimized or dismissed. When work opportunities are scarce for women, they are afraid to press for their rights.

SEWA now took an aggressive stand by raising its demands for better wages, bonus payment, logbook entries, and a provident fund. The Labor Department issued a notice to each of the employers we listed. The 200 workers who had been discharged were reinstated. SEWA filed a case in the Labor Court on behalf of twenty-four women who were not reinstated. The employers remained absent from court and sought frequent adjournments to the hearing of the case. While the workers suffered unemployment and SEWA waited for the court's judgment, the employers changed their company names to avoid the court summons. SEWA appealed to the Gujarat High Court for justice toward workers. Members organized a *dharana* in front of the employers' shops. Our energies were being burned at both ends—local and legal.

Internally, a demoralizing incident occurred. During the litigation on wages rates for petticoat stitchers, one of the SEWA leaders was bribed by an employer to solicit information regarding our strategy in order to break our unity. When this was discovered, the members were furious and the woman was forced to resign from SEWA's executive committee. However, the damage to the unity of the women had already been done.

As invariably happens, the price of thread shot up as soon as the minimum wage notification was announced. The stitching rate for a dozen petticoats was 8 rupees, out of which the cost of thread rose from 2 to 4 rupees. So SEWA insisted that henceforth the supply of thread would have to come only from the employers. Finally, to accommodate the new price of thread, the rate of petticoat stitching was raised from 8 to 10 rupees and then 14 rupees per dozen. The discharged workers were reinstated at the new rate. Although SEWA has a tradition of celebrating every success, big or small, no one was in any mood to celebrate the reinstatement. The price of thread had risen yet again. The general feeling in SEWA was that we were doing nothing but treading water.

In 1995, the Labor Minister was pressed for an enforcement of the minimum wage law. Garment workers were included in the law on paper only. For the next two years, SEWA accompanied labor officers and worked jointly with them to conduct inspections in garment units and ensure that proper identity cards were issued, minimum wages were paid, an attendance register was being maintained, and the dues of the workers were being paid. Twenty thousand garment workers were now members of SEWA.

The number of garment stitchers taking loans from SEWA Bank surged as they sought to replace old sewing machines with new electric ones. Members were joining the Bank's insurance scheme. They were renovating their small houses, or buying houses in their neighborhood with SEWA housing loans.

The times were changing. During the 1990s, retail trade boomed, as did the garment industry. Production occurred in small factories as well as in homes. Both types of workers were paid on a piece-rate basis according to output, with no written contract between employers and workers. Demand for products like *salwar kameez, lengah,* fancy kids' wear, cushion covers, and *chania choli* dominated over frocks and petticoats in the market. Every month, SEWA Bank lent money for buying new machines or installing electric motors in the old ones to cope with the new demand.

In the beginning of 2000, a severe earthquake shook Gujarat. At the same time, the state's economy too suffered a shock. Again, in a changing economic scene influenced by liberalization and globalization, the world of the home-based workers underwent major changes. In September 2003, when I attended a SEWA garment workers' trade committee, I felt like that old spider again, struggling to climb a wall. A quick survey revealed that asset ownership had declined among the eighty-four members in the meeting. Only fifty-five women owned their sewing machines; the rest worked on rented ones, and only twenty-five worked on electric machines. The rent on sewing machines had risen from 50 to 150 rupees in five years. Sixty women were assisted in stitching by daughters younger than age fifteen. Sixty-three workers lived in rented houses, and the average net income was around 30 to 50 rupees per day. The legal minimum wage of

89.60 rupees per day was only a dream. The workers sighed, "Where is the work that we may demand wages?" One of them reported that in Revadi Bazar, out of eighty-four shops that sold petticoats, only nine or ten are open—the rest having closed down.

The problem garment workers face today is not merely that of exploitation. Locally, work availability has declined sharply since the city suffered communal violence in 2001. Muslims, who are predominantly home-based workers, have been affected the worst. The riots were so devastating that the entire city was paralyzed under a spell of fear, threat, and loss. The toll on the economic lives of the city's poor was enormous. The city's informal economy suffered losses amounting to approximately 179 crore rupees just in forty days' time, according to the Gujarat Institute of Development Research (GIDR) study. About 257,000 home-based workers—around 80 percent of the workers in manufacturing—were badly affected.[3]

This time, SEWA was a direct victim of violence and hatred. Out of 100,000 SEWA members in the city, 40,000—most of them Muslim—were in relief camps. Two live bombs were found on the steps of our building but, due to timely information, were later defused by the police. Two of SEWA's branch offices were burned down. We all began working in the five relief camps, maintaining health and sanitation and linking the women and their employers so they could resume earning. Five hundred sewing machines were put in the camps for producing garments that were sold in SEWA shops in the city. Work and income could to some extent distract the women's minds from the unspeakable horrors they had witnessed. The prime minister entrusted us with the rehabilitation of the widows and orphaned victims of the violence.

Over time, the women have returned to their homes—some repaired, some rebuilt. Some were not allowed to return by their landlords. Those who feared to return moved away to live with their own community in another part of the city. They have had difficulty finding work, far from their old neighborhoods.

Just as the industry seemed to be reviving, the employers stopped work for months in protest against a new value-added tax levied by the

3. Jeemol Unni. "Loss of Income among Informal Sector Workers in Ahmedabad During the Period 28 February to 8 April 2002." Ahmedabad, India: Gujarat Institute of Developmental Research. Unpublished report, 2002.

central government on industries. This was followed by a strike of truck drivers all over India that brought major industries in Gujarat to a standstill for months. There was work for six or seven days a month instead of an earlier twenty-day average. There was despair. It seemed that every macro policy affected the poor, self-employed women in one way or another.

A major problem for those living in rented houses is the attitudes of their landlords. To save on the cost of electricity, he controls the main switch, preventing the woman tenant from working late at night. "That is the only time I can work fast," says Faridaben, one of the committee members. "During the day, with my four children and an old man to attend to, I can hardly work."

The women are also angrier. "The indifferent attitude of my contractor angers me," said Zubedaben. "I have worked for him for so many years, yet I dare not ask him for anything. His response is, 'You are free to go where you can get more.' He knows I have nowhere to go. We continue to suffer in silence." Her old fighting spirit has gone. The stress of unemployment wears on everything in the women's lives. Amirjahan confides, "I beat my children when anything goes wrong"; while Sharifabibi admits, "I get very angry with my machine when it fails me at peak times." Zulekhaben becomes angry with her husband: "If he were earning enough, I would not have to work so hard. This is a do-or-die situation for me." And yet they find the strength to continue.

Manali, the head of SEWA union, has dealt with labor disputes for many long years. She has less faith in the legal structure than ever before. "In cases where I have dealt directly with employers through meetings and negotiations, they have brought some positive results. But in court cases, workers have mostly lost. Or they may have received some compensation or favorable orders, but ultimately they have lost their jobs." An understanding of the employers' capacity to pay the workers, combined with a willingness to approach amicably any disputes between employers and workers, are the basic elements for resolving labor disputes. Laws do not bring justice to the workers, so why do we resort to legal recourse again and again?

The only faith the women have is in their togetherness. The other day, Saira, the young secretary of the garment committee, was reporting to the members on new activities. She said that a newly appointed thread committee has successfully explored the possibility of buying thread in bulk directly from the manufacturers. They will collaborate with SEWA's rural embroiderers who were facing the same problem of the ever-rising cost of thread. A batch of young stitchers is being trained in sewing machine maintenance to better serve the stitching community. A housing committee has been set up to help those living in rented houses install separate electric meters in their homes, and SEWA Bank has begun providing financial services to them. Saira also reported that almost ninety-two riot widows have collaborated with the National Institute of Fashion Technology to create high-fashion garments. The prospect of developing their skills still excites the women. The spider climbs, falls, but does not lose hope. She is not alone.

4

Vendors

Three generations ago, Lakshmiben Teta's family grew melons and pumpkins on the Sabarmati riverbed and sold their produce in Manekchowk, Ahmedabad's vegetable market. They lived outside the walled city in Chamanpura, an area that has long since become a working-class slum. Farmers, weavers, potters, cobblers, and other producers from the neighboring villages came into the city to sell their wares. With the advent of textile mills and other industry in Ahmedabad, the river water had so many industrial effluents that it could no longer support crops. While the men looked for work in the textile mills, the women continued to sell vegetables in the market, although they now bought the vegetables from wholesalers. As the market continued to grow, new houses and retail shops gradually began to occupy the once-open plaza of Manekchowk.

Manekchowk is the heart of Ahmedabad. The major market of the city, it throbs with activity today, just as it has for more than a century. It began, in fact, as a conglomeration of markets—the commodities market, the gold and silver market, retail cloth, grain, and the spices markets, the brass and steel utensils market, and, dominating them all by the sheer number of customers it attracts, the fresh fruit and vegetable market. The commodities market has since moved, and the jewelry merchants have opened larger shops on the other side of the river in new middle-class neighborhoods, but the vegetable market continues to thrive in Manekchowk.

The original market consisted of a large building where fruit and vegetable sellers sold produce from stalls. Those stalls are premium real estate today. Demand for stalls in this vibrant market has so far outstripped supply that the market has long since spilled out of the building's confines and onto the sidewalk and side alleys. There are specialty corners—the lemon and green chilly vendors cluster at one end of the street, while piles of shelled peas are sold at another; the over-ripe fruit sellers who cater to the poor sit along the building wall. On the sidewalks, the vendors are predominantly women and children. Each vendor occupies enough space for herself and her two baskets. They typically sell only one or two kinds of seasonal vegetables, and they do brisk business because their prices are low and they have the advantage of immediate accessibility—the fresh greens are, quite literally, at the feet of the passersby.

The entire area is nothing but small businesses and smaller shops: stalls along the walls, pushcart vendors, pavement vendors, and basket vendors line the streets with their wares. Most customers shop on foot, but there is a constant stream of traffic—rickshaws, cars, and scooters whiz past, leaving a cloud of exhaust in their wake. The streets are old and narrow, and the throng of customers is so great that automobiles must honk their way through the crowds. By any logic, this city center should have been declared a pedestrian zone a long time ago.

Currently about 313 women sell vegetables on the pavement at Manekchowk. Many have been there for generations, like their mothers or mothers-in-law before them. Most, like Lakshmiben Teta, belong to the *vaghari* community. All around them, the city has grown—more shops, more traffic, more buildings, and more people. However, very little of this economic expansion has benefited the vegetable vendors; it has only served to elbow them into the margins or displace them. The vendors *are* the market, but not according to the municipality. It views the street vendors as an uncontrollable group that is too poor, too ragtag, and too "backward" to deserve a place in the market. City planners would rather they did not exist. The police see them as an obstruction to traffic although ironically, the vendors have been there since before the advent of the automobile. What matters to the municipality is that they have no legal claim on their place of work and are therefore guilty of encroachment.

And yet the market exists because the vendors exist. Caught in legal limbo, the street vendors are vulnerable to all forms of exploitation. The retail shops do not want them on the sidewalk; the police do not want them

Vegetable vendors at the Manekchowk market. (SEWA Academy)

on the street. But both are ready to look the other way, day after day, year after year, if they are monetarily compensated for averting their eyes.

The real issue is not one of a territorial war between street vendors and vehicles; rather, it is how to answer the needs of the traditional, small-scale economy that is still the backbone of Indian life—rural or urban—if its very existence is in denial. Vendors the world over are struggling to find a way for the individual entrepreneur, the worker-producer-marketer, to operate and contribute in a market environment that is designed only to meet the needs of a large-scale industrial economy. In the case of many developing nations, there is a gap between ground reality and the state's concept of the economic infrastructure it supports.

Lakshmiben Teta's family has been selling in the market for several generations. Her attachment to her place on the pavement is particularly understandable—she gave birth to one of her seven children right there, on the pavement! She is old now and can no longer sell because years of breathing exhaust from passing cars has given her asthma. Her daughter-in-law, however, occupies her seat in the market every day.

It was Lakshmiben who first approached SEWA with the problems of the women vendors of Manekchowk, and their biggest problem was the police. By law, the women were encroaching on public space, and the police used their "illegal" status to extort all kinds of bribes in cash and kind. If the vendors failed to pay, they were beaten up and their goods were confiscated. Those that failed to placate the police were summoned before the traffic court, a process that was terrifying for women who could neither read nor write. Their families had to intervene, and in the end it all cost them even more in both bribes and lost work time.

Initially, SEWA's efforts focused on helping the women retrieve their confiscated goods. Because most of the women did not have ready money, they bought vegetables from the wholesale market in the morning and agreed to pay for them with interest at the end of the day. When the police confiscated their goods, the women's troubles doubled: they still owed the wholesaler money plus the mounting interest. After only a few such days of trouble, the women were forever in debt to the wholesaler. The women needed credit—not only to run their day-to-day business but also to tide them over in times of difficulty. SEWA Bank began to look more closely at the women's lives. The women were hard workers, they had a large and steady clientele, and they had great business acumen. All they needed was capital to buy their goods at a competitive rate and legal space from which to conduct their business. The bank could help them with the former, and the SEWA Union could tackle the latter.

Dealing with the police was not easy. Long used to a free run of fruit and vegetables, not to mention some "tea money" for their pockets, the police stepped up their intimidation hoping that any efforts to organize the women would fail. I approached the police commissioner several times on behalf of the women to explore ways in which the women's presence in the market could be legitimized, but nothing seemed to work.

In 1977, a new state government came into power, and with it came large-scale transfers in the police department. The new police officers took a particularly harsh view of the vegetable vendors. "Too loud and too many" was their opinion. On Independence Day, August 15, 1978, SEWA held a protest demonstration in the city. Our voices must have been heard, because the municipal corporation drew four-by-four-foot squares on the pavement—enough space for a vendor and two baskets: *"Bay topla-ni jagah."* Of course, this was in no way a pitch license for the space, but we were still delighted!

But the forces against the street vendors' presence were quite strong. The police and the municipal corporation were unhappy about the con-

gestion, and the shopkeepers resented the competition the vendors presented. The situation finally came to a head in January 1980. A cyclist died
in a fight between two rival gangs at the steps of a bank in Manekchowk.
Tensions in the area were high, so as a precautionary measure, the police
declared a curfew and closed off the Manekchowk area. This presented a
good opportunity for the traffic police to get rid of the street vendors, even
though they had nothing to do with the accident. When the curfew was
lifted, business and traffic moved along as normal but the vendors were
not allowed to set up.

The women were very agitated. Being daily earners, they could not
bear the loss of income. Most were already treading water financially, so
each day without work meant further losses and serious consequences.
SEWA approached the municipal authorities with ardent pleas to allow
the vendors to sit on the spots chalked out for them, but all they did was
shuttle us between the offices of the police and the municipal corporation.
The officials listened to us very respectfully but offered no solution. Seven
days of peaceful negotiations brought no results; it was like hitting one's
head against a wall.

The last meeting with the police commissioner was especially exas-
perating. Sixteen of us were arguing the case for legalized vending, when
the police commissioner began lecturing us on the importance of family
planning. Like a schoolteacher, he went one by one, around the room, and
asked each woman how many children she had. I suppose he meant to
put us on the defensive. But our leader, Lakshmiben, who has seen it all,
piped up and said, "Sahib, so now you tell us, how many children did your
mother have?" "Oh, my mother? I am fifth of seven children," he replied
sheepishly. That was the end of our negotiations.

Late on the evening of January 28, we decided that the vendors would
occupy their chalked positions in Manekchowk the next morning, and we
informed the authorities of our decision in writing. The mayor called me,
urging me to overturn the decision, but he gave me no assurance that he
was willing to intervene to solve the problem. SEWA was then part of the
TLA, and much to our dismay, even its president tried to dissuade me from
such direct action. I told him I would stand by my members because their
demands were justified—this was civil disobedience against a law that was
anti-poor. Everyone has a right to earn a livelihood, especially the poor!

The following morning, the vendors and SEWA organizers arrived
at the market at eight o'clock. Two police vans were already stationed

there—as if we were going to be violent! By ten o'clock, more police had arrived. Crowds gathered at the sight, and there was tension in the air. The police seemed uncertain as to what should happen next, but the SEWA women had no such doubts. The shopkeepers looked on curiously. The police asked me to tell the women to withdraw from the street, but I argued back and kept the police busy talking with me. In the meantime, the vendors quickly brought their produce and took their seats. Other SEWA members and organizers stood by to defend the vendors in case the police decided to swing their truncheons at the women.

The police could have treated this as a law-and-order problem; they could have taken the vendors into custody or clamped down a curfew again. But as soon as the women sat down, the morning customers clustered around them, saying, "Oh, good! So glad you all are back!" Within seconds, chillies and tomatoes were being weighed and money was changing hands. Business resumed and normalcy returned. There was little for the police to do.

By midday, the police decided to withdraw from the scene. "So you think you don't need us! Fine, now you handle the situation!" And with this parting shot, they all departed, leaving not even one policeman to direct the traffic. We rose to that challenge as well. SEWA members and staff directed the traffic and crowds in Manekchowk for almost a week. After the first day, the women's determination and efficiency must have impressed the other traders in the market, for surprisingly, the men volunteered their help and gave their full support to the women they once looked down on. The cooperative spirit in the market was unprecedented. In fact, even today, the women say that they have never earned more than they did in those six days of disobedience—there was no one around to collect kickbacks. Manekchowk was back to normal.

Although the vendors were back in place, they were still illegal and so the crux of our problem remained. Written petitions to all relevant authorities went unanswered. We tried to shake things up with another demonstration, larger than the previous one, and we invited the chief minister to address the vendors' rally. We felt that as a people's representative, he needed to hear what the people had to say. But after hearing the women out, Chief Minister Shri Babubhai Patel began instead to admonish them. "Why did you leave your villages and come to the city? Don't you see that is the root of your problem?" But despite his attitude, he had registered the women's message. Two days later, he called us to a meeting in his chamber. The municipal commissioner and the police commissioner were waiting there for us. Then the home minister, the law minister, and the labor minister joined in to discuss the vendors' issue. Only Lakshmiben and I represented SEWA. Both sides were keen to see an end to hostilities, so we worked out a temporary solution in no time. The SEWA identity card would be treated as a valid vending license for the women in Manekchowk. The card already contained all the necessary relevant information: the vendor's name and picture, the place where she sold her wares, and my signature as General Secretary of SEWA. For more than two years, until that government fell, the SEWA identity card remained valid, and the police harassment decreased. The following government, however, had other plans.

1981 was a difficult year for the city's poor. There were large-scale demonstrations and riots on the issue of reserved seats for "scheduled caste and tribes" in the medical school. Unrest in the city always means loss of income to the self-employed poor. Spirits at SEWA were also low because of internal tensions with the TLA leaders. Around this time, I received an invitation from Supreme Court Justice and Chair of the Free Legal Aid Committee P. N. Bhagwati to attend a seminar in Delhi. I replied to this invitation in an agitated mood, saying I had come across far too many laws that were anti-poor, and I proceeded to write an account of the injustices done to the Manekchowk vendors in the name of the law.

I also mentioned in my letter that Lakshmiben had been selling vegetables in Manekchowk for the past forty years, sitting in the same place where her mother-in-law had sat before her. Her income of 10 rupees per day supported her family because her husband had been sick and unemployed for twelve years. Each time she was fined—which was three or four times a week—she had to pay 12.50 rupees. She had receipts of the fines she had paid for past six years. Shakriben too had been vending in Manekchowk for the past forty years, and she too had the receipts to prove it. Deviben had been vending for twenty years in the Danapith section of Manekchowk; again, she had receipts for the fines she had paid over the past eight years. There were many women who could demonstrate continuous presence at that market over many years.

Justice Bhagwati decided to turn my letter into a public interest petition and advised us to engage a lawyer. We found Indira Jaising, a young lawyer who had won the case of Bombay pavement dwellers, to fight for the rights of our street vendors. On January 7, 1982, with SEWA as an organization and Lakshmiben, Shakriben, Deviben, and myself as petitioners, we filed the case in the Supreme Court of India against the municipal commissioner, the police commissioner, and the state of Gujarat. The petition claimed that by denying licenses to the petitioners, the vendors' fundamental constitutional right to trade was being violated by the municipality. The defense's reaction was silence, and the police department did not attend. The two-judge bench ordered a "stay" on the prosecution of vendors. The Court ordered the municipal commissioner to protect all SEWA members in the Manekchowk area and to work out a permanent solution for accommodating street vendors in consultation with SEWA. Until such time, the vendors of Manekchowk would get temporary certificates to sit and vend from their current places. SEWA's second plea was to make the Manekchowk market a pedestrian zone, but the Court did not accept it on the grounds that it inconvenienced existing private and public residences, shops, and offices in the area.

Initially, our negotiations with the municipal corporation concluded with plans for long-term collaboration to settle these issues. The corporation agreed to provide special buses for headloaders to transport their wares, a cold-storage facility for the wholesale market, and special vending spaces for women in every new shopping complex built by the municipality. Unfortunately, the following year, the ruling government in the city fell and all our plans came to naught. The court order regarding Manekchowk survives today as just a document. The municipality drags its feet at every step, even as the next generation of vendors takes its place, plying their trade in the name of their parents—some dead, some alive.

Harassment at the local level continues in Manekchowk. Vested interests are deep and pervasive—space in this thriving market is at a premium, and the poor are bound to get the short end of the stick unless they can band together to protect their interests. Through SEWA, the women have access to legal aid and a voice for effective and at times not so effective communication with the government.

In 1986, the President of India nominated me as a member of the Upper House of Parliament—the Rajya Sabha. On August 5, 1988, I moved a resolution on vendors—the first time in Indian Parliament history that street vendors came under discussion.

In my resolution, I urged upon the Government "to formulate a national policy for hawkers and vendors by making them a part of the broader structural policies aimed at improving their standard of living." I also urged "to protect their existing livelihood and provide legal access to the

Four Supreme Court petitioners: Deviben, Laxmiben, Shakriben, Elaben.
(Anand Patel)

use of available space in urban areas." I had argued through my resolution "to make them a special component of the plans for urban development, by treating them as an integral part of the urban distribution system. Give them legal status by issuing licenses, by providing exclusive hawking zones, and issuing guidelines for action at local levels."

In his response, the minister of urban affairs promised sympathetic consideration to the vendor issue. The resolution to formulate a national policy for hawkers and vendors was passed unanimously. But without political clout to bring pressure on the ruling party, a private member's resolution has no mandatory strength. That is the price one pays for keeping one's distance from all political parties; but we would have it no other way.

Over the years, SEWA's membership of vendors has grown to 41,000 in Ahmedabad. The situation in Manekchowk has improved, but only marginally; fines continue, but they are lower and less frequent than before. SEWA organizers go to the police station on their members' behalf. This saves the vendors' working time, and the legal procedure is followed without kickbacks. The women are no longer subject to the terror tactics of earlier days; such tactics no longer work because the women are stronger, knowing they are so many, and that many will come to the aid of one, so they can stand up for themselves and can get legal representation.

Unfortunately, the anti-encroachment authorities that confiscate their cart and goods still continue to be a threat. A confiscated cart may not be released for several days, which means the vendor is unable to go out and earn. Often, the cart that is returned is damaged or broken. Before, the anti-encroachment officers used to take the cart as well as the goods on it; now they dump the goods before the vendor and take just the cart. Small mercies, indeed!

Meanwhile, the number of city vendors has grown steadily. It is difficult to get definite numbers in the case of street vendors because they are mobile and market driven. However, a 2001 survey conducted by SEWA in Ahmedabad revealed that there were about 80,000 vendors in the city engaged in 100 different trades in 140 major markets. Twenty-five years ago, in the Jamalpur market, for example, there were 125 vendors. Today, there are close to 1,000. Half of them are first-generation vendors. The police made arrangements to accommodate two rows of fruit carts in the market, but a third row of vendors cropped up quickly. Conflict is inevitable unless the municipality is willing to address the growing vendor population and formulate a system for issuing them proper space and licenses.

Clearly, an increase in unemployment in the formal economy is the cause of the swelling numbers of those seeking to make ends meet in the informal economy. The vendors are just one such group. In Ahmedabad, the steady demise of the city's textile mills from 1980 through 1990 left more than 100,000 mill hands, including the contract labor, without work.[1] Most of the unemployed were men; many waited for years for a new factory job to materialize during which time the challenge of feeding and clothing the family fell on the women. Some mill workers have turned to the informal economy for work—setting up small businesses and very often competing with the women at jobs that were once considered unskilled and low paying. For many women, vending is their only source of income;

1. Jan Bremen and Parthiv Shah. *Working in the Mill No More.* New Delhi: Oxford University Press, 2004.

about a third of the women vendors are the sole earners in their families. In the early 1990s, the municipal authorities announced that they would stop issuing pitch licenses altogether. Over the years, around 1,000 vendors had been issued such licenses intermittently. Now only mobile vendors can hope to get a license.

In a growing urban population, when the pressures for land ownership are huge, the authorities fear that, once legitimized, street vendors will lay claim to a space and build permanent structures over it. This fear is not entirely invalid. The key, however, is to work with the vendors to build a system that allows for the poor to earn a living, and for the authorities to maintain order in the markets. The current system is built on distrust and pig-headedness, which gives rise to abuse and corruption.

With so many operations occurring in gray areas, systems of corruption have become deeply rooted. Retail stores owners and larger businessmen can afford to bribe or intimidate the policemen, but the poor are at their mercy. A bangle seller outside the Bhadra temple must pay the policeman 3 rupees per cart per day as her fee. If she pays up this amount, she will be left to earn in peace for the rest of the day. In areas where vendors are more visible, because they *are* the market, the amounts they pay out are larger. Toward the evening, especially on festival days when customers throng the markets, the air is heavy with tension; the power brokers move among the customers taking note of how much business each vendor conducts because that will determine how much each woman will pay for that day!

Apart from the police, there are the dons of the underworld who control the area by taking a cut of the business as well. When SEWA workers go to new neighborhoods to organize vendors, the women sometimes say that they cannot make the decision to join any organization without permission from the *"bhai."* When the SEWA organizer meets with this bhai, he inevitably boasts that he could easily get all the vendors in his area to enroll in the union, but what is in it for him? Working around these power mongers requires courage, diplomacy, and, most importantly, the cooperation of the women themselves.

In some markets in working-class suburbs, the don's daily charge is 20 to 25 rupees per cart. In other places, the dons have devised a novel method of extortion. They come and place a cup of tea at the vendor's stall three times a day and demand 10 rupees per cup. They do this whether the vendor wants the tea or not.

One exploiter the vendors particularly dislike is the *mehta*, the billing clerk in the city's wholesale vegetable market where the vendors buy their goods. The vendors pay a commission of 10 percent to 16 percent to the mehta for vegetables they purchase, although the official rate is 6 percent. Moreover, they end up paying another 4 to 5 percent of the value of the goods in transportation costs. On goods worth 1,000 rupees, a vendor could spend about 150 rupees as an aggregate overcharge.

Moneylenders too play a major role. When SEWA started working with the street vendors, they borrowed capital to buy their daily stock of vegetables, paying interest rates as high as 10 percent per day. If they were unable to repay the same day, they had to pay back money the next day with 20-percent interest. After the SEWA Bank formed, vendors were able to borrow at affordable rates, and those who are members of the bank continue to do so. However, the cost of credit in the market remains unchanged; even today, vendors who are not members of SEWA Bank continue to borrow at these high rates.

In the older markets like Manekchowk, Danapith, and Saraspur, the vendors face less trouble from the authorities. The status quo has enabled some sort of mutual understanding. Although the struggles remain the same as before, the scene of the battle has shifted to the new urban neighborhoods where markets are springing up almost spontaneously. Demand from new residents for daily necessities is met with prompt supply by vendors, hawkers, and pushcart sellers who are quick to recognize new business opportunities and are able to act on it. The municipality, however, has little on its blueprints for new markets—vendors are still invisible, and making space for them in newly developing markets is still out of the question. The municipality is caught flat-footed in far too many areas of urban growth in Ahmedabad—whether it is providing water, sewage, electricity, or transportation services to new neighborhoods, or ensuring that adequate commercial, financial, or social institutions reach the new suburbs. Urban development becomes a process of fait accompli. As services crop up in a neighborhood in response to local need, the role of the authorities seems to be limited to bestowing on them a legal or illegal status. Sometimes, entire marble-floored shopping plazas are built before the municipality acknowledges their existence. How do the poor stand a chance?

The struggle to reclaim the city has yielded some minor results. Access to water and sanitation has improved marginally, compared to what it was thirty-five years ago. After many petitions and delegations, some public toilets have been built in market areas. However, they are few in number and far away from the vendors' place of work. "You *sahibs*, don't you ever need to go to the toilet?" Maniben once asked the municipal corporator of her area. Sometimes such simple questions are the only reminders to the authorities that their job is to provide basic public services to the people.

Middle-class attitudes toward vendors are still ambivalent. While they certainly enjoy buying fresh produce at low prices, there is an aversion to the vendors' poor clothes and rough speech, as well as a tendency to distrust people who seem so keen on selling and so willing to bargain. Ironically, one of the biggest fears of the middle class is that they will be cheated or taken advantage of by these lowly businesswomen. The vendors just laugh and take it in stride—such attitudes are hardly new to them.

Over time, some officials do come to develop some sympathy for the vendors. As if to prove it, junior staff at the municipality sometimes call ahead and warn the women that an anti-encroachment raid is about to take place on a certain site. Anti-encroachment authorities too sometimes admit to being tired of this constant and futile confrontation. "Why don't you SEWA people find a solution to this problem?" they ask the vendors. They too see the absurdity of the situation.

It is clear from our Ahmedabad experience that street vendors in the cities of India need a comprehensive policy that will integrate their livelihood and their concerns for market space, licenses, and financial and civic services into urban planning. To be effective, such a policy must be formulated with substantial input from the vendors themselves; their voice and representation are crucial.

To begin with, we need to recognize the significant economic contribution vendors make to India's cities. Their role in the distribution of basic goods and services cannot be underestimated. In India, more than 50 percent of the lower-income population in the city purchases most of its daily necessities from street vendors, while the financially better off also buy a significant portion of their supplies from such vendors.

Not only do hawkers and street vendors provide a valued service to consumers, but it is also an important means of employment for large numbers of the urban poor who would otherwise be unable to maintain themselves and their families. With the number of jobs in the formal economy shrinking, vending offers an earning opportunity with low-capital requirements and relatively easy entry. Moreover, both large- and small-scale producers depend on the vendors' services for retail distribution.

Estimates vary with regard to the actual numbers of vendors and hawkers. According to the draft National Policy for Street Vendors, India has approximately 10 million vendors, of which about a third are women. A recent study of Ahmedabad vendors estimates that street vending operations represent nearly one out of five informal enterprises (17 percent).[2] Street vendors constitute 2 percent of the urban population; that is, there is one vendor to every thirty-five to fifty people.

In 1985, in *Bombay Hawkers Union vs. Bombay Municipal Corporation*, the Supreme Court directed that each city should demarcate "hawking" and "no hawking" zones to enable vendors and hawkers to carry out their business. Two years later, the Supreme Court judgment (*Saudan Singh vs. New Delhi Municipal Corporation*) declared hawking to be a fundamental right and stated that "if properly regulated, according to the exigency of the circumstances, the small traders on the sidewalks can considerably add to the convenience of the general public, by making available ordinary articles of everyday use at comparatively lesser price . . . the right to carry on trade or business mentioned in Article 19(1)g of the Constitution, on street pavements, if properly regulated, cannot be denied on the ground that the streets are meant exclusively for passing or re-passing and no other use."

However, despite the fact that vending provides a vital service to urban consumers, despite its role in livelihood generation, and despite the Supreme Court rulings in its favor, vendors and hawkers face daily struggles to ply their trade in all cities across India.

Dr. Sharat Bhowmik of Bombay University conducted a study of the problems of hawkers in Bombay, Delhi, Ahmedabad, Patna, Imphal, Bangalore, and Bhubaneshwar on behalf of SEWA.[3] His study found that only

2. Jeemol Unni and Uma Rani. *Urban Informal Sector: Size and Income Generation Processes in Gujarat.* New Delhi: National Council of Applied Economic Research, 2000.
3. Sharat K. Bhowmik. "Hawkers and the Informal Sector: A Report." Mumbai, India. Unpublished report, 2002.

two cities—Imphal and Bhubaneshwar—had made some provisions for including street vendors in their civic plans and that Imphal is the only city that has clearly stated rules on street vending. Manipur's State Planning Act stipulates that there should be provision in residential areas for four to six shops and ten hawkers for every thousand residents. The Bhubaneshwar development authority has reserved 3 percent of public space as a commercial zone within which space is also reserved on pavements for street vendors. Though Bangalore is a large city, street vending is not as widespread there as in other cities. In Calcutta, the state government and the municipal corporation are strongly biased against hawkers, while the general public and the media have expressed their support for the cause of the hawkers. According to the Bhowmik study, 82 percent of consumers in Calcutta prefer to buy from hawkers.

The study also reported that street vendors in Imphal were exclusively women. The women had waged a three-year battle against private builders and stood their ground. In Ahmedabad, as well, 40 percent of the vendors are women who have a strong union in SEWA. Since vendors are self-employed and scattered, the formal trade union movement is not very interested in them. Only the formation of vendors' organizations will have the power to democratize the market place and secure legal rights for street vendors. To date, however, their unions, cooperatives, and associations do not have a strong enough voice to make an impact.

Dr. Bhowmik's study noted that after the large-scale raids on hawkers in Mumbai in 2001, the amount of bribes paid to the police and municipal authorities increased sharply—in some cases, tenfold. Desperate street vendors are willing to pay any amount to be left in peace to carry on their business and to be forewarned about impending police raids. Vendors in Mumbai pay good money for these "protection" services.

When the British brought Indian cities under regulatory control, the laws that were formulated in 1882 formed the basis for the Bombay Provincial Municipal Corporations Act of 1949. This law continues to be followed to this day without major amendments.

As of 2004, the Ahmedabad Municipal Corporation has issued licenses to only about 1,000 vendors while the city currently has close to 80,000 vendors and hawkers working on the streets. Municipalities in many cities have limited the number of licenses issued to street vendors, despite the fact that one cannot effectively control the numbers of vendors by simply denying them licenses. This only creates large numbers of "illegal" vendors who do nothing but fill the coffers of the underworld in the form of bribes.

The situation is the same in most cities. The demand for licenses far exceeds supply, which puts the officials issuing licenses in a position to exploit vendors. According to a study by the feminist publication "Manushi" in Delhi, officials collect "rents" worth 5 million rupees per month while processing, issuing, and enforcing licenses. Legal fines to Ahmedabad City for traffic violations or the release of confiscated goods totaled nearly 8 million rupees, while bribes paid to police, city officials, and others totaled an estimated 35.5 million rupees! A second look is needed to see how this amount is budgeted in the municipal and government books.

The demarcation of vendor zones is a good beginning but poses two main problems. One of the vendors' main assets is their mobility. Most zoning plans fail to recognize that markets tend to grow in an organic fashion. They can arise in various neighborhoods at certain times of day, finely tuned to the needs of the customers living or working in the area. Whenever specific areas are designated for vendors, invariably, neither vendors nor consumers are consulted. When provisions do not correspond to the needs of the people involved, they are either ignored or abused. Effective forums for dialogue between vendors, citizens, planners, and the municipality are desperately needed.

Transporting large amounts of fresh produce to the market is a major issue for vendors. Vendors of vegetables, fruits, fish, and other perishables must buy and transport their goods daily. Unfortunately, the city transportation system does not allow vendors to carry goods on public buses, trains, or subways. This forces most of the poor to walk very long distances with heavy loads on their heads or to spend money on hiring pushcarts or rickshaws to take them to market. Public transportation geared to the needs of the working population would not only provide services where they are needed but also generate substantial revenue. Mumbai has separate compartments in local trains for fish vendors; Trivendrum has buses that serve fish vendors traveling every morning from rural areas. These efforts need to be duplicated on a large scale across the country.

It seems as if urban planners design cities to follow some grand scheme in which there are no working poor. They give full consideration to the neat and tidy formal economy, but they are completely at sea regarding the needs of the working masses. The poor are not part of anyone's grand vision.

Part of the problem is our concept of space itself. Land valuation, and the economic viability of certain kinds of land use, raises the question of who gets to use what land. Unfortunately, the balance is tilted in favor of powerful, vested interests. A land use plan has to integrate both the informal and formal economies of the city because that is India's reality. Both are complementary and capable of coexisting peacefully. Vendors weave color, life, and vibrancy into markets. If planners could rise to the challenge and consult the vendors when making decisions concerning the location, relocation, and design of new markets, they would be well rewarded. Vendors are willing and fully capable of contributing financially toward the maintenance and upkeep of marketplaces. After all, the bribes they are currently forced to pay are not cheap.

The media, particularly the press, is unaware and at times unclear about the significant role that vendors play in the mainstream economy. Public perceptions cannot change until the media plays a positive and active part in reporting the role of vendors in society. Studies on vendors—from an economic, social, historical, or anthropological point of view—are rare indeed.

I was heartened to see the recognition vendors receive in Italy. In Milan, the Chamber of Commerce issues licenses to vendors after they complete compulsory training courses. Each vendor receives a ten-year renewable license and pays taxes. There are 1,500 daily markets and 8,000 weekly markets in Milan. The labor unions represent their grievances to the authorities. Every three years, they hold a vendors' convention.

Everywhere I have traveled in the world, I have talked to vendors and observed that the issues are not that different from those of the street vendors of Manekchowk. I had long dreamed of getting vendors from different parts of the world together to share their experiences and exchange ideas. Such an opportunity arrived in June 1995, when the Rockefeller Foundation offered its facility in Bellagio, a small village on Lake Como in Italy, to SEWA to conduct an international workshop on the legal status of street vendors. Participants came from ten cities—Accra, Ahmedabad, Milan, Manila, Durban, Nairobi, New York, Rio de Janeiro, Santa Cruz, and Vera Cruz. Three representatives—one male vendor, one female vendor, and one union organizer represented each city. Our stories were remarkably similar. Most vendors had been to jail more than once for vending. They agreed that street vendors, among all occupations, are the most regulated and least protected by law in their respective countries. The legal issues too were similar: not enough licenses, inadequate space, and unsupportive policies. Police harassment was a daily affair. City planners ignored them; banks did not trust them. Their trade organization had trouble getting results.

The conference concluded with a proclamation of vendors' rights. The representatives formed an informal international alliance. Eventually, in November 2002, StreetNet International was formed in Durban. The road from Manekchowk to Durban via Bellagio was full of surprises, stops, and sometimes detours, but to us it seemed that what was once only a little footpath was turning into a paved road.

Following the Bellagio International Declaration of Street Vendors of 1995, SEWA mobilized its efforts to organize vendors' groups in several Indian cities. In 1996, SEWA initiated a census survey of vendors in four-teen major cities in coordination with local voluntary organizations and trade unions. The groups met in Ahmedabad to form a strategic alliance to represent vendors in one voice at the national level. The result was the National Alliance of Street Vendors, India (NASVI), whose headquarters were based in Patna. Its newsletter, *Footpath-ki-Awaz*, or Voice of the Foot-path, has since served as the vendors' voice.

In collaboration with the Urban Development Ministry, NASVI orga-nized a national policy dialogue in Delhi to move toward formulating a national policy. Vendors' associations from thirty cities discussed their concerns with the government and policy makers, who finally set up a national task force to prepare a draft policy paper. The final draft is now with the various state governments for endorsement.

The state of Gujarat has prepared its own draft policy with the same basic objectives as those stated in the national policy: "to give vendors legal status by amending, enacting, repealing, and implementing appropriate laws and providing hawking zones in urban development/zoning plans." The chief minister has yet to give his stamp of approval on this policy, which would legalize the status of vendors in the state of Gujarat. We all wait with bated breath; but until then, *Bay topla-ni jagah* is still just a dream.

5

Banking

From the beginning, the need for financial services among poor but economically active women was glaringly apparent. Almost all the women were in debt to private moneylenders, touts, pawnshops, grocers, or landlords who, although quick to hand out cash or credit on demand, charged interest rates ranging from 10 percent per day to 25 percent per month for their services. The women also had no safe place to save—their living conditions did not allow for much privacy from needy or greedy eyes.

The formal banking system in India was nationalized in 1969 with pressure from the central government on the local banks "to serve the poor." In 1972, SEWA took this opportunity to approach the banks on behalf of our members. Since the banks had no idea how to reach the poor, let alone how to assess their creditworthiness, they were keen to use SEWA as an intermediary.

But it was not so simple. First, it was difficult for banks to think of lending to anyone without some form of collateral, and the absence of assets among the working poor was a problem. Illiteracy was another. Not only could the women not sign their own names, but they also did not see any need to confine themselves to an official name and surname. Some women used their father's name as their middle name because they were too shy to utter their husband's name in public; others followed the traditional working-class convention of using one's first name followed by either one's father's or husband's name and dispensed with the relatively modern use of surnames. The bank staff did not look kindly on the women's efforts to arrive at an official identity—to them, these were nothing more than attempts at deceit.

If the banks were inexperienced, so were we. The women felt intimidated by the formal office atmosphere, and not without reason. The bank tellers rolled their eyes at their loud, uncultured speech or their body odors, and they turned their noses up at the crumpled pile of small-denomination notes the women produced from their *cholis*. In essence, our members were not the type of clientele that the banks usually liked to welcome. Although one can attribute it to lack of experience, underlying this attitude was distrust of the poor and condescension toward their economic activities.

The women too faced some very practical difficulties. Busy at work all day, they had difficulty getting to the bank during normal banking hours. At the day's end, if the cash meant for deposit did not get to the bank on time, it was spent. It was also common for them to give their savings for safekeeping to the same wholesaler or contractor from whose clutches they had to escape.

At a SEWA members' meeting at Naranghat in December 1973, Chandaben, a used garment dealer from Poori Bazar, asked me, "Ben, why can't we have our own bank?" "Because we have no money," I replied patiently. "You need a very large amount of capital to start a bank!" "Well, we may be poor, but we are so many," Chandaben replied. I was taken aback! She had such faith in our group's ability that she thought we could move mountains! Chandaben's words started everyone at the meeting thinking, "Why ever not? We have to have our own bank!" The more we dreamed aloud, the more real the idea appeared. It was worth investigating.

In our true and tried fashion, we conducted a survey of our proposed bank's potential clientele.[1] We learned the following:

- The level of illiteracy among headloaders, cart pullers, basket weavers, rag pickers, and junksmiths was 90 percent.
- Women in all twelve trades surveyed lived in slums.
- The homes of headloaders, rag pickers, and vegetable vendors did not have *pucca* walls.

1. *SEWA Report, 1988*. Ahmedabad, India: Self-Employed Women's Association.

- All the block printers, bidi rollers, incense stick rollers, and papad rollers worked in their homes.
- Ten percent of the garment makers worked in their contractors' shed.
- Eighty-two percent of the women were married.
- More than 80 percent of the headloaders and cart pullers and 65 percent of vendors took their children to their worksite.
- Ninety-six percent of the block printers worked on rented tables and verandas.
- Sixty-five percent of the cart pullers and fifty-nine percent of the vegetable vendors had rented carts.
- Eighty percent of garment makers had rented sewing machines.
- Among service providers, cart pullers earned the most of all the trades, with a monthly average income of 300 rupees.
- Among vendors of different wares, vegetable vendors had the highest income at 300 rupees per month.
- Home-based workers had a lower income, among whom the lowest income was that of the garment makers, who earned 100 rupees per month.
- The lowest income of all the trades surveyed was that of rag pickers, who earned 82 rupees per month.
- The most indebted of those surveyed were the handcart pullers, vegetable vendors, rag pickers, and block printers who did not know about the family's financial dealings.

Each trade worker was indebted to the extent of 700 rupees on average at the time of the survey. In short, the women were all economically active; they lived and worked in slum conditions; they were predominantly illiterate; and their economic contribution was crucial to the family's survival.

With this reality in mind, we set out to form a bank of our own in 1974. Bank shares were 10 rupees each. Within six months, the initial share capital of 71,320 rupees was collected from 6,287 members. Shri Mahila SEWA Sahakari Bank Ltd. or the SEWA Women's Cooperative Bank was established on May 20, 1974.

We had found the capital, but the Registrar of Cooperatives would not register our bank. Because the applicants were women, poor, illiterate, "in scattered occupations" and of "lower community," the registrar considered them unqualified. The Urban Cooperative Bank Act of course does not disqualify anyone for any of the above reasons; the real block was just the middle-class, bureaucratic mindset. Taking me aside, the registrar told me with genuine concern, "Elaben, consider me your elder brother, and believe me when I tell you to forget this bank idea. These poor ladies will never repay your loans, and in the end, you will find yourself considering suicide! Put such ideas out of your head!" But I knew my sisters well. Was it not their idea to begin with? Had they not just raised the share capital for their bank? Had I not been a daily witness to the women working and earning, having cash income in their hands, and their pressing need to save and borrow, I might have paused at his words.

The registrar then took another course of argument. "How can you ever do banking with illiterates?" He had a point. Not one of the fifteen promoters of the proposed bank could sign their names. That evening, I taught each one of them to sign their names. They practiced long into the night, until they could do it without error. However, the registrar was not impressed. Then I suggested that we use photographs on bank passbooks for identification. He agreed to this, and so SEWA Bank was registered as a cooperative bank.

After that, there was no looking back. The women completely shattered the myth that the poor are not bankable. The illiterate, the slum dwellers, and the self-employed not only proved themselves creditworthy, but they turned their bank into a viable, profitable, financial venture, without the aid of any subsidy. And year after year, since its inception, SEWA Bank shareholders have received dividends without fail. Few banks, commercial or otherwise, can boast of that!

It is the clients who make a bank, not the money. We were not just another bank; we were different. Our bank had to provide an integrated set of banking services to poor women, but more important, the bank's management had to comprise the poor women themselves. The SEWA Bank was a cooperative in name, and it aimed to stay cooperative in spirit as well. The mission of the Bank was outlined in 1974 as follows:

> Credit must further the productive and earning capabilities of the poor self-employed women. Our Bank will aim at extending technical and management assistance in production, storage, procuring, designing, and sale of their goods and services. The Bank will give loans to redeem the women's pawned jewelry, mortgaged house or land, redeem old debts

from brokers, moneylenders or landholders. SEWA Bank will aim to adopt procedures and design schemes suitable to poor self employed women like collecting daily savings from their homes or workplaces, and giving training and assistance to make their loans and savings productive.

Enlisting the support and services of the union was also key. Step by step, the union could extend the Bank's role in providing legal aid, as well as linking support services like childcare, skills development, and medical insurance. A deposit-linked group insurance program was envisaged. The overall objective was that savings and credit facilities be available to all self-employed women members and that the Bank and its services would grow at their pace, in the direction of their needs.

The early months were full of new experiences for the women. Having been told that no amount was too small to deposit, and that they would build up assets if they deposited even a rupee every time they came to the bank, the women began to bring in small amounts of cash at a steady rate. To any woman who complained, "I have no money, I cannot save," Chandaben would say, "You wouldn't go empty-handed to a temple, would you? You can always find a rupee in your pocket if you have to! So just remember to deposit something, however small, every time you come to the bank!" Mindful of that, many women would come in, stand in line to deposit, say five rupees, and then go to the other end of the counter and stand in line to withdraw ten rupees from their account! Such transactions were typical in the early days when the Bank was a learning experience for all concerned.

Wherever possible, we devised symbols and color codes in place of written information, to help the women who could neither read nor write. Each passbook had an identity photo of the account holder in lieu of a signature, but printed in the back was a page of the Gujarati alphabet and numerals, so that the women would have the tools to read with if they wanted. We also made sure that anyone coming to the bank could find someone to teach her how to sign her name or read her passbook entries.

For a long time, SEWA Bank was known as the "*foto* bank" among working women. In a corner of the room, a staff photographer was on duty all day, taking pictures of new account holders displaying a slate with their name and account number written on it. Behind him was a wall of steel

cupboards containing stacks of passbooks given to the bank for safekeeping by women who did not want their families to learn of their personal
finances. Women gathered at the bank as if at the village well, exchang-
ing news and gossip and ordering endless rounds of tea. At the end of the
day, the tiled floor was covered with tea stains and bidi stubs, all evidence
of increasing activity.

By the end of 1976, SEWA Bank had 11,038 member-depositors, a
working capital of 1,198,872 rupees, and a profit of 21,623 rupees, which
yielded a 9-percent dividend for the 6,945 shareholders. Well begun was
half done!

Banking is a serious business; there is not much room for error. So how
is a bank for the poor different from other banks? And how does it function? Arriving at these answers took a lot of unconventional thinking and
a constant evaluation of the women's real needs. By keeping a tight focus
on the women themselves, we could build a banking system that worked
for its clientele.

SEWA Bank is both similar to and different from other banking institutions. As a cooperative bank, SEWA Bank is a highly regulated, deposit-
taking institution owned by its members, who also make up its customer
base. The bank operates under the dual supervision of the Reserve Bank
of India and the State Registrar of Cooperatives and is a mainstream formal financial institution for the poor.

An elected governing board of twenty-five trade-wise representatives
of the member-customers governs the bank. This keeps SEWA Bank constantly focused on the poor and self-employed women it serves. There is
a strong alignment of interests and objectives between the board, the
management, and the bank customers.

The women who constitute SEWA Bank are also the women for whom
the Bank was constituted. So in a sense, there is no "they" or "we"; lines
between owners, management, and clients are quite blurred. Those who
demand the service and those who supply the service are inherently the
same critical mass of women. In sum, SEWA Bank grows out of the needs
of working-class women from the informal, self-employed sector, where
their needs are not met by the country's banking services at large.

To begin with, the Bank had to go to the women—it could not wait
for the women to come to it. Given the kind of labor-intensive work the
women engage in, they have no time to bring their earnings to the bank at
the end of the day. Furthermore, it is uneconomical for them to spend

money on transportation to the bank—the amount they have for deposit is small, but the need to make deposits is frequent. In fact, the Bank needed to not only devise door-to-door services, but also to set up a daily collecting schedule to match the saving needs of the women. Consistent contact with the clients was key to the Bank's credibility and success.

Once a client's saving pattern is established, it is a lot easier for the Bank to assess her creditworthiness. It was also imperative that the loan application process be simple and streamlined so that it is easy for all to understand. The women, being illiterate, need constant verbal explanations and assurances as well as assistance in filling out the forms. They need information about banking options available to them and what products or services might better suit their needs. The women are eager to learn about financial planning because most of their experience is with hand-to-mouth living. The Bank, therefore, holds training and counseling sessions in integrated financial planning to meet women's needs over a life cycle. Because the poor are vulnerable, providing support services like medical and legal aid, insurance, capacity building, or marketing know-how becomes a vital and integral part of the Bank's functions.

SEWA Bank is also different in the way it evaluates its clients and their credit-worthiness. A self-employed woman is essentially a risk-taking entrepreneur. Her entrepreneurial skills are most evident in how she manages her assets—as she perceives them—against the odds she faces.

Of tangible assets, the women have few—perhaps some cash savings or some silver jewelry that can be sold or pawned. If she has a roof over her head, she can work at home, so that is her real estate. She may have a cow or own a weaving loom inherited from her family; she may have a pushcart or a sewing machine—such are her means of production. Even a food ration card is an asset because it allows her to buy food at a fair price from a government shop. In fact, among poor women, any identity card, paper certificate, or license is a very valuable asset because it establishes her place in some sort of a system. The Bank takes all this into consideration.

But there are also intangible assets that, though unconventional, play a major role in the women's lives and in their ability to function in a financially responsible fashion. Education is an asset that few women possess, but even basic literacy can be turned to good advantage. Children are enormous assets, because the more hands for working, the higher the income in the family. Husbands can be assets or liabilities. A husband that does not have a drinking problem, for example, is an asset; in-laws that will allow a woman to work outside the house are assets; the goodwill of one's caste is an asset. The women are very good at turning such intangibles into real assets in order to earn a livelihood.

A woman with few skills and no money still has her body for an asset. She sells her labor pulling carts, carrying loads, or working at construction sites. Good health is an asset. Women with traditional skills like basket making or junk smithy make wares at home and sell them in the market. Some communities like the vaghari are traditionally vendors dominating the vegetable, fruit, and used-garment markets. Muslim women, whose cultural norms do not allow them to work outside the home, turn to sewing, block printing, and tie-dyeing, which are traditional, home-based occupations. The Bank follows the lead of the women in identifying their strengths. Bank field workers, known as *banksathis,* look carefully into the women's lives and identify those assets that they can turn into capital.

Banksathis are the Bank's frontline workers. They come from the same communities as the customers and live alongside them in the same neighborhoods. They typically also pursue the same trades as the women while working in conjunction with the Bank. A banksathi is usually someone who has experience at maintaining a bank account; is a local leader with good credibility; is strong, energetic, and alert; is active within SEWA; and can preferably read and write. Banksathis have fixed deposits of 15,000 rupees in SEWA Bank—the amount that is taken as a "security deposit," a safeguard against any misappropriation. (Recently, the Reserve Bank of India has suggested raising the amount.) She may borrow from the bank and deposit the amount in her fixed-deposit account. A capable banksathi can serve around 400 borrowers of the bank. A bank staff in-charge monitors the banksathi.

Although the women do want to build up some savings, this is difficult for several reasons. A common complaint is, of course, "I have no money, how can I save?" One banksathi's response to this argument was, "Try this! Every time you knead dough to make roti, take two small fistfuls of flour and put it aside. If you do it for six days in a row, on the seventh day you will have enough flour to cook a day's roti without reaching for new flour! Saving is the same thing!" And then she added, "For that matter, I should tell you how to cook vegetables as well—lots of water for

Banksathi Dilshad mobile banking in Dariapur with chindi and garment workers. (Rahul)

gravy, and lots of chillies for spice—if it's too spicy hot, people eat less! You need fewer vegetables, and it tastes so good!"

Food is the very first thing that poor women economize on. The other is sleep—less sleep means more working hours and hence more income. Used to a lifetime of making do, going without, and constant self-denial, the women see frugality and saving as a form of suffering, an inescapable part of their lives. This explains why they preferred the precarious but relatively less demanding cycle of earning and spending on a daily basis. The question for the Bank was how to channel the women's innate sense of frugality toward exercising financial discipline without adding to their suffering.

By focusing on building programs that maintain constant and continuous contact with its clients, the Bank is better able to gauge the women's needs and capacities. The Bank takes interest not only in how the client spends her loan amount, but also assists her in finding the best deal for her money, whether it is buying pushcarts, sewing machines, or a one-room home. The Bank also intervenes on the women's behalf if they have heavy debts with moneylenders, pawnshops, or property owners. Of all the banking services, redemption of old debts is the first and most vital activity. It frees the women from life-long indebtedness and consequently increases their bargaining power with wholesalers and suppliers.

A sea change comes over the women once they see money building in their bank accounts. They feel more self-confident knowing they have a cushion to fall back on. When financial tensions ease, the women say that their husband's attitude softens—the men are more willing to consider women as partners instead of an economic burden. The women begin to have a voice in the family.

Savings and insurance services are an integral part of providing credit facility because risk plays a large role in their lives. SEWA Bank offers inflation-protected savings, like mutual funds invested in safe securities, and life-cycle savings for old-age pensions, children's education, weddings, or housing.[2] Similarly, on the insurance front, SEWA Bank offers health, life, and asset insurance. SEWA Bank's deposit-linked Group Insurance Policy with the Life Insurance Corporation and General Insurance Corporation covers the depositors in case of maternity, widowhood, accident, hospitalization, loss of life, and exigencies like flood, fire, and riots. This has enabled the women to withstand the chronic risks to a considerable extent.

Credit is by far the biggest reason why self-employed women flock to SEWA Bank. Over time, the Bank's loan procedure has become simpler and more decentralized. It takes less than ten days from submitting the application to receiving the money in hand. What takes time is following up on the end use of the loan money, which calls for a lot of fieldwork on the part of the Bank. Of all the loans awarded by the Bank, 77 percent are unsecured loans.

The loan procedure is relatively simple. The banksathi first assesses the applicant. Before coming to a decision, she takes notes on several points: irregularity of income, unpaid debt installments, number of dependents in the family, number of children working at home, regularity in savings, absence of a steel cupboard in the house for storing valuables, the legal

2. *Annual Report of SEWA Bank, 2004*. Ahmedabad, India: Self-Employed Women's Association.

status of the slum she lives in, the general safety of the neighborhood, involvement in police cases, and also the whiteness of teeth—a sure sign of tobacco addiction that indicates a steady expense. The presence of any one or more of these factors does not disqualify a candidate—such mitigating circumstances are, after all, a part of the women's lives. The banksathi's role is to note potential areas of trouble, but also to note areas where supplementary help can be provided to the women—access to *crèche*, to legal services, or to medical attention. Assessing the creditworthiness of a woman whose husband drinks or who is a widow without family support, for example, requires taking into consideration a lot of other factors and making certain allowances.

A bank facilitator then follows up on the banksathi's recommendation and probes deeper into an applicant's business activities. She notes the level of competition in the business, the family's finances and their productive assets, the woman's entrepreneurial skills, and her overall participation in the Bank's savings programs.

The facilitator then asks the banksathi to explain the loan application process, the repayment rules, and the implications of overdue payments to the potential member. Only after there is no doubt that the woman has thoroughly understood the process will the banksathi sign the form recommending the woman. The application is then presented to the Loan Committee, which meets every third day and makes its sanctions. If approved, the loan is disbursed through the main office of the Bank within a week to ten days. The banksathi then informs the woman whether her loan has been accepted or rejected. The banksathi earns approximately 1 percent on savings and 3 percent on loans over the total business she has transacted.

Sometimes, when the Bank hesitates to lend to women living in such poor conditions that even their identity cannot be verified, a board member sometimes steps in to help such women get a ration card, a voting card, or an electricity connection so that they can establish a legal identity. Since the Bank board is made up of members who can identify with such cases, they are quick to note the need for merging all kinds of support services— be they legal, medical, childcare, or housing related.

Today, the Bank runs four sub-centers in areas of Ahmedabad where large numbers of our members work or reside. About seventy banksathis are engaged in keeping the contact between the Bank and the women alive and healthy. The center in Rakhial, for example—the second largest of the four centers—is situated in the thick of an industrial labor area, in a narrow, three-story building. Every house in the neighborhood is teeming with factory workers, contract laborers, or home-based workers rolling bidis or incense sticks or stitching garments for factories linked with the global market. At the center, financial transactions take place on the ground floor; there is a lounge on the second floor where the women can talk to each other, hold meetings, make friends, or simply rest; while the third floor serves as a training room.

A team of three facilitators appointed by SEWA Bank work at the Rakhial center. Parul and Alka are college graduates with a background in commerce, while Maniben completed her education through the seventh grade. She worked in an ice factory before she joined the staff of SEWA Bank. The center also serves three other neighboring labor areas—Bapunagar, Odhav, and Naroda—where eleven banksathis, residents of those neighborhoods, operate.

On average, each month at the Rakhial center close to 3,000 women deposit anywhere from 5 to 1,000 rupees in their savings account and close to 2,000 women receive loans every month, most of whom are repeat borrowers. Around 300 new bank accounts are opened each month at this center, and they receive close to 100 new loan applications at the recommendation of banksathis.

A good way to understand the scope of the Bank is perhaps to look to its activity on a given day. Besides coming to deposit money into their regular savings accounts, the women also put away money under various savings schemes. They can save in a recurring fixed-deposit account, or they can take advantage of a saving scheme that would allow them to borrow small amounts promptly. One can deposit money in regular monthly installments of 250, 500, or 750 rupees for a period of five years toward the purchase of a new home. Women can also save in installments for auspicious occasions like weddings. They can participate in a pension scheme where they save small amounts regularly until the age of fifty-eight, though the amount can be withdrawn after ten years, if they choose.

Loan repayment transactions are constant throughout the day, taken to buy back gold ornaments from moneylenders or to rebuild homes destroyed in the earthquake, floods, or riots; to purchase new tools of their trade like carts, or machines or raw materials to expand their current business or to start a new one. More recently, loan applications to buy cell phones (called *theliphone* by our women because they are carried around in fabric pouches called *thelis*) have poured in. Women who run their businesses single-handedly have shown keen interest in the cell phone as a production tool—they can order supplies from the wholesale market by phone without leaving their retail site. Regular telephone lines from the government are difficult to get, especially for people living in slums. So one can thank the technological revolution for such democratic tools as the cell phone that leapfrogs barriers like middlemen and bureaucratic red tape!

In an effort to equip the women for making sound financial choices at every stage in life, the Bank conducts a training course that the women can attend weekly for eight weeks. The women learn about financial planning for all eventualities in life—for emergency needs, such as at the time of death, accident, sickness, disasters, or even maternity, one needs good insurance; for consumption needs, like day-to-day living, children's education, marriage, or old age, one needs savings; and for productive needs like getting the most return for your hard work and business acumen, one needs a loan. As women come to learn the different roles of savings and loans, they become better money managers.

During extended class discussions, the women talk about every aspect of their financial needs in an effort to arrive at what is essential and what is extraneous in life. Then each woman makes a budget plan for her family. They take this home to discuss with other family members who have their own opinions of what is essential and what is wasteful. Frequent cups of tea, bidi, chewing tobacco, alcohol, and entertainment like television and movies all come under attack until the family agrees on what stays and what goes. It is interesting that wedding expenses are considered nonnegotiable—everyone agrees that they cannot be touched!

This exercise opens up many doors in a woman's life. It helps her think more carefully about what her real assets and her real needs are, and by pulling together a budget for the family, she is able to open channels of discussion at home. Even their husbands, in proxy, attend the course. Shardaben, a shopkeeper, said that one week she had some important guests coming home for dinner, so she planned to miss her class that evening. Her husband, however, was so keen to learn the next lesson that he insisted she not miss a minute—he promised to cook for the guests and make apologies! Although it is possible to involve the husbands in these classes, we have found it better to empower the woman herself. Once she has a good understanding of her family's finances, she is able to implement changes at her own pace, in her own way, instead of having to give in to her husband's decisions.

The women love the certificate they receive at the end of any training course. Each woman takes a simple test in family budgeting at the end of her eighth session, but they all receive a certificate that they take home quite proudly.

The training sessions teach the Bank a lot. For example, old age is a cause for great anxiety among the women because their earning capacity diminishes and their dependence on others for survival increases. The knowledge that money is fungible really excites them—a 100-rupee note can be spent on food or medicine, or it can be spent on buying equipment— the effect of whether it is spent on consumption or on production can make a difference in one's life. The women find such ways of seeing fascinating. They realize they *do* have options. Sometimes they cry out, "If only you had told us this earlier, when we were still young!"

Individual counseling follows classroom counseling. Just emphasizing what instances warrant using one's savings, and in what case it is advisable to borrow, the women can avoid a lot of pitfalls. For the poor, who take loans to make ends meet, their repayment capacity is so limited that the debt trap consumes their life till its end. Simple advice, such as "do not borrow more than two or three times what you have," allows them to consider other options.

Roopaben, the wife of a factory worker earning 800 rupees per month, sold *cholaphali* (a chickpeas snack) on the street during the day. At night, she stitched quilts. On average, she earned 10 rupees a day. Her days of adversity started with her husband's illness. She borrowed 2,000 rupees at the interest rate of 5 percent per month to pay for his medical expenses. There was almost no income coming in during the period—he could not go to work for two months, so he brought in no money, while she lost her income selling snacks on the street, because she had to stay home and tend to his health. All she could attend to were her quilts, which unfortunately brought in very little money. When her husband was rehired, his new salary was lowered to 500 rupees per month for the same job. To make ends meet, their oldest son quit school and started working in a garage. Soon, her second son also joined his brother—together they earned a little more than 600 rupees per month. Roopaben worked hard, but her own health was getting weaker. She had contracted tuberculosis. To pay for her medical bills, her older son borrowed 2,000 rupees from his employer, who then deducted 200 rupees from his pay every month. To make matters worse, that monsoon season, heavy rains caused great damage to their rickety house and a wall collapsed. The family had to borrow 10,000 rupees at 5 percent interest to pay for emergency repairs. The enormous debt load and dwindling cash flow were a source of constant worry. Her stomach always seemed tied up in knots, until eventually the pain in her belly was so acute, she had to stay seated even when selling her street snack. Her daily income was no more than 25 rupees. The doctor said she needed a hysterectomy, so she borrowed 12,000 rupees by pawning the jewelry her father had given her upon her marriage to pay for the operation. Her second son also took an advance of 5,000 rupees against his salary to cover debt payments and the loss of her income. It was at this stage that Roopaben was introduced to SEWA Bank. She began by opening a savings account. As her health started improving, she could work more and more. She saved 50 rupees every month in her account. With the help of her now grown daughters, she could make and sell more cholaphali, so her business grew. She could then sign up to save 10 rupees a day in one of SEWA's daily-saving schemes.

She was well on the road to recovery when the 2000 earthquake shook the whole of Gujarat. It shook Roopaben's life as well. Although her house survived, there was very little work for almost a month. Her savings were depleted. As normal life resumed, she once again began saving 10 rupees a day until she had built up 2,000 rupees in her account. Against that, she took a loan of 10,000 rupees from SEWA Bank to help her sons buy equipment to set up a new auto rickshaw repair shop. She felt very grateful to her sons who had helped her in her struggles, so she wanted to help them in their enterprise. But as luck would have it, the following year, there were communal riots in the city and all work came to a standstill for weeks on end. It was hardly a good time to start a new garage business. Her husband's factory, which was in a riot-torn area, had suffered huge losses, and all the workmen were laid off. Her husband was once again unemployed. Her own business was small and her income was inadequate to support the family. Roopaben began to default on her SEWA Bank installments. Although she had suffered a setback, the Bank was willing to work with her because she had shown a capacity for perseverance in the past. She was well aware of her financial responsibility and was more than willing to work toward repaying the amount. As a qualified foreman in a machine shop, given the opportunity, her son was well able to run a good workshop. The Bank continues to work with Roopaben so that she can get back on her feet yet again.

Mangariben Ranaji is a handsome young woman who owns ten donkeys bought with money she borrowed from SEWA Bank. Her father was
a donkey trader, so she grew up taking care of them. At fifteen, she was
married to a man who drove his uncle's truck. But when that job vanished,
the two of them found work in the building construction industry. They
borrowed money to buy four donkeys at 3 percent interest and transported
sand from the riverbank to the construction site. When the new SEWA
Bank building was being constructed, they were supplying sand to the
builder. Mangariben did not fail to notice that all day long, poor women
like herself went in and out of the old building. One day she stopped to
ask what the women were doing there. "You can get loans here!" someone explained. "But first they want you to start saving." Mangariben
opened an account and started saving regularly. Eventually, taking a loan
of 5,000 rupees, to which she added 1,000 rupees of her savings, she bought
four donkeys—two for her husband and two for herself. Her husband
would leave home at 4 o'clock in the morning and dig sand from the river.
She would arrive at 8 o'clock, carrying his meal, with their two little daughters and four donkeys in tow. All day long they would load the donkeys
and walk to the worksite, delivering the sand. "We would work till we
made 100 rupees," she said. Usually by midday they made enough money
to return home and rest their donkeys. On their way, Mangariben would
often stop at SEWA Bank to operate her account. With her second loan of
6,500 rupees, she repaired her home and bought two more donkeys. After
several loans, and her extensive connections in the building industry, today
she has a pucca house to accommodate their family of fourteen—which
includes her ten donkeys.

The notoriously dry riverbed of the Sabarmati is now no longer dry—
the newly constructed Narmada Dam has brought water to the Sabarmati.
The water flows along the two banks so the sand is no longer easily accessible. With her current loan of 35,000 rupees added to her savings,
Mangariben bought a tractor. She plans to transport bricks and steel to builders on the outskirts of the city and to rural areas. It is only a matter of time
before Mangariben will be driving her tractor instead of herding donkeys.

The role of SEWA Bank's governing board is pivotal to the functioning
and scope of the Bank. The board meets every month and keeps the Bank's

feet firmly planted on the ground. The members discuss the latest developments and changing trends in their trades, but also guide the Bank toward or away from certain areas of operation. It is a powerful position to be in, and the women know it. In fact, it seems that once a board member of SEWA Bank, always a board member! Even a decade after their term on the board has expired, the women still introduce themselves as board members. This enormous sense of pride has more to do with intense identification with the mission of the Bank, and the maturity and broader understanding of their own role within it, than to any clinging to status. Retired board members continue to play a very active role at the grassroots level, interacting with their trade community on current issues, supporting and monitoring the banksathis in their work so that they do not abuse their considerable power, and visiting newer slum neighborhoods that need banking services. Besides, all ideas for the Bank's new financial products usually originate from the board members.

Because a lot of the urban poor have strong ties with their villages, they often invest their savings in reconstructing their village homes, or they remit money to family members struggling to survive. A great many return to the village to perform weddings and other religious ceremonies. Because banking services in rural areas are minimal, very often the village family depends on their urban relatives to take loans on their behalf.

Traditionally, Indians save in gold. Gold jewelry—as ornaments for the rich or as security for the poor, is part of most marriage transactions, and it is very often the only form of wealth a woman possesses. Either way, it is seen as the safest investment that can serve a family's need "in the middle of the night." In times of need, gold jewelry can be mortgaged; it is easily transportable, and it never loses value.

A SEWA study found that as soon as the women had some savings, 83 percent of the women bought gold for their own use—as a nest egg for their own future; and 36 percent bought gold to give to their daughters as a wedding gift.[3] Since a good deal of their cash savings go into purchasing gold, the Bank has been looking more closely at how best to accommodate this need. To tell the women that gold is a nonperforming asset is doing them a disservice. The poor have frequent and firsthand experience of all sorts of crises—financial and otherwise, and at such times gold has

3. Virginia Petrova. "Gold Product Research and Loan Product Research." Unpublished report, 2003.

proven to be failsafe time and again, while other economic systems like banks and insurance companies are slow to the rescue. So until we have an economic infrastructure that can provide a security safety net for the poor in our country, gold continues to be a good form of savings. The challenge for SEWA Bank is to make sure that the women diversify their assets through loans and savings and to provide service to the women in their time of need.

When SEWA Bank celebrated its twenty-fifth anniversary, the governing board decided to use the resources of a special fund to buy a small souvenir for all the shareholders of the Bank. Several ideas were tossed around—a wall clock, a transistor radio, a silk sari, educational scholarships for children, bank shares . . . but the only one that met universal approval was a gold nose ring! "So we can hold our nose high!" they clarified.

One of the biggest causes of indebtedness among the poor is the marriage ceremony. Huge amounts of money are borrowed to pay for gifts to the in-laws, to feed wedding guests, and to fulfill all sorts of social obligations in the community. It takes years for the family to repay the debt, but there is a common belief that if the wedding is sufficiently lavish, no one will have cause for complaint and the couple will have a worry-free married life. Out of twenty SEWA members who were all heavily indebted, sixteen had incurred the debts to marry their sons and daughters and half of the women had spent more than 50,000 rupees. All sixteen women belonged to different castes. Ironically, their castes did have provision for group marriages to minimize wedding expenses—each family needed to contribute less than 2,000 rupees to participate—but most women had looked away from that option. Out of the sixteen, only three women had taken a loan from SEWA Bank for the marriage—besides, one cannot presume that it was their only loan; twelve had borrowed from relatives and other unrevealed sources. Seven of them were paying an interest of 5 percent per month, and five of 3 percent per month. Only one of them had managed to pay off her debt— she worked as a domestic maid, and her son was married in a group ceremony organized by her caste.

"Instead of spending all that money on the ceremony, gifts, and food, would it not be easier to have a simple ceremony and deposit the money in a fixed-deposit account in your son's or daughter's name as a gift?" I'd argue. "People cannot 'see' the fixed deposit account. But a lavish wedding—no one could fail to notice that!" is the usual reply. "My daughter will be able to hold her head high in her in-laws' home," is another common response.

In 1986, the working capital of SEWA Bank crossed the 1 crore rupee mark. Usha Jumani, who had been the Bank's managing director and who was so instrumental in developing the Bank's unique identity, had stepped down. The Bank's foundation was now strong; it was time to look to the future. Looking around for a mid-career woman banker who would be interested in taking the Bank to the next level, I found Jayshree Vyas. Or rather, she found us! She was a senior loan officer at the Central Bank and her job involved evaluating all loans worth 10 million rupees and up. The irony did not escape anyone. Jayshree insisted that it was the power of the minuscule loans at SEWA Bank that really fascinated her. She was ready to work with us, in whatever capacity she could. I liked her enthusiasm and introduced her to the board. We all felt that her considerable experience in mainstream commercial banking would be an asset to us as our numbers grew, year after year. "I may have to unlearn a lot before I can learn," she smiled, and she was hired.

Jayshree brought a new, professional touch to the Bank that it badly needed. She streamlined the banking process and found ways to put our working capital to better use, without losing sight of the women's needs for an instant. During the 1990s, she introduced the Gold Card, a card that entitled good, repeat clients to quicker loan processing and preferred service at the Bank. It was the women who made the choice—quick loan approval was determined more important than a better interest rate, or even larger loan amounts. Jayshree also introduced the mobile van to serve those members living in far-away slums. Jayshree's life-cycle approach to a poor woman's banking needs has had an enormous impact on the Bank and its ability to reach out to more women.

The introduction of computers in 1987 simplified and sped up banking operations. Of course, the transition was neither easy nor quick. While it did not take long to master the machines, it took the staff almost two years to trust them! The movement of papers from table to table, seeking entries and approvals, was no longer necessary. Before, it took fifteen days to prepare a list of overdue loans; now it took less than a minute of just one staff member's time to pull up the report with any kind of breakdown one needed. Analyzing data became easier; decision making faster. The only problem, to this day, continues to be language. A lot of the reports need to be translated into Gujarati for the benefit of the members. English language classes are becoming essential for a lot of the bank staff. In the field, computer printouts of balances will not do for the women; they still prefer hand-written entries in the passbooks. Trusting any kind of system takes time, and only time can validate its trustworthiness.

Computers have accelerated the decentralization process at SEWA Bank. The instantaneous transfer of data from the sub-centers to the main office allows for more accurate accounting. It also helps the financial counselors pull up all the various accounts a person holds to get a better picture of their finances. Although the banksathis are not yet able to use the computers, it is only a matter of time before they do. They have taken quite a liking to cell phones, which they carry everywhere in their *thelis*. "Why is everyone smiling here?" the President of India, Dr. Abdul Kalam, asked the women at the bank counter when he came to visit SEWA. The reason was that the women's applications for loans to buy mobile phones had just been approved. The banksathis are now gradually requesting handheld devices to assist them in their work. But in order to achieve more efficiency, we need to customize the software to meet their needs.

Despite serving low-income women's groups, or perhaps because of it, SEWA Bank is a profitable venture distributing on average 15 percent of dividend each year to its members. Since it holds a large amount of deposits, it is sustainable and is not dependent on external funds or grants to meet its business and social objectives. At the same time, it has a profitable loan portfolio that provides it with the revenue stream to fund further growth.

The Bank that saw its humble beginnings in the cellar of the TLA moved to a new building in 1997. For years, the Bank was on the ground floor of the SEWA office building located at one end of the oldest bridge in the city—Ellis Bridge. Bursting at the seams, SEWA Bank now had to find new premises. We were looking in the working-class neighborhoods of the old city without finding anything that suited our needs. In 1997, a brand new set of buildings was being built at the other end of the bridge, and the tenants included the Export Import Bank of India, the Bank of Paris, and other mainstream financial institutions. SEWA Bank was offered the opportunity to purchase a floor. Much to my surprise, the board visited the site and approved heartily. "Who says a poor women's bank cannot sit next to a rich man's bank? We like marble floors too, you know!"

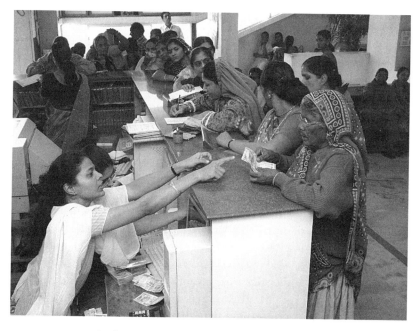

At the SEWA Bank counter. (Narendra Otia)

The Bank board has faced many challenges over the years. In 1998, the Reserve Bank of India liberalized the banking sector. SEWA Bank could determine what interest rates to charge its clients for lending and what interest to offer for saving. For the board to come to an informed decision, Jayshree first explained the parameters within which the board could base its decision. Details of the cost of funds, operating expenses, returns on assets, bad debts, and margin of profits were presented so that they could be analyzed and weighed before arriving at a number. One of the board members, Rehmatbibi (who was illiterate), said, "Let's stay close to the going market rate for savings and lending. Because if our savings interest rate is lower than the market rate, no one will deposit their money here, and if our lending interest rate is far lower than the market rate, the women will just turn around and sub-lend their loan money."

The strong links between the SEWA union, the federation of cooperatives, SEWA Insurance, and the Mahila Housing Trust enable SEWA Bank to deliver housing finance, insurance, pensions, and other social security schemes to its clients, in addition to banking products and services. The Bank takes a comprehensive view of the needs of its clients. This life-cycle approach has been crucial to the Bank's success.

Most of the clients of the Bank are new to banking. Over the years, after some experience and some exposure to savings accounts, successive loans, and SEWA Bank's services, the women are able to go from an uncertain livelihood and *kuchha* housing to a more secure livelihood and pucca brick structures. The women are able to survive small crises and financial uncertainties better with the support of the Bank and each other. During large-scale disasters, like the recent earthquake, when trade suffers and the economy breaks down, the women suffer enormously. At such times, SEWA Bank tries very hard to make sure that it remains stable in the face of disturbances. The Bank would like to assist the victims in many ways by playing the role of a buffer by providing small, quick loans that would be repayable at their convenience, or at least on a looser schedule. But regulating authorities are quite inflexible in their requirements— they will not permit such "aberrations" on the part of any bank or the design of a special product other than the standard one.

During the recent riots, SEWA Bank tried to build up a stabilization fund, independent from the regular bank finance. Our objective was to relieve the borrowers from the interest burden while still following the financial discipline. But the regulating inspectorate saw this in a different light; they feared that the Bank was devising a way to bring down its percentage of nonperforming assets. Banking rules do—and rightly so—ban any funds created to write off bank loans, but that was certainly not our intention. When national banks incur losses during such large disasters, the government of India comes to their rescue by pumping thousands of rupees into the bank's capital fund. But a small bank serving a totally poor clientele has no such recourse. There is to date no viable policy that keeps smaller banks sustainable in times of disaster.

The Bank is constantly trying to balance risk and security. When the women and their families face multiple and frequent disasters, when they incur expenses beyond their means or losses in their business, or when they are faced with chronic risks like low income, unemployment, or sickness, they turn to the Bank for help. The Bank has been able to provide help in so many areas by essentially sharing the risk that expectations have risen. "Why can't we have our own doctors, our own hospital?" many ask, in the hope that the Bank will undertake health insurance in addition to the group insurance that covers hospitalization, death, widowhood, and maternity for its 200,000 members.

Similarly, SEWA Bank and the SEWA union have entered into a partnership with the Ahmedabad Municipal Corporation to attend to the problem of housing for the poor because the house is also a work place for many informal-sector workers. The "Parivartan" housing program is designed to upgrade the slums in the city. Slums located on municipal land are first identified; then SEWA mobilizes the women slum dwellers to form a residents' association. Every household deposits 2,100 rupees with the municipal corporation, which entitles them to a toilet, a sewage system, water supply, and electricity in their new pucca house. The women may borrow the amount from SEWA Bank if they are unable to pay with savings. The title to the house is issued in the SEWA member's name, and it is entered into the official municipal record. Local SEWA leaders play a significant role in making this happen. Once the project is completed, the neighborhood tends to acquire a more respectable name—such and such colony or so and so *nagar*. However, working in collaboration with outside agencies, especially a government of any sort, is not without problems.

The municipality is quick in collecting funds, but slow to start the building process. Meanwhile, the women are impatient—they are paying interest on a loan that has yet to see any results. They feel frustrated and turn to the Bank for help, even though the Bank has no control over the government and other power structures. The overlap in the roles of SEWA and SEWA Bank also causes some confusion at times. By intervening on behalf of the women in dealing with the government, the municipality, or with insurance companies, the Bank often bears the brunt of the women's frustration. When, for example, an insurance company makes a low assessment of the damage to a riot victim's house, she is devastated. While the insurance company takes a limited view of what constitutes damage and how it occurred, for the woman, the loss continues to haunt her for years after the incident. Rebuilding a life, regaining trust, and recovering one's livelihood against overwhelming odds is a daunting task; while the Bank can play a crucial supportive role in recovery, it can by no means solve all problems. The clients' needs are greater than what an economic entity like a bank can provide. Yet the women see the Bank as "our bank," a provider, a sort of "mother" that provides shelter, is caring, understanding, forgiving, trusting, and "all-powerful." While admittedly SEWA Bank has tried to "mother" its clients, that is not its mission. Its mission is to empower the women themselves. For a formal financial body, serving clients who have grown in the traditional, nonformal culture of unwritten mutual trust, this is a challenge.

Time and again, the women say that SEWA should start a factory so that their children can find work, or start a hospital so that their health can be better taken care of at less expense, or to establish "our own insurance company" for better protection and quick compensation. True enough. Having a savings account or having the ability to take repeat loans does not necessarily mean that a woman's children will find work or that the education loan will equip them to face a slump in the employment market. Loans taken for specific purposes that are supposed to yield fruit do not come with any such guarantees. "Our own" SEWA Bank is not able to control the macro structural factors, and this is a reality to reckon with.

Poverty can be removed not by charity but by raising the earnings of the poor, by productive work, and by providing financial services that suit their needs. There is also a need to weave financial services with employment and livelihoods. Credit is not a quick fix to poverty. Credit is not the end, but the means. Ensuring livelihood security against the onslaught of the commercial and large industrial global competitors requires policy intervention through collective action by producers, entrepreneurs, and their organizations. These organizations have yet to build up their capacities and plan in a strategic way.

The Bank brings the women together—as workers, as businesswomen, as sisters; it makes them more mobile; it helps them learn to take charge of their finances, to plan for their future; it gives them an incentive to embrace new knowledge, including basic literacy; and above all, it teaches them about independence.

I have heard the women call their new, money-generated strength *"powershakti."* This powershakti can have a mixed effect on the women's lives. Increasing financial independence is significantly empowering to her as an individual, and it also increases her value within the family and her standing in the community. But as soon as the status quo is upset, she invariably has to face hostilities from both the family and the community. At such times, her slowly and steadily developing inner courage comes to her rescue. Once that happens, then the self-confidence and self-esteem are there to stay.

6

Health Care

In 1977, I was reviewing the reasons why some women had defaulted on their SEWA Bank loans. Out of five hundred, twenty women had defaulted on their loans because they died. Of these twenty, fifteen had died in childbirth. Just two years earlier, I had seen them, loan applications in hand, active and alive and enthusiastic about expanding their business. To die in childbirth in this day and age? I felt upset and rather angry with myself. How could we have been so preoccupied with the economic needs of the women that we were blind to their basic health needs?

Sickness is a recurring crisis in the lives of poor women. They are illness-prone because their living, working, and financial conditions make them vulnerable to disease and malnutrition. Few have ready access to clean drinking water, or to an adequate supply of water for washing. Their living conditions are often unsanitary because municipal services like sewage and drainage are nonexistent or outdated. Their diet is inadequate for lack of money; they have limited knowledge of how to prevent or take precautions against disease; and medical help is often out of reach—both financially and in terms of distance. Medicines are expensive, and the financial need to keep working despite their illness gives their weakened bodies no time to rest and recuperate.

Apart from illness caused by cramped and unsanitary living conditions, SEWA members, who work in a variety of trades, also suffer from occupation-specific health problems. Street vendors suffer from asthma and lung diseases because they breathe the exhaust from cars and buses all day long; they are also prone to traffic accidents and injuries. Cart pullers too suffer a high degree of traffic injuries, but miscarriages are even more common, caused by the constant strain on their back and stomach muscles from pulling carts and lifting loads. Bidi rollers and their family members breathe tobacco dust that also causes respiratory problems. Rag pickers looking for recyclables in garbage dumps are vulnerable to all kinds of skin diseases, stomach ailments, and tetanus. Because women are commonly found in jobs that require repetitive, labor-intensive work and use low-grade tools and materials, chronic, work-related aches and pains are a part of their daily lives.

Pregnancy—a time when upper- and middle-class women take special care of their diet and enjoy especially good health—is a difficult time for poor, working women who suffer from anemia, malnutrition, and physical strain. For the sake of economy, many suffer gynecological problems in silence and place a low priority on their own health, postponing medical help until it is often too late. In fact, the poor may well consider pregnancy a life-threatening illness. Maternal and infant mortality looms large among the poor.

First we looked into tapping any existing medical network that we could direct the women to. Although government-run clinics were affordable, the poor tended to avoid them. The lines at these clinics were long, and the women could ill-afford so much time away from work. The staff's attitude toward the women was often unsympathetic—they considered the women dirty, ignorant, and unreliable when it came to following medical advice, and this attitude reflected in the kind of care the women received. The women too had little confidence in the municipal doctors: middle-class men and women whose medical advice seemed so impractical to them—prescribing medication and operations they could not afford, recommending diets they were completely unfamiliar with, and talking of proper rest and exercise when their only option was work. Some women turned to private doctors who had a reputation for quick fixes, in the hope that a little extra money in fees would rid them of their problems once and for all. But during pregnancy, almost 70 percent of poor women turned to the dai—the midwife—for help and advice.

The dai lives in the community and knows its people well. As a member of the community, she is aware of the general health of the women and of their chronic problems. She also knows who has had a tough time delivering babies and how many of a woman's children have survived; she knows which woman can afford to eat well, and who has a good support network in times of need. We took a closer look at the role of the dai and found a hard-working woman, whose vast experience and traditional knowledge could be built upon. By upgrading her traditional skills and learning about more modern medical practices, the dai had the potential of playing a wider role as a health care provider in the community.

SEWA's interest in the dai arose for a second, equally important reason—she is self-employed. While valued for her work, she receives no fixed income for her services. Traditionally, her needs were taken care of by the entire village, in cash and in kind. But with changing times, her professional status and income have declined. Modern medicine has rendered her services undervalued and outdated. While the current generation of dais is getting old and infirm, few young women are stepping into the profession. This was a dying, indigenous institution that deserved to be rejuvenated.

Ranjanben Desai, a senior organizer at SEWA who was working with rag pickers, conducted the first survey of dais in Gandhinagar district. The knowledge and skill base of dais desperately needed upgrading. Even more important, certain harmful and risky traditional practices had to be stopped. SEWA set up a dai school to train the women in modern and safe methods of child delivery. Initially, SEWA's efforts were predominantly focused on training the local dais, who could take care of 80 percent of the day-to-day illnesses and health problems of women and children. The women were also trained in dispensing basic medicines, initially under the supervision of a medical doctor and a team of medical interns. The training was thorough but unconventional; the women's extensive hands-on experience in the field and the wide theoretical knowledge of the doctors made for a rich and lively give-and-take form of learning. This group of women developed into a fairly large team of sixty *arogya sevikas*, or health workers, in rural districts. Eventually, we were faced with the question: What direction should this health initiative take?

It is SEWA policy that all its services should be run, owned, managed, and used by the worker-members themselves. They must ultimately be economically viable and self-supporting. Although such economic initiatives are born as a result of trade union activity, I feel they have no place within the structure of a trade union. Economic enterprises therefore become independent cooperatives that function independent of the union.

It was not until we found some seed money and good leadership in the person of Mirai Chatterjee that we could launch a health cooperative. Mirai came to SEWA in 1984, having earned a degree in Public Health from Johns Hopkins University. She brought with her not only a first-class intellect, but also an enormous willingness to listen. Whether it is due to her sparkling personality, or because she likes to put flowers in her hair, the women opened up to her easily, and called her Meeraben. But building the Health Cooperative was a slow process.

It was not until May 1990 that the People's Health Cooperative, called the Lokswasthya Cooperative, was finally allowed to register. As always, the issue was the viability of our venture—poor, ignorant women running a health cooperative? And you think you can do it without doctors, but with dais? Because we had no model to copy, the officials took a long time to approve of our aims and bylaws.

In an effort to introduce the idea of dai-run health cooperatives to the state government, we invited the health minister to attend a meeting of more than 700 rural agewans from several rural districts. I began by lecturing to him that it would be a great mistake to ignore the importance of dais in the health infrastructure of India—it would be like ignoring the wisdom of your grandmother in the family. Then I turned to the women and asked them, "How many of you were delivered at the hands of a dai?" An overwhelming number of hands went up, including the minister's! "In fact," he said, "my widowed mother was a village dai!" I was duly chastened; I was one of the very few delivered by a medical doctor. The minister, however, agreed to provide funds for a dai school.

Dai training involves a lot of learning and unlearning. Six twelve-day sessions begin with a general discussion between the dais and their medical trainer about common gynecological practices and the reasons why they do or do not work. This initial discussion is fundamental to understanding the strengths and weaknesses of prevalent practices, and it gives the trainer an indication of where she can fill in the gaps in their understanding. Invariably, it all begins with an introduction to male and female anatomy. Most dais have just a rudimentary idea of human anatomy, so physiological charts and diagrams hold great fascination for them. The process of reproduction, the growth of the fetus at every trimester, and the changes in the mother month after month are discussed at length. The women are best able to retain new information when they can see the process as whole—complementing, supplementing, or supplanting what they already know. The women learn why sterilized tools and clean hands are important, but they also learn why the strenuous massaging of the uterus to induce labor is harmful. Postnatal care of the mother, which is generally neglected, is also emphasized.

As new professionals, the dais are encouraged to charge fees for their services; in villages, they may charge a land-owning family 101 rupees, but a landless family may be asked to pay 51 rupees. Although each caste usually has its own dai, when the dais are well-trained, women from upper castes do not hesitate to call trained lower-caste dais for their deliveries. At such times, the men too treat the dais with due respect, no matter what her caste.

Because of their role as helpers in time of need, dais are respected in the community, and they often take on leadership roles. Nanduben from Anasan village is now a dai trainer, although just a few years ago, her only identity was that of a dalit, a low-caste woman. Recently, Nanduben sat on an expert panel at a World Health Organization (WHO) conference in Mexico, an experience that has given her great encouragement. Back in her village, she is now a strong candidate for the position of Sarpanch, the village head.

Although dai cooperatives are viable institutions for implementing various reproductive and child health programs, the government has yet to see the potential of the role the dai can play in the nation's health system. SEWA has been advocating, in every possible forum, its confidence in dais and in positioning them at the center of all community-level health activities.

In the government's revised Reproductive and Child Health Policy, the role of the dai is missing. The policy envisions that 80 percent of the births will occur at an institution, where a nurse will replace the dai. How the formal health system of clinics and nurses will actually reach the people is still unclear. The health system does not favor the untrained; the challenge then is to make a strategic alliance between the trained and the traditional, the nurse and the dai, to work together in communities.

By 1987, the demand for health education from SEWA's growing membership increased, and our focus shifted to health information and education. As word of our health efforts spread in the surrounding villages, three

Shakriben explaining
the reproductive
process with the help
of a multi-flapped
apron.
(Amit Dave)

more health cooperatives were formed in Gandhinagar, Kheda, and
Mehsana districts. Each cooperative runs health centers that provide primary health care. Every cooperative also runs health camps quite regularly, with a special focus on gynecological and pediatric problems. The
health workers organize the camps with the support of government medical officers from the Primary Health Centres and private doctors in their
area. The patients pay for medicines and laboratory tests.

The health camp in village Jakhda in Sanand taluka is a typical example. It is a day-long women's event, held in the two-room panchayat
building. At the entrance, a health worker registers each woman's name
and health details on a card and explains the medical check-up process
to her. Women then wait their turn in a long queue to see the doctor.
Two female physicians examine the patients in one room, while a nurse-

technician conducts diagnostic tests, including Pap smears, in the second room. Outside on the veranda, a pediatrician examines any children that come along. Close by, a group of village women watch video tapes on subjects like "Know Your Body" with a mix of curiosity and embarrassment. There is also a medicine counter filling the doctors' prescriptions. The government provides subsidized medicines at such mobile camps held in interior villages that are far from any public health centers.

There are also small group discussion sessions where the women can ask and receive all sorts of information on nutrition or health care. Varsha, a young and relatively inexperienced health worker, explains why it is important to keep sanitary rags clean and not hidden in dusty places. The women listen in silence. She also tells the women to eat green leafy vegetables to prevent anemia. "We don't bother to grow vegetables around here," the women say. "The water is too saline." Varsha then suggests they put jaggery and not sugar in their tea, because it has more nutritional value. The women quickly argue, "Jaggery increases bleeding during menstruation. Don't you know that?" Varsha then suggests that sprouting increases the nutritional value of a *dal* like *moong*. But the women retort, "Who has the time for such fancy cooking?" However, when Varsha produces the sprouted moong salad she has prepared, they crowd around her for a taste. Some immediately ask her for the recipe and others wrap some salad to take home to share with their family. Most of the women eat roti with tea during the day and *khichdi* for supper. Vegetables and rice appear on their plates hardly once or twice a week.

There are no men around the camp, so the women look relaxed. In the evening, they rush home to cook the evening meal and report the day's events to their family and friends. Some put their newfound knowledge to use; others think about what they learned but continue as always. The health workers notice that not all women can come to the camp; some cannot afford to miss a day's work. Regrettably, this is how the poorest miss out.

Over time, we came to realize that such camps are quite effective because they save time and money all around. The women welcome them because they are local, and because they can go in the company of other women of their community, so they feel comfortable asking questions. At the end of the day, patients with serious illnesses are referred to a "bigger doctor" in town. The health workers keep track of the follow-up. "If only the health workers would visit our village everyday!" the women sigh.

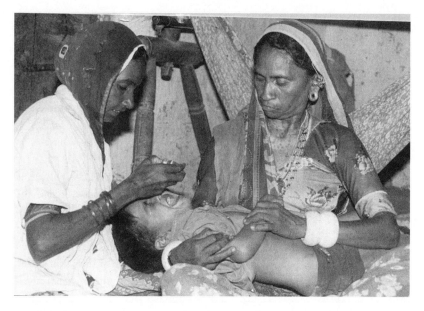

Midwife Kaliben administering polio vaccines at a village health center.
(SEWA Academy)

Health camps in urban areas face a different set of problems. Tuberculosis (TB) is a major killer of poor people living in crowded, unhygienic
slums. The treatment is expensive and drawn out; a TB patient requires
50 rupees a day for medication, while her daily income may range from
30 to 80 rupees. As a result, the patient does not even initiate treatment or
may not complete the course. The uncured are most likely to infect others
in the family, and thus TB spreads fast in slums.

SEWA health organizers work in collaboration with the Ahmedabad
Municipal Corporation to provide information and education about TB,
to identify suspected TB patients, and to refer them to microscopy centers
for sputum and other tests. They may also provide supervised treatment,
take care of the tight follow-up, and ensure completion of treatment.

A lot of this work is done in the labor areas of the city, Chamanpura
and Amraiwadi. This collaboration, which started in 1999, goes by the
acronym DOTS (Directly Observed Treatment, Short Course). The treatment is assigned to SEWA's health cooperative, which manages the TB
centers with a laboratory facility and eleven barefoot doctors. The pa-

tients—men and women—often come on their own, with complaints of chronic cough, but mostly they are identified at local health camps, at education classes, or at SEWA meetings. The treatment is funded by the WHO and the Indian government. About 4,000 patients have been treated through SEWA's program; almost all TB patients have completed the course of treatment.

The latest method of TB detection is not by an X-ray but through three periodic sputum tests. The patient is treated with a daily dose of seven to ten tablets. The DOTS worker has to be very regular and persuasive with the patient and must administer the dose with her own hands. Often she has to be tactful; since TB carries a social stigma, patients like to keep the treatment secret from neighbors and relatives. Large doses of medicines have to be taken with food, and that is a problem. "This stomach wants seven rotis, not seven pills," complains the patient. Milk is seldom an option.

TB is an airborne disease. The crowded city slums are getting more crowded every day. A slum like Shankarbhavan in the old city of Ahmedabad has 1,413 houses, with an average of seven persons sleeping in one room. Thirty percent of the families share their sleeping space with goats, chickens, dogs, and birds, breathing the same air.

The Muslim areas like Raofni-chali and Rabia-ni-chali are even more crowded. No wonder these slums have the highest incidence of TB. In the Jamalpur and Dariapur areas, men are pushed out to sleep on street pavements or in mosques. In Bhaipura, there are very few women; mostly men live there. They are cart pullers and casual daily-wage earners who drink in the night and forget to take their dose. The DOTS worker goes early in the morning to administer the pills, before the men leave for work. The liquor interferes with the TB medication, but there is little the health worker can do except remind them.

The latest TB medicines are very effective, but when a patient defaults on the dosage, the relapse is severe. There are more men than women among the patients, but there are more women than men among the cured.

SEWA health workers work hard in the neighborhood. Of all the TB centers in the city, we have the highest conversion rate (91 percent), the highest cured rate (87.5 percent), and the lowest (4 percent) dropout rate.[1] This wins us no awards, however. The municipal staff complains, half in

1. TB Control Society. *Revised National TB Control Programme, Ahmedabad City.* 2004.

jest, "Why do you find so many new patients day after day? You SEWA-
wallahs spoil our numbers!" With a growing reputation for good health
care, the city has begun to attract increasing numbers of TB patients from
Rajasthan.

The sale of medicines at the village health centers was generating only a
modest income for the Cooperative because the drugs were sold on a no-
profit basis. In order to be sustainable, the Health Cooperative needed to
expand its activities. With an initial capital investment of 70,000 rupees, a
small drug shop was opened near the SEWA office in Ahmedabad. Its sales
of 3,000 rupees a month were encouraging, but inadequate.

The head of L.G. Municipal Hospital in Ahmedabad visited our small
medicine shop and saw our efforts at providing cheap generic medicines
to the poor. He encouraged us to scale up our activities by serving larger
numbers of poor families through the municipal hospitals. At the invitation of the Ahmedabad Municipal Corporation, SEWA's Health Cooperative was asked to run a round-the-clock, low-cost drug counter at the L.G.
Municipal Hospital. The municipal corporation also advanced us, interest free, 500,000 rupees as seed money.

Fortunately, we already had three years of experience running such a
low-cost medicine outlet. A bright young pharmacist named Mittal Shah
took on the new responsibility of running the medicine counter at the
hospital. With her energy and enthusiasm, the counter was open and running in no time. The hospital staff was also supportive of our efforts, and
the doctors supported our presence by prescribing generic drugs instead
of brand-name medicines. Success, however, was still elusive.

The other more serious problem in the early months was the hostility
we faced from the neighboring drug stores. The huge difference between
our prices and theirs was a real threat to their business. One shop, located
right outside the hospital gates, which had done so well in the past, had
to shut down, due to competition from us. Seven others located around
the hospital had to discontinue their night shift. One of their men, posing
as a patient, tried to frighten the customers by yelling loudly that we were
keeping poor quality medicines. The following week, late at night, the
shopkeepers dispatched a group of thugs to frighten our team of young
girls on the night shift. But although they initially succeeded, other SEWA

sisters rallied to their rescue. Union leaders like Chandaben and Sumanben, lionesses when provoked, had faced such intimidation tactics before, and they spent several nights at the drug counter to boost the spirits of the young team. Eventually, the crisis subsided.

Two years later, the municipality invited the Health Cooperative to open a counter in Shardabai Hospital, located in another vast working-class area of Saraspur. We readily accepted the offer, as Saraspur was home to a great many SEWA members. Ila Shah was our new manager and pharmacist.

The low-cost drug counters of our Health Cooperative in Ahmedabad faced another boycott, this time from the city's chemists' association. They felt that our low prices distorted the entire drug market. This boycott was more serious than our earlier crises, and continued in force for over a year, despite numerous representations by us before the State Health Department. It was a difficult period. The chemists' association tried their best to choke off our medicine supply. However, because of our high volume of sales, many small wholesalers continued to supply to us surreptitiously. There were some traders, however, who were supportive of our cause, and in the end, we managed to pull through with their support.

The main purpose in our retail vending effort was to promote the use of cheaper, generic drugs. But because the doctors of Shardabai Hospital did not always prescribe generic drugs, we were forced to carry brand medicines as well. We took the initiative of trying to convince the doctors to prescribe generic drugs, as we had done in the case of L.G. Hospital, but to no avail. We received no support from the doctors.

Our agreement with the L.G. Hospital expired in 1999, and the municipality decided not to renew it. Those doctors who had supported the use of generic drugs had since retired or were transferred to other hospitals. The superintendent doctor, who had initially invited us to the L.G. Hospital, had left the country. The Health Cooperative looked around for a suitable retail space in the neighborhood, but local landlords were reluctant to rent to us for fear of pressure from other shops. The agreement at the Shardabai Hospital, however, has been renewed twice; on average, 400 customers are served every day.

It is regrettable that we are caught up in the politics of curative medicines. Better nutrition, clean water, better housing, good rest, and fresh air are preventive medicines that have a lasting impact on health, and I wish we could turn our attention to those areas as well.

Housing is a health issue for the poor. Ever-sprawling slums devoid of basic civic amenities are a hot bed for illnesses. Forty-one percent of Ahmedabad's population lives in slums. This population accounts for 77 percent of the city's employment and contributes 46 percent of the income generated in the city.[2] The population of Ahmedabad slums has been growing faster than the overall population.

In 1997, the number of people per public waterstand was 133, and only 26 percent of the slums had a household toilet. In twelve slums where many SEWA members reside, 35 percent of the residents reported that there was no garbage collection service by the city.[3]

In 1995, a program called Parivartan, meaning "change" was launched by the Ahmedabad Municipal Corporation in active partnership with SEWA. The Parivartan Project aimed at improving the basic physical infrastructure of certain slums located on municipal and government lands. It also identified certain necessary internal home improvements. The slum dwellers formed a residents' association. Cost sharing was equally divided between the municipal corporation, the private sector, and the residents' association. Each household paid one third of the total on-site capital cost of the services provided, including water supply to the home, a sewage connection, paved internal roads, lanes and by-lanes, storm water drainage, street lighting, solid waste management, and landscaping. SEWA Bank was the financial institution for the community project.

The slum improvement project has had a direct impact on the health of the slum dwellers. A 2002 SEWA study found that with access to water and drainage, the proportion of people bathing daily increased from 74 percent to 96 percent.[4] This resulted in a marked improvement in women's ability to take care of personal hygiene, as well as a dramatic reduction in water-borne diseases like malaria, gastroenteritis, skin infections, typhoid, and jaundice. The average monthly medical expense of the families decreased from 131 rupees to 74 rupees.

2. SEWA Academy. "Parivartan and Its Impact: A Partnership Programme of Infrastructure Development in the Slums of Ahmedabad City." Unpublished report, 2002.
3. Mihir Bhatt. *Assessing the Performance of Municipal Services for the Poor in Ahmedabad: The Report Card Project.* 1999.
4. SEWA Academy. "Parivartan and Its Impact: A Partnership Programme of Infrastructure Development in the Slums of Ahmedabad City." Unpublished report, 2002.

Chhagan Ratna na Chhapra, a name that means hutments owned by Chhagan Ratna, the landlord, was a slum that received municipal services under our project. Its dignified new name is Sinheshwarinagar. The change from *chhapra* to nagar is not just one in name. Compared with the neighboring Madrasi ni Chali, which was unfortunately not included in the project because it is on private land, the difference in living conditions is clearly apparent—in Madrasi ni Chali, only 58 percent of the residents are able to take daily baths because they do not have a municipal water connection.

Babuben, a vegetable vendor and SEWA member who lives in Sinheshwarinagar, has a two-room house now registered in her own name. Although suffering since childhood from a fungal skin infection, she managed to bathe just once every two or three days. "We hardly ever washed our bed spreads and quilts because they consume so much water in washing! During my first pregnancy, I still had to fetch water from a public tap quite far away. Walking with a day's supply of water was not easy in my condition. I took a bad fall and almost lost my baby. And in those days, the only place to defecate was to squat by the railway tracks after dark. Women did not have an easy time. Today it seems like I am a new person in a new place. Even the worm that has lived in my belly for as long as I can remember is gone. These are the blessings of Goddess Sinheshwari!"

Infrastructure development in poor neighborhoods has had a direct and positive impact not only on health, but also education, nutrition, and social relationships. Electric lighting in the home has made it possible for children to study at night, because many work after school to supplement some of the family income. With increased light and fans during the summer months, productivity for home-based producers like bidi rollers goes up considerably. As Jiviben, with her dramatic flair puts it, *"Ghar badla, dooniya badli!"* meaning, "A changed house, a world transformed!" Slum improvement is poverty alleviation. The women all agree that having better amenities at home has even improved their social status—their relatives like to visit them, and the community no longer thinks twice before marrying a daughter into their neighborhood.

Under the Parivartan program, twelve out of fifty slums have been upgraded; the rest are still waiting eagerly for changes. Bureaucratic procedures and incessant delays impede progress at every step, yet the women do not give up hope—they know they can make a difference.

Despite the relative success of the Parivartan Project, its future depends on what kind of priority the municipality puts on it. In today's soaring real estate markets, urban land is a political issue. The Slum Clearance Board and the Housing Board, initially constituted for the purpose of uplifting the poor and their living conditions, are on the verge of being dismantled. The land, earmarked for the poor, will soon be on sale in the open market.

But we have long since learned that although government policies and attitudes have a significant impact on the lives of the poor, what has an even greater impact is change from within the community. So on the health front, building up a community-based cadre of barefoot doctors-cum-midwives is an exercise in capacity building and community development. Already, slowly but surely, the health workers are changing lives, changing neighborhoods, and spreading knowledge and awareness.

The Shankarbhuvan slum, on the bank of Sabarmati River, is one of the oldest and the worst in the city. Shardaben, an inhabitant of Shankarbhuvan, was among the first batch of health care trainees. Although still in her teens, Shardaben had already been through a lot; her husband had not only abandoned her, but had taken their little daughter with him. The health worker training was a godsend; she enjoyed what she learned and her spirits revived. Working in the community as a barefoot doctor gave her the confidence she needed to begin afresh. Today, she trains both health workers and *dais*.

Because of her active leadership, every child born in Shankarbhuvan in the past fifteen years has been immunized, and her role in reducing malaria in the community is not insignificant. Shardaben is not coy about teaching men and women about safe sex and talking to newlyweds about family planning.

Drainage is her community's biggest problem. The residents' demand for a gutter line in Shankarbhavan has so far been unsuccessful. Even after five consultation meetings, the municipality keeps demanding more and more data from them. Because the slums are on illegally occupied land, they have few basic services. Garbage is not cleared regularly; toilets are in the open, on the riverbank, without any privacy. One nongovernmental organization did build a toilet complex for the residents, but the women's toilet was closed down because no one kept it clean. "The backyards are so dirty that you have to watch where you put your foot on the ground. No one likes to visit my house because the whole area smells," Shardaben laments. Her fight for municipal services continues.

Raising the awareness of health issues in the community is a slow process; but small successes show through in many different ways. There is no longer a blind faith in or blind fear of doctors; the reason behind how and when to take medicines becomes clearer, and where to turn to for affordable treatment and medicines becomes common knowledge.

There are many examples of such transformations. The process of receiving and giving health education becomes a lifeline for numerous SEWA members, and many later become active leaders. The Health Cooperative has elected many of these strong leaders to a three-year term on the board. Of the seven board members, six are from the working class. This has kept the Cooperative focused on poor women and their needs.

Health insurance for the poor does not exist, yet they are the ones that need it the most. Rehmatben, a block printer, had an appendectomy that cost 3,000 rupees. As a result, she had no income for one month. Kankuben hurt her back when her buffalo kicked her during milking. Three months later she had not recovered enough to be able to work again. Being the breadwinner of the house, she had to borrow money for daily expenses from a moneylender. Her downward spiral had begun.

SEWA tried to address this issue by looking into the possibility of group insurance for poor, self-employed women. Poor women are considered "bad risks" because they are always in a crisis of one sort or another. Besides, the insurers believe that transaction costs would be too high. Apart from the Life Insurance Corporation, none of the insurance companies would agree to insure SEWA members. But since the mid-nineties, the insurance sector is gradually being liberalized and times are changing for the better. Today, some insurance companies are prepared to insure poor self-employed women, even though it is only in the case of hospitalization.

But when there are no hospitals near the village, when transportation to and from her village is irregular, not available or unaffordable, when a woman cannot afford to lose even a single work day, when children must be left unattended so a woman can work, when cattle and the housework have to be attended to no matter what the circumstances, most medical problems get neglected until they turn into crises. Common long-term sicknesses like tuberculosis, cancer, piles, high and low blood pressure, and diabetes are particularly damaging. They rapidly drain the family budget, yet unless the woman is hospitalized, she has no medical insurance.

Until 1980, the concepts of group insurance and risk pooling were virtually unknown to us at SEWA. The idea was new and puzzling. "I have been well most of this year, so since I did not have an emergency, will I get my insurance premium back?" was a common question in the beginning. Vimo SEWA, SEWA's insurance plan, is not yet self-financed because of a considerable dropout rate and high operational costs for maintaining constant field contact with a large membership. It covers the members' risks related to natural and accidental death, widowhood, hospitalization, and loss of assets. A special deposit-linked scheme covers benefits like maternity, dentures, and hearing aids. In 2003, we introduced children's health insurance under the family insurance package. Vimo SEWA also covers all members for cataract operations. The most widely sought-after risk coverage is for life and health insurance. The current rate of death claims is 3.5 per 1,000 members a year. Accidental death claims are 14.5 percent, but the cause is sometimes difficult to determine. When municipal officials do not know the real cause of death, it is their habit to write "heart attack" on death certificates. Vimo SEWA's claims committee takes, on average, forty-five days from death to reimburse the insurance payment. Vimo SEWA pays upfront and the insurance company reimburses us. Health claims take fifteen days for reimbursement.[5]

SEWA members are now preparing to establish Vimo SEWA as a SEWA Insurance Cooperative, much like the SEWA Cooperative Bank. Today, a total of 106,479 men, women, and children are insured under a comprehensive group insurance scheme for life and for nonlife risks. Two of the most important outcomes of health insurance have been stronger links with local doctors and more responsive referral services for SEWA members.

Working with larger entities like insurance companies or the municipality has its advantages and disadvantages. Tensions rise over the government's "family planning mindset" that still perceives poor women as candidates for population control and sterilization. Although this is slowly giving way to a more holistic approach, it is only because SEWA has insisted that government policy makers and medical service providers conduct a dialogue with the health worker and the community at every turn. This has eventually led to a healthy respect for the abilities and understanding of the humble health care worker.

5. Denis Gerrad. "Paper for the Ministry of Finance." Ahmedabad, India. Unpublished paper, 2003.

The government increasingly wants to take up large-scale campaigns to eradicate TB, malaria, and HIV/AIDS by using SEWA's close links with the community. However, tensions build when our health care workers are transferred from programs directly administered by SEWA to government-linked programs. When Padma, one of our best primary health care workers, was transferred to a government-run AIDS team, the loss became obvious. Working under the straitjacket system, there was no room to use her excellent interpersonal skills, which were great for communicating nutrition, hygiene, and primary care to poor women. It is difficult for people's organizations to adjust to the kind of vertical programs that the WHO and similar international organizations demand.

However, the focus of the SEWA Health Cooperative has shifted from direct primary health care to service provision through camps and referrals. By working in collaboration with the municipal corporation and the government health system, our effort is focused on revitalizing an existing system and making it accountable to the people it purports to serve. The hope is to be able to reach out to a larger number of people.

Being a trade union with a growing membership, there is always a huge demand for health information and services. As SEWA grows, so, justifiably, does the demand for health care. However, maintaining quality while at the same time accommodating expansion is difficult. Building strong, capable people takes time, and it will be a while before we have a critical pool of health care workers who are both good service providers and good leaders—they cannot evolve overnight. SEWA's strong organizers are not necessarily strong managers. The pace of our self-development and capacity building has to match the growing demand.

For SEWA's health cooperatives, the key issue remains to be sustainable and still serve the poor. One way is to bring new medical technology and products to the doorsteps of the poor. Of course, they need to be both appropriate and affordable. Properly trained health workers can learn to conduct eye examinations; administer pregnancy, urine, and sugar tests; or test for anemia.

The issue of occupational health hazards, which was one of the primary reasons for the formation of SEWA's health care program, is regrettably still largely unexplored. Rag pickers, stitchers, and junksmiths need better-designed tools that will not endanger their health. Although we have developed tool prototypes in partnership with the National Institute of Design and the National Institute of Occupational Health, they are still expensive and out of reach of workers. Technical solutions like changes in the use of equipment or changing production processes require skills our health team does not have, so we have concentrated our efforts in the area of primary health and health education. We have managed to introduce ergonomically designed sickles among agricultural workers, tables among incense-stick rollers, gloves among tobacco workers, for example, but these efforts are still small and modest.

For women, whose first priority is employment, studies that show how dangerous or toxic their work is have little impact because they have few alternatives. While more studies and research are needed on their work-related illnesses, we also need to find work alternatives, skill upgrading, and technical solutions simultaneously. By putting up signs and posters about how to recognize and deal with pesticides and toxic products and what emergency actions can be taken, we are able to raise awareness. Health education has the capacity to set in motion changes that are far-reaching.

Gutka, or chewing tobacco, which has spread like wildfire among all classes and cuts across age and gender lines, is consumed by the poor to kill hunger and to help them remain alert through long hours of work. Its use is so widespread that bonus packets of gutka are part of the wage negotiations of agriculture workers today. HIV/AIDS and other sexually transmitted diseases are also spreading fast. Community-based health education can play a vital role in the transmission of educational information to the poor so that they do not become hapless victims of a preventable disease or health condition.

7

Embroiderers

The Radhanpur and Santhalpur talukas of the Banaskantha district in northern Gujarat are some of the poorest and underdeveloped districts of Gujarat. The district is essentially a scrub desert, where some 200,000 people live in about 110 villages under harsh climatic conditions. The area has an average annual rainfall of about twenty inches. The soil and water are saline. The ground water table is sinking at an alarming rate every year. Chronic droughts alternate with flash floods year after year, relentlessly devastating the land and its population.

In 1987, I visited the interior villages of Santhalpur and Radhanpur with a team of SEWA members to look into a proposed Indo-Dutch program of supplying drinking water through pipelines to these villages. Rajiben, our Danapith vendor-member, whose family came from Radhanpur, often talked about the area, and she told me how their families had migrated from Pakistan, before partition, in search of land and water. When we visited these desert districts, they had suffered three consecutive years of drought. Village after village in this vast arid land was enveloped by blowing winds that deposited the desert at every doorstep. Men were absent from their homes—most had left in search of work. Older men sat quietly, smoking bidis, in the shade. We sat with the women as they talked about their lives steeped in scarcity. And even as they talked, their hands were busy with a needle and thread, their heads bent over some embroidery. Their homes were bare, their possessions few, but still their houses gleamed. The mud walls were encrusted with tiny mirrors that reflected sunlight into the dark, shady interiors. Everywhere one looked, the mirrors glistened. Richly embroidered fabrics hung over doorways, welcoming visitors; the bedspread we sat on was embroidered, as was the child's crib cloth, the shopping bag that hung from a wooden peg, their clothes, the men's shoes, and even the horns of their oxen were covered with embroidery. Tiny mirrors sparkled and winked and twinkled among the colorful threads. The sharp contrast between the beauty and the poverty in this desert land was glaring. The strong, dignified women had created riches with just thread and needle. How could such hard-working, tenacious, and highly skilled women be so poor? Every home we visited seemed to be dually inhabited by both beauty and poverty.

The women belonged to many communities: Ahir, Rabari, Mochi, Bharvad, some Hindu, and some Muslim. Each community was still predominantly engaged in the traditional occupations of their fathers and forefathers, like cattle-rearing, leather-working, farming, coarse cotton weaving, carding, and wool spinning. Each caste and community had its own distinct form of embroidery—stitches taught by mother to daughter, generation after generation.

While the women's embroidery has not changed much over many decades, the land they live in has. The desert, like a blanket of sand, spreads wider each year, and any greenery that once surrounded the village has receded further and further away. The wells run dry because groundwater has sunk deeper underground. Families can no longer sustain many cattle, traditionally a major source of income and a form of wealth.

With scanty rain, droughts in the area are frequent. Families migrate to Kutch and Kathiawad in search of work. The average wage for a migratory worker is around 20 rupees for men and 15 rupees for women—if they are lucky enough to find work. It is a hand-to-mouth existence. If there is no monsoon that year, they do not return home to their villages. Sometimes, if they receive word that the government has set up relief work sites in their district, they return.

Slowly and silently, droughts strip away a family's precious assets in rural areas—their cattle, bullocks, livelihoods, savings, and health. Without rains, they are forced to buy fodder instead of growing it. If fodder is inaccessible, or expensive, the family is forced to migrate with their cattle. Often, their only alternative is the temporary, low-paid, contractor-managed relief work set up by the government.

Puriben, a woman from Vauva village in Banaskantha, said that she walked six kilometers every day with one child on her hip, one on her back, and another on the way to get to work. She would spend the day in burning heat, digging pits and carrying heavy loads of earth on her head to build public roads. Because the site was such a long way from home, and traveling with small children was difficult, sometimes they would stay overnight at the work site, eating *rotlo* and drinking black tea for their evening meal.

Even as a carpenter, Umiyaben's husband was dependent on the rains. Most of his business was making plows and other agricultural implements for the farmers. But without rains, he too would bundle up a thick bed sheet and a couple of pots and take his family on the road. Sometimes they only earned enough for one meal a day; finding work was a recurring struggle.

Very quickly, we realized that the women wanted relief from migration and regular work in their own villages. With the help of the Foundation for Public Interest, a development research organization, SEWA surveyed the skill base of the women in Radhanpur and Santhalpur talukas. The survey also brought to light the fact that 80 percent of the women had embroidery skills. We needed to find a way in which the women could be home-based and still earn a regular income. This would allow the local ecology as well as the economy a chance to regenerate. We all needed to come together to devise a program that aimed broadly at providing an assured water supply and income to the communities through their active participation in its implementation.

The Ahirs are a rustic community of tall, sturdy people who are predominantly cattle breeders. They believe they have descended from God Krishna, who led his people from Mathura to his new capital in Dwarka, in western Gujarat. The Ahirs were among those that settled along the way, in north Gujarat.

Cattle and embroidery are the two mainstays of their daily life. The women's clothes are heavily embroidered—their skirts, blouses, and the *odhni* they cover their heads with. They embroider all through their lives. By the age of five, a young girl learns to handle a needle and thread and begins embroidering with a simple chain stitch. Until her daughter turns eighteen, when it is time for her to go to her husband's house, a mother embroiders her daughter's dowry—a dozen skirts and two dozen blouses, each lovingly, painstakingly, and exquisitely embroidered to clothe her daughter for several years.

Each year, a woman needs two sets of skirts, blouses, and odhni for daily wear. The same two pairs are worn, day in and day out, over the course of the year, until they need to be replaced. Whether toiling in the fields, or in the dust and mud, breaking stones or clearing thorns, they still dress in the same, gorgeous clothing. As a result, wear and tear on their clothes is heavy, and they constantly need repairing. When a blouse is torn or too tight, the embroidered panel is carefully taken out at the seams and sewn on to a new cloth backing.

Hansiba is ninety-two years old and can still demonstrate nineteen different embroidery stitches. Each stitch has a name: *kaach mogru, kangri, badam, barjali, khapkhaukdi, bandni kharekdi, rathodio, jaalee,* and so on. Hansiba is Puriben's mother. "In my day, I could get the cloth made to my specifications. I carded the cotton, made loops, spun the yarn, and took the hanks of yarn to the local weaver who would weave me a cloth of my choice—plain, bordered, lined, or with checks. The weaver's wife would bring the beam to my home and prepare the weft under my very eyes," she recalls.

Hansiba learned dyeing from her mother. "I boiled the bark of the babul tree in a big pot. When the water turned red, I would add a small portion of the dye powder that I bought from the *khatri,* the dyer. My colors are always fast because I used natural dyeing processes that used *baval* and tamarind, and I avoided any contact with sunlight while processing. It is a skill, you know!" Hansiba says, as she smiles a toothless smile.

The women take their embroidery with them to the fields. While the men rest in the shade after lunch and smoke a *chalam,* the women's hands are never still. They embroider every spare moment they can seize. At home, embroidery is a means for girls to escape from tedious housework and their mother's nagging. In embroidery, women find companionship and comfort, an activity both stimulating and soothing, a creative outlet, but also a labor of love of a mother for her daughter. A new bride living with her in-laws has little time to embroider. Her life is crowded with housework, cattle, and field labor. It is not until she is in her last months of pregnancy and home again at her mother's side preparing to deliver the baby that she finds time to embroider. On the fifth day of the fifth month of pregnancy, according to tradition, her sister (and never herself) starts embroidering a *topi* for the newcomer. Eventually, after the safe birth of her child, the young mother begins embroidering in preparation for her daughter's dowry.

During the first monsoon showers, when there is a lot of work to be done in the fields, the women take along small, thin pieces of fabric that require fine needle work because in the damp, monsoon air, it is tougher to put a needle through a thick fabric. The fabrics also tend to be dark-colored in this season, to avoid showing much dirt. But during harvest, when they are busiest, the women bring along *sadu bharat* embroidery, which is relatively simple and quick. In the wintertime, the women embroider skirts using thick *gajia* cloth to keep them warm. In the summer, when the sun is hot, they embroider home decorations on white cloth—colored fabrics would just fade under the intense gaze of the sun. This is also the season when they are not busy in the fields and there is plenty of time to embroider intricate designs on larger pieces, like skirts.

There are also times when embroidery is difficult. According to the women, "When there is too much housework; when the air is full of mosquitoes buzzing around; when the buffalo is about to deliver a young one; when there are unexpected, unwanted guests (like moneylenders) in the house; when children bother you too much; or when there is unbearable pain in your heart—as when you learn that your daughter is unhappy in her husband's home. . . . These are the times when a woman cannot concentrate." "*Bharat sookhnu ye chhay ne dookhnoo ye chhay*," say the women, meaning "Embroidery serves us in happy times, and it sustains us in hard times." So embroidery is tied into a woman's identity, her culture, and her very sense of self.

During hard times, when the family is forced to sell their valuables, traders go from village to village buying up the women's embroidered dowries. Stories of distress selling abound—no woman can forget being forced to part with her embroidery. Each piece is a record of many years of love, labor, and memories. Umiyaben from Vauva sorely remembers the drought when she let go of all her best embroideries for a mere hundred-rupee note.

Large brass and steel pots gleam in every household in these villages. They are a source of great pride among the women—a status symbol of sorts. Gauriben of Bakutra village remembers the trader who came to her village with modern, stainless steel vessels with a mirror shine. She was so enamored of these new vessels that she decided to invest in them for her daughter's dowry. She bartered some of her best embroidered skirts for a few stainless steel vessels. She carefully wrapped them in cloth and stored them up high, out of everyone's reach. A few years later, as her

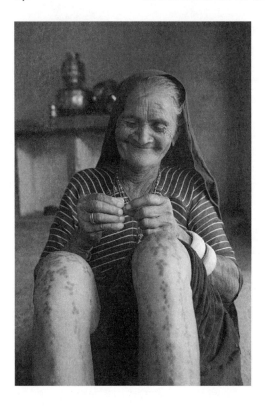

"Embroidery serves us in happy times, and it sustains us in hard times." Bhachiben threading a needle. (Amit Dave)

daughter's wedding day was approaching, she took them down to clean them. When she undid the wraps, she discovered to her horror nothing but a heap of black, rusted junk! She had been thoroughly cheated by the trader. But what still lingers in her memory is how her humiliation was compounded by the beating she got from her angry husband.

One reason the women are cheated and exploited by the traders is that the women do not travel much. They hardly ever leave their villages, and when they do—such as when they migrate—the men in their family always accompany them. The women are largely ignorant of the market value of their embroideries, particularly because the buyers are in faraway cities. The traders have a monopoly. The women accept the prices the trader dictates because in hard times, they are grateful they have a buyer at all.

Puriben had never stepped outside her community on her own. The men did all the shopping in her family. Even when they migrated in search of work, she never went to the worksite without her husband by her side.

The question of looking around for a better price for her embroidery was out of the question.

But even if the women did know the fair price, their isolation and insecurity reduced their options considerably. The traders are well aware of the women's desperation to sell, while the women do not have the economic cushion to wait for a better price. At the back of their minds is the fear: "What if the next trader never comes? What if he doesn't come soon enough? Then, what will I do?" Ready cash is of unparalleled value in tough times. And their embroideries have good cash value.

On the basis of our survey, the State Water Board became active in the area. However, the main refrain we heard from the village women was for work. So we at SEWA decided that generating work and income would be a major component of the project primarily aimed at water supply. We began looking for a young woman who was willing to live and work in the villages and to take charge. Reema Nanavaty was just twenty-one years old, but she had a Master's degree in microbiology and had just passed the prestigious Indian Administration Service examinations. Still waiting for her government appointment, she came to work on our project. She traveled to remote villages with the water board, noting living conditions, water scarcity, occupations, incomes, and the women's skills, looking for ways for the women to earn cash income. This was her first exposure to life in India's villages. Unbeknownst to us, when the appointment in the Indian civil service came, she turned it down. She said that working with the women in Banaskantha had changed her outlook on life forever.

Puriben too describes those early days that changed her life. "On a winter day in 1989, a young woman visited our village Vauva. She said she wanted to talk with the village women. She introduced herself as Reema and said she was an organizer at SEWA."

Of course, the village women had no idea what SEWA was. At the small meeting, Reema said that she had brought them some work; she needed a dozen *kurtas* embroidered. But only four women were willing to take her offer. When Reema said she would be providing both the cloth and the thread, the women felt that they had little to lose. Gauriben was one of the four women. A few days later, when Reema returned to collect the finished items, none of the women would show her their completed work. First, they wanted to see the money. "Reemaben produced the cash— a 150 rupees per kurta—and paid them on the spot!" Puriben said she could not believe her eyes. In a village where most men earn 175 rupees in an entire month, such earnings were too good to be true. More women came forward and offered to embroider for her. It was not easy for SEWA to pay out cash every time, because arrangements to sell the embroidered kurtas were not yet set up. However, we were determined to take the initial risk to establish credibility.

The next order was for twenty kurtas. Gauriben secretly kept two kurtas for herself—one she worked on during the day, and one at night. This way, no one would know that she had been greedy. In her mind, her need for money overrode any qualms about giving equal earning opportunity to everyone. When she received a full 300 rupees for her work, the earning power of this new opportunity became clear. "That evening, my supper tasted sweeter than ever before," she said.

As the work became regular, the orders bigger, and the women's trust in the SEWA organizer grew, they were willing to wait for one week for their payment. Just the slightest economic cushion enabled the women to trust. For SEWA, managing the cash flow became a little easier. Reema hired two team members, Sukruti and Neelam (in Ahmedabad), to manage embroidery sales.

One by one, the neighboring villages also heard of the work and the prices that SEWA women earned, and they began inviting our team to bring them work and to talk to them. Each caste and community had its own unique style of embroidery—*Ahir, Rabari, Jat, Mochi*—and the women of all communities were needy, though not to the same degree. Our priority was to reach the poorest women in every village.

At the meetings, the SEWA team asked the embroiderers to show their work and offered to buy any finished pieces if they needed cash. Such pieces formed the core of SEWA's sample library of stitches. Reema explained to the women that the reason she paid them more than the traders was not out of charity but because she was giving them the fair market value for their goods. This awakened the women's curiosity about the outside world, which valued their craft.

SEWA's actions spoke louder than words—the prices Reema offered for the embroidery were high, payment was timely, and she kept coming back with more work. The SEWA team helped the women to organize into small embroidery groups. Under a national government program called Development of Women and Children in Rural Areas, popularly known as DWCRA, such groups could obtain a revolving fund of 15,200 rupees combined with a small grant for training. The amount, deposited in a local bank, was to be solely controlled by the women's group. "We formed the group for one simple reason. We wanted the work," said Bhachiben. As long as there were work and payment in cash, the women were ready to join anything! Few women realized that by coming together, they were building more than an economic structure that would give them a sustainable livelihood.

Initially, when the SEWA team came to the village, the women would shove, push, and fight for work because they were so very needy. At times, up to 200 women would crowd around. When it was time to collect payments, the rush would be even more frantic out of fear that money would run out. But when the SEWA teams kept coming, and coming, sometimes arriving before the women had even gotten out of bed in the morning, the frenzy eventually calmed down. The frequent visits, combined with consistent, reliable, well-compensated work, won their trust. "For sure, she is not a trader," the women would say to each other about the SEWA organizer. "Did you notice she conducts all business in the open, when all the women are present? Everyone knows who got the work and who got paid how much."

SEWA's small office was in the nearby town of Radhanpur, though very few of the village women had been there. In order to bring women from different villages together, meetings were sometimes called at the Radhanpur office. But the women were wary of venturing into town. Umiyaben, a group leader, was one of them. What was she supposed to do at a meeting, she wondered. She did not go. The next time, she was invited to go to the Ahmedabad office to attend an orientation class. Curious about the big city, but unsure about her role in the venture, she took along a few friends for company.

At the SEWA office, there were women everywhere. A group of women rag pickers was discussing the ins and outs of their trade rather loudly. They were talking about contracts and traders, and the price of everything! Umiyaben was impressed. All these women, coming and going around the office, behaving as if they all belonged there. And there were women sitting in chairs behind tables, talking on the telephone, typing papers, and yet they were all just like her—a little citified, but still no different than her. And they were all so busy.

Umiyaben and the women of Radhanpur and Santhalpur districts were in Ahmedabad to attend an orientation meeting at the SEWA Academy. Its purpose was to raise awareness regarding women and work.

Sitting in a circle, in a small room, Namrata, a SEWA organizer, asked the women to introduce themselves and to talk about their life and work. Every woman there worked; every woman had a trade that she lived by, and every woman had plenty to share about the struggles she faced. When Namrata pointed out that women the world over worked for long hours, that they earned relatively little, and that very few women owned assets in their own names, heads began to nod. Every woman knew exactly what those words meant. The meeting had one motive—to introduce the idea that a woman's work had value. The other purpose of the meeting was to impress upon the women that embroidery was *their* work and that *they* would be running their own business. SEWA would not do it for them. The women nodded, but they had little idea of what that implied.

Namrata Bali initially came to SEWA as a student of textile design. Lalita Krishnaswamy, then in charge of SEWA's economic activities, saw the rapport she had with the women and hired her in 1984. Namrata was quiet, efficient, and had great interest and respect for the indigenous knowledge of the women. Much later, when SEWA Academy was formed as a training and research arm of SEWA, she seemed the most obvious choice to run it. Namrata loved nothing more than to get the women talking and questioning and discussing new ideas.

Very early in SEWA's history, not long after we were ousted from the TLA, Lalita had recognized the enormous potential of the craft skills of the women. She worked with the block printers of Ahmedabad—an old Muslim community of printers and dyers who were fast losing their traditional skills and helped them set up a cooperative to revive their craft and turn it into a source of livelihood. She also set up SEWA's first retail store to market chindi quilts, block-printed fabrics, and tie-dyed scarves made by SEWA's increasingly diverse crafts membership. The women from Banaskantha did not know it, but the seeds of their venture were sown by Lalita many, many years ago.

In the jeep, on their return journey, fired up after all the frank talk, the women concluded that "[they] will all eat the same rotla." Meaning that they would come together and share. They left with a new feeling that work and opportunity were within their reach if they are willing to take some initiative. Excited, they shared the idea with other women in their villages.

When venturing into the embroidery business, we at SEWA had pledged to ourselves three things. One, any woman seeking embroidery work will be given work and will not be turned away; two, all payments for work will be made in cash within ten days' time and no later; and third, that at least 60 percent of the price of the product will go directly into the hands of the embroiderer. These guiding principles became the backbone of SEWA's efforts to organize the rural poor women of Banaskantha.

For the women, embroidery took on another, wider role. It was a group effort at earning a livelihood, where the opportunity to talk, share, and exchange ideas, opinions, and skills became an important element. With SEWA's help, other DWCRA groups formed in the region. Women who did not embroider but had other skills formed groups of salt farmers, gum collectors, forestry and agriculture workers, marginal farmers, as well as savings and credit groups. Within four years, a large number of groups had sprouted all over the district. In 1993, 91 groups with a total membership of about 40,000 women formed a district-level federation called the Banaskantha DWCRA Mahila SEWA Association (BDMSA), which was often shortened to simply "the Association."

In every group, the first battle every woman faced was simply for mobility. The task of distributing new work, collecting finished work, and making regular payments involved frequent travel between their villages and the SEWA office in Radhanpur. At times, there were training sessions in account keeping or team building that would allow them to take on more managerial, financial, and organizational responsibilities. There were also frequent sales and exhibitions of their embroidery in large cities like Ahmedabad, Delhi, and Bombay that they were asked to attend. The women were excited by the possibility of travel and of seeing the world they had only heard about. But to travel outside of their homes, villages, and districts was not easy. First, they had to overcome their own diffidence, and second, mounting resistance from their communities.

To Puriben, Radhanpur was just a name, even though she lived just an hour away by bus. When she was elected to the managing committee of the Association, Puriben was needed at the SEWA office in Radhanpur to meet with representatives from other villages. Although she was aware of the importance of her presence at such meetings, she also knew that her village community frowned upon women who "roamed around on their own." She could not decide whom to disappoint. On the day of the meeting, when her SEWA colleagues came to pick her up, she hid in the fields. They left without her. According to her, she did this several times; it was months before she found the courage to attend her first meeting in town.

The first time Gauriben—another managing committee member—
went to Radhanpur, she lied to her family that she was off to visit her
mother. Some relatives, who found out the truth, told her family and
warned her in-laws that if she was allowed to go to town to meet "people
in offices," one day she would not come back; she was bound to be ab-
ducted and sold in the city. Luckily for Gauriben, her family had faith in
her and her work. However, their faith was tested when Gauriben was
asked to represent the Association at a large craft exhibition in Delhi. She
was gone for six days, and today she laughs and says that her family prayed
fervently every single day she was gone, begging for her safe return. Most
village women faced and braved much opposition in the early days of their
organizing. But they persisted. Rasuben was the first person from her village—man or woman, young or old—to see Delhi. The whole village came
out to hear her stories when she returned.

Community elders fined Umiyaben's family 10,000 rupees because
they had allowed their daughter-in-law to leave the house "for no reason."
Relatives descended on Umiyaben, scolding her for risking her family's
reputation. Although at times she was tempted to put an end to it all by
quitting her work organizing and managing the embroidery group, her
husband remained supportive and reassuring. He would cook and feed
the children so she would have time to travel and mobilize other groups.
Slowly, when the men in the community saw that the women's association was growing, they realized that things were beyond their control. If
they fined one woman, they would have to fine them all—including
women in their own households. Umiyaben's fine was never paid and was
eventually forgotten.

Rasuben had no trouble going to Radhanpur, but her challenge came
when she was assigned to purchase embroidery threads in bulk from Patan
city. She laughs at her inexperience today, but it must have been frighten-
ing to stare at the station clock, unable to tell the time, not knowing when
the bus would depart. Nor could she read the names of destinations on
the buses, so she hardly knew which bus to chase in case she was late. But
with the grit and perseverance that strong women like her possess, she
managed to reach her destination, bargain a good price with the trader,
and return with the threads. She says that the trip was one of the most liberating events of her life.

In the early days, the women had a lot to learn in order to manage
their embroidery production, their group, and their office effectively.

Always having been on the receiving end of directives, the women were afraid of taking the initiative. Most had no formal education, and hardly anyone could read and write. But as the women took on more responsibilities of collecting materials from the district office, printing the design on the materials, distributing them to the members in the village, collecting the embroidered products when they were finished, and delivering them to the Association office, they gained more confidence. There was room for all kinds of talents. Saviben, who had an excellent eye for color and design, soon began preparing samples and experimenting with various combinations of threads, colors, and stitches.

Being unable to read or write was a handicap each woman faced in a new way. Hansaben, who had to keep an account of how many finished products each women deposited, and how much payment each should get, could neither read nor write. But she enlisted her young, school-going daughter to write down the figures for her in her account notebook. Then, after her daughter read aloud what she had written, Hansaben signed off with her newly learned signature. Similarly, Puriben, responsible for keeping the payment records of embroiderers from six different villages, handled somewhere between 30,000 rupees to 1 lakh rupees every fifteen days despite being unable to read or write. But her sharp mind would not miss a beat—she had a memory for every transaction, and her accounts tallied perfectly at the end of the day.

Even those who did not take on leadership roles in their village had to develop new skills, particularly time management. Some of the most lucrative orders are for export, but export orders are highly time-bound. In the early days, an order for 5,000 mirror-work wall hangings had to be embroidered and dispatched within twenty days. Excited at getting such a large order, the women agreed to deliver them on time, but the work was more than they could handle. Despite the hard work, they failed to fulfill the order in time and they lost it. Time and again, fearful of unemployment, the women found themselves unable to turn down work. But their capacity to work on a tight schedule was low, and very often they failed.

Yet demand for their embroidery was growing. Orders for their products started streaming in. What was a quiet women's activity had now turned into a streamlined production process. For better or worse, this was the direction their success had led them. It was all too soon and all too perplexing. "At first we never understood why there was so much insistence on quality and keeping track of each thread. We felt pressured for no reason," Umiyaben said. But when failed orders began to pile up, the women began to get worried.

The demands of the outside market were often incomprehensible to the women. They were used to stitching what they liked, using traditional patterns on thick fabric, using stitches and colors that pleased them. However, orders were placed by an urban market, which demanded paler colors on finer fabric. "My hands refuse to do that kind of embroidery. Such sickly *angreji* colors!" some complained. When they rebelled and added a touch of bright color or a favorite motif to their work, their piece was rejected. This upset the women no end, and understandably so.

Saddened as we were to see the creative process of embroidery become a homogenized product for an urban market, the women were glad to have work. They were glad they were not migrating in search of work year after year. They were glad they could work in the comfort of their homes on a schedule of their choice. They were glad their embroidery had material worth and that *they* were the beneficiaries of their labor, rather than a middleman. For these reasons and many more, they welcomed the dictates of the urban market. Once in a while, they were commissioned to produce something typical, traditional, and close to their hearts. One such product, a large wall hanging, is on display at the Victoria and Albert Museum in London.

In the meantime, we had a crisis on our hands. Finished products worth 20 lakh rupees were piled up at the Radhanpur office, some unsold and others unsaleable. Some orders had missed their deadlines. Some were of poor quality. Some looked like complete novices had made them. Some had been rejected because midway in a design, a mismatching thread had been used. In trying to ensure that no woman who came seeking embroidery work was turned away, SEWA had taken on a challenge it had only partially mastered. Enormous amount of funds were tied up in products that could find no market. For a full three months in 1992, all production was stopped.

What did not stop was the effort to understand what to do differently. Perhaps such a crisis brings out the best in everyone, and women in the villages rose to the challenge. First, we felt it was necessary to conduct a complete census of all embroiderers in seventy villages, testing and recording their skills, graded in three levels. Those that were highly skilled could work on new orders; those with middling skills would get further training before working on new orders, and those with minimal embroidery skills would get more thorough grounding in basic embroidery. Samples of different stitches were prepared; the peculiarities of each embroidery tradition noted. Differences in the styles of each village, community, and group were also noted. The emphasis was on quality and authenticity.

Continuous planning, implementing, and monitoring were deemed essential, so an embroidery spearhead team was formed. This team was composed of eight *aagewans*, or group leaders, and two paid, local organizers. At the first meeting of the embroidery team, all the tasks of embroidery production were broken down in great detail. The tasks of printing, sewing, monitoring, collecting finished products, checking, sorting, grading, and packing were addressed. Keeping written records, however, was still very difficult for the women.

Training team members was an elusive activity because the team members kept changing. If a woman could not attend the training session, she would send her mother-in-law instead! So at every session, the trainees kept changing. Some arrived late, having walked great distances, stopping along the way for rest; others left early to catch public buses that kept unpredictable schedules. Few managed to attend a full day's session. It took two and a half years for the team to settle down, take on responsibility, and perform effectively. This time, though long, was a worthwhile investment. When the women were willing to face so many odds to come together to build a quality control system, it was imperative to not lose patience but rather to allow the women to set their speed and style of learning. This was the only way to real change.

Ninety-one DWCRA groups engaged in different economic activities like embroidery, savings and credit, watershed, forestry, and salt production were operating in the villages. Since the embroidery group was the largest, a good part of the office bearers of the Association were elected from among them. This often led to discontent, and the Association's general body meetings invariably became stormy. Eventually, the women came to a mutual understanding—if the president was from the embroidery group, the secretary would be from the watershed, savings, nursery raising, or some other group, and vice versa. Political awareness among the women was growing.

Building infrastructure was slow and full of pitfalls. Because the Association had no storage facility, all purchases were made in small quantities. Fabrics or threads would often run out, and Rasuben would have to rush to the local market to buy substandard products at high prices to meet demand. A storage facility was eventually built with some help from the Craft Development Council with Rasuben in charge of her beloved threads, which she arranged so meticulously that she boasted she could put her finger on any color thread, "even in the dark."

Apart from a grading scale, the team also devised a system of distributing the work. Each team would collect the material, monitor the tailoring, put together the kits for the embroiderers, and ensure the timely implementation of the tasks.

From this point on, each piece was graded and the embroiderer paid according to the quality of work. The grading was done by a team of their peers, respected for their embroidery expertise and fairness, who graded each piece in front of everyone, openly, so that every woman knew what grade her work was given, why, and how it compared to work that was graded at a higher level. A system of samples was devised for reference.

On the design front, Laila Taibji came to our rescue. For days, Laila sat with the embroidery women in their homes and work centers, discussing color, thread, and patterns and developing designs. She lent support in marketing through Dastkar, a Delhi-based organization that she founded, which is devoted to promoting Indian crafts and supporting artisans through design, marketing help, and publicity.

The opening of Banascraft, a retail shop in Ahmedabad to sell products made by the Banaskantha and Kutch women's groups, was a great boost. But while the shop has high visibility, good recognition, a reputation for quality, and a steady consumer base, financially, it is the least productive. It requires a large investment of both time and money for the amount of revenue it generates. Yet its role is vital to the women as their rural presence in an urban environment.

Producing items on order from buyers is by far the more lucrative option because it requires smaller investment, and the capital rotates faster. There is no fear of overstocking. However, it is demanding in terms of high quality and timely delivery.

Craft exhibitions in some of the larger cities of India are also a good source of income. With good publicity, demand can be extremely high for Gujarati embroidery products. Every year, ten to twelve exhibitions, on average, are organized with the help of Dastkar.

The best publicity is often the artisans themselves. When the women represent their embroidery work at an exhibition or sale, their presence lends the product an authenticity, and it validates the woman's work and identity. This transparency accounts for a lot. The women producers get first-hand experience in facing customers at the point of sale, where they can witness the success or failure of their product design and learn about the price structure they are operating within. Such exposure is invaluable, and every detail of it is noted and repeated back at home in the villages and in the courtyards where the women gather to embroider.

The general socioeconomic climate in the district is changing too. With a steady income, the women are able to look up and out into the world. They know they can make choices, and they know they can bring about change. They realize the power of collective strength and an individual's potential for tapping it. One by one, they begin to exercise their rights, because they become aware of their rights. It is a process of empowerment—a political process—that cannot be taught, but can only come from within. It is a slow but irrevocable process.

Since the formation of their groups, poor families in the Radhanpur and Santhalpur taluka are no longer forced to migrate in search of work. During droughts, only those families with big herds of cattle move in search of fodder. Without the need to leave in search of work every year, the village schools begin to fill up with children. Gauriben says, "When we went looking for work outside, our children went with us. Who can study with an empty belly? We never sent our daughters to school; we were in a hurry to marry them off. But now we let them to see a bit of the world before marriage. Of course, we still promise them in marriage when they are little girls. That is our custom."

But that, too, is changing, though very quietly. Groups that have a high number of young women and girls are the most productive. This fact is not lost on the community. Girls are also particularly dependable when it comes to fulfilling time-bound orders. In 1998, a large order for cushion covers was being prepared for an exhibition in Paris. Unfortunately, the pressure on the women was compounded by the fact that the one and only day of the year when all marriages in their community take place fell during this period of work frenzy. If they missed the auspicious day, the families would have to wait a full year for the wedding. But many of the young girls were of the opinion that they would rather wait a year than lose good income. It is no surprise that the elders were of the same opinion. Under the leadership of Jomiben, Kankuben, and Subhadraben, an unprecedented decision to postpone the girls' marriages was taken that year.

Appreciation of the fact that the women's embroidery work is supporting a large number of families of the community, especially during
the hot, drought-ridden period of the year, is growing. Restrictions on
women's travel too are gradually wearing away, and families and communities are beginning to respect and accommodate the demands of their
work. When the young and very talented Hiraben was awarded the
Kamladevi Chattopadhyaya Mastercraftsman Award in Delhi for her
embroidery skills, the village Panchayat hosted a grand reception in her
honor when she returned. Daughters and wives and sisters and mothers
are emerging out of the shadows.

The women are conscious that they are beginning to matter. "Now
everyone in the village knows my name and anyone can give directions
to my home," boasts Hansaben. "Even in the bank, the officer knows me
well by name and signature. I have my own account and I am a signatory
on the group's account." "We have been transformed from 'bahu' (bride)
to 'ben' (sister)," laughs Puriben. "My son calls me as 'saab' (boss)!" says
Gauriben. "And when my telephone rings, my husband runs around telling everybody to keep quiet so I can talk on the phone."

Most of the women believe that changes in the family's power structure do not lead to more friction with their husbands. In fact, they said,
they quarrel less because there is less financial stress on the family. "Normally our husbands are not the source of our troubles. After all, he is the
father of my children," says Umiyaben. "The real problem is with our
young sons. They have no earnings of their own, and they constantly pes-
ter their mothers for money. Our young men need work."

Their growing self-confidence begins to reflect in the women's ability to intervene in matters that affect their lives. "We are not afraid to talk
to men or with government officials," Gauriben says proudly. "Very often
we have to pull and push them to work with us. If a government official
ignores me, I just go to his boss. If his boss does not listen, I turn to someone else, until someone hears me out." Gauriben was fighting to build a
water tank in her village, so she approached the Talati, the village secretary, to write her an official letter recommending the need for construction. He refused to write it. The next time Gauriben took a few women
with her. They told him how difficult it was to fetch drinking water from
several kilometers away every day, but to no avail. "Sahib, why would
you refuse to write a letter that could result in bringing water to our village? Is it because I am an illiterate woman dressed in a *ghaghra*, and you

are a big man? But I have shakti to convince you." With that Gauriben produced her SEWA membership card and the Association's passbook and placed them in his hands. This was her way of letting him know that she spoke for many, and that she carried financial weight. One glance at the documents and the Talati said, "So now I know you," and he wrote the letter.

In 2001, following the devastation of the earthquake, the women of Bakutra village wanted to build new houses with the help of their Association, but the men of the village were not in favor. The men felt that taking the government compensation of 50,000 rupees was the better deal. Still, at the women's insistence, the Association began rebuilding five low-cost houses. The men were angry but silent. The construction of houses continued. By the end of 2002, eighty-seven rebuilt houses with earthquake-resistant construction were ready for inhabitation. The promised government funds never came. Had the women not spoken out, they would still be without homes.

The groups' political impact had increased in the villages. Saviben, independent of any political party, was unanimously elected Sarpanch (head of the village council) for a cluster of five villages. Obviously, her service to the region was well appreciated. She said, "People trust me because they see us working. I get my shakti from my work."

Puriben was on the SEWA delegation that went to Delhi to meet the Prime Minister of India, Atal Behari Bajpai, regarding the severe drought in Gujarat. The prime minister listened attentively as she spoke about the drought conditions in her region and the urgent need for fair-priced fodder for the cattle that are so important to the local economy. Having had plenty of experience with talking to local government officials, Puriben felt that making her case in front of the prime minister was "easy." SEWA's fodder security program was born as a result of her persuasion of the government.

When SEWA first started working with the women of Banaskantha district, the two main concerns the women had were employment and water. SEWA's economic activities took off relatively easily, but bringing water to the region has not been easy. Although the women have been actively trying to introduce a watershed project in their village, they have met with little success to date. For their initiative to see any results, it must be approved by the village Panchayat and there the matter stalls. In Puriben's village, the Sarpanch felt that women shouldn't be involved in any serious undertaking. "It is our work to handle the government grants that come to the village," he said. Puriben and her team were not allowed on the water project committee. It was clearly an issue of gender and power. The tension has lasted for ten years. Despite realizing that if the women's efforts are blocked it is a loss for everyone in the village, the Sarpanch clings to his power. Puriben's village is nothing but a name on a long government waiting list of villages in need of piped water. There are still people in the village that believe water is not a women's issue. Embroidery activities that can be done in the confines of the home are fine, but activities that involve getting out into the world and involve bigger money, like watershed development, have to be left to the men.

One area where the women did meet with some success was in drought relief. Year after year, the embroidery-skilled hands of women were condemned to manual labor, digging in the scorching heat of summer. We urged the state government to recognize skill as a durable asset and include skill development in its public works program. Finally, in 2000, our plea to the chief minister was heard. The government recognized embroidery as an employment activity that would be paid the same minimum wage as other workers on public worksites; women embroiderers and their children no longer need to go digging at relief sites in Gujarat.

The collectively developed assets of the Association are a source of pride and security for the women. "Whatever you see here is in 'our' name," says Rasuben, pointing to the office furniture, computers, raw materials, vehicles, nurseries, water pumps, and bankbooks. As shareholders in the SEWA Trade Facilitation Centre, a newly formed trading body, the women are full of plans for the future. The Radhanpur SEWA office is fast becoming computerized. Three embroidery organizers—Chandrika, Ayesha, and Rashida—were chosen for computer training. The young girls had some high school–level education and were keen to learn a new skill. It was not easy. They attended computer lessons from eight to ten o'clock in the morning, then set off on their rounds in the villages, and then at the end of the day, from eight to ten o'clock again, they returned to the office to practice on the computer. This continued for four months; first they worked on design and color manipulation on the computer, and then on the accounts. After the training, their biggest satisfaction was that they no longer had to carry the heavy accounts register to the Ahmedabad office every month—they simply emailed them!

As the Association has grown, it has developed the capacity to take a broader, integrated approach to social security, both on a day-to-day basis as well as in times of crises. The Association provides social security services like health care, child care, housing, and insurance services. There is a mobile health van that travels to villages in the district; the women pay half the cost for medical care, and the other half is paid by the Association. There are a few daycare centers for children, but they are not enough. Functional literacy classes, which are offered through SEWA's Jeevanshala schools, are increasingly popular but their reach is limited because good teachers are hard to find.

Time and again, natural disasters have devastated the arid regions of Kutch and Banaskantha. Cyclones ripped across Kutch in 1998 and 1999. Close on their heels, on January 26, 2001, a deadly earthquake measuring 6.9 on the Richter scale struck a large part of the state, leaving more than 20,000 people dead. Four years of crippling drought also took its toll on the lives and livestock of the embroidery workers and their families. During all of these crises, the women have been able to give and receive support to other women within the Association. When they were most vulnerable and had lost everything, the women felt that they would be able to get back on their feet with the help of their sisters.

The women make a distinction between this immediate help and long-term disaster relief. On the third day after the earthquake, when roads were repaired, the SEWA team reached the members with food. The first words out of Gauriben's mouth were, "Ben, have you brought us work?" Sitting in their temporary tents, Gauriben and the women in her village started their embroidery work almost immediately. "Keeping our hands busy is the one thing that helps us get back our lives. It is our livelihood."

The women's savings and insurance programs were key in replacing roofs after the cyclone and rebuilding earthquake-proof homes after the earthquake. Eight thousand houses were rebuilt, with the women as primary owners. Most of the houses have attached roof rainwater harvesting tanks. Toilets were their second priority.

Roof rainwater harvesting is one of the most welcome interventions. Water shortage is a constant concern. Through the Association, the women's groups have constructed a large number of rainwater harvesting tanks, community tanks, and plastic-lined village ponds and have recharged several village wells. Moreover, after some basic training, one group has taken over the repair and maintenance of hand pumps in the villages.

Water tanks cost 18,000 rupees, and 30 percent of the expense has to be borne by the member, which amounts to more than 5,000 rupees, which they simply don't have. Embroidery work does not pay enough for them to take a loan of this size. At a 2–percent monthly interest, it is far too expensive for many women. In the fourth year of drought, people did not feel confident that the year would bring rain and that there would be ample employment through agriculture. If there was no employment, then how would they be able to pay back their loan? Or even have enough rainwater to fill their new expensive tank? While the women are able to form small assets, they need a higher income. They do save regularly, but savings last through only one year of drought.

Though every poor woman in Vauva—the first village to form a DWCRA group—is a member, not all 500 members are able to enjoy "full employment." In other villages, like in Bakutra, there are definitely women that the Association has been unable to reach. In spite of the most vigilant efforts, the poorest of the poor still get left out because they do not embroider. Many of them are engaged in construction work. Some of them are compelled to go to work on salt farms in coastal districts. Another group that is slipping through the cracks to some extent is the very old. Members that were elderly when Reema's team first went to Bakutra are now too old to embroider, so they have no secure income. However, they are benefiting to some extent from their savings, insurance, and health care.

In part, the inability of the Association to ensure full employment to embroiderers demonstrates the need to take advantage of broader and changing markets. With the recently developed Trade Facilitation Center, whose goal it is to reach the global market, strong marketing efforts are underway.[1]

---

1. SEWA Trade Facilitation Centre (Unnat Bazzar) is a company, perhaps the first of its kind in India, formed by more than 15,000 artisan shareholders who are the suppliers and producers of the company. The company has been incorporated with a planned turnover of 62.5 crore rupees. SEWA, the Kutch Craft Association, and Banaskantha DWCRA Association are the promoters of the company. At present, in the initial period, the share of retail sale is 28 percent in the total turnover and that of indirect sales is 72 percent. The STFC has started implementing the process for ISO 9001 certification. It plans to become a Buying House for internationally organized retailers. The total sales target is 428 crore rupees. The present sales stand at 1.25 crore rupees (2004).

Testing foreign markets is expensive, though well worth the money and experience, because it compensates well. Exhibition sales through museums and arts and crafts organizations in Europe and the United States are generating a lot of interest in the indigenous embroideries of Gujarat. Reaching a bigger market with more purchasing power is a challenge. They insist on quality, variety, and exclusivity for every product, which is a challenge for the 15,000 embroiderers of Banaskantha.

The women feel limited in planning on a bigger scale, monitoring global market trends, speaking the business language, and honing special negotiating skills. The Association is able to develop contacts, technical support, and market information to some extent, but it needs more professional expertise. Professionals and experts are expensive; besides, when they work with village women, they often need to unlearn a few biases and learn new concepts and practices by using a participatory approach.

In a big-scale modern market, some product standardization is necessary. This is a big challenge for the women who work with their hands, sitting in their homes, in seventy scattered villages. The other challenge is preserving the women's traditional heritage. SEWA has encouraged the embroiderers to use their traditional skills as an income-earning activity to create marketable products with traditional stitches and motifs. While care has been taken to keep the *aari* stitch of the *Mochi* distinct from the *soy* stitch of the *Ahirs*, or the motifs of the *Jat* from the *pako* of the *Sodhas*, mass production itself has a leveling effect beyond anyone's control.

Yet nothing is static, not even tradition. The women's foremothers wore *Kamakho* blouses of silk that changed to *mashroo* over time and eventually into the cotton-*mashroo* as we know it. The *heer* silk thread they embroidered with does not exist any more. Sadly, because the women are busy with the embroidery that earns, they have less time to embroider their personal clothes. The Association encourages the production of traditional clothes that are the women's everyday wear to avoid turning toward ugly designs on polyester.

Another activity of the Association is to maintain a sample library that buys old, well-preserved, representative embroidered pieces from the women at market rate. The traditional piece is copied faithfully in every possible detail in an effort to retain traditional forms, but also to give the women a chance to keep up a living tradition. Once the new piece is finished, the old embroidery is returned to the woman. The sample library is unique and fast becoming a source of great pride for the women.

Basraben Fakir (right), Sarpanch of Muhadi village, with a model at
an embroidery fashion show organized by SEWA and the National
Institute of Fashion Technology. (SEWA Trade Facilitation Center)

As fabric and thread become more and more expensive, and because
professional design and marketing expertise costs heavily, the basic prin-
ciple of delivering 60 percent of the price of the product into the hands of
the producer poses a big challenge. Small products like cushion covers still
put more than 60 percent of the income in the woman's hands, but for large
products that require more raw materials—like clothing, bed sheets, or wall
pieces—the woman only gets about 50 percent of the profit. This is an area
the Association is working hard to maintain.

SEWA's goal of regenerating the economy and the ecology of the region has only partially succeeded. The ecology of this region is degener-
ating at a steady rate. Communities that depend on cattle breeding, fodder
raising, and subsistence agriculture are suffering a slow and silent loss of

livelihood. Forced migration in search of fodder and work hinders ecological or economic regeneration because in their absence, the region deteriorates further. It is only the local people who can regenerate the environment of their region. By staying, they are better motivated to conserve and harvest rain water, build communal water tanks, grow fodder, raise nurseries, plant saplings, and thus enliven their environment. Women have been the leaders of change in this region.

Embroidery is one tiny part of the vast panorama of India's myriad arts and crafts that are struggling to stay alive in the hands of the women. An enormous skill base of our country is discarded, ignored, and unrecognized. There are thousands of weavers, potters, and carpenters carrying generations-old traditions within themselves, but they are condemned to work as unskilled labor at roadsides. If embroidery can establish the status of women as workers, producers, and entrepreneurs, so can a number of other quiet, skilled economic activities carried out by the rural people of India. Ignoring them is our nation's loss.

8

Gram Haat

The Gum Collectors

During our meetings with the embroidery groups, the women often talked about women poorer than themselves. These women collected gum from the thorny scrub called *gando baval (prosopis juliflora)* or the "mad tree," a species introduced some decades ago by the forest department as a species that could supposedly desalinate desert land but also had multiple other uses. The baval or gum tree gum is edible, and it is used in making sweets; the pods are fed to cattle, and the branches can be burnt to make charcoal. The baval, however, has proliferated with abandon, decimating local fauna in the process. The plant is called mesquite in its native South America.

The thirsty villages of Antarnesh and Aewal in Banaskantha are among the last villages before the border to Pakistan. Gum collection is the only source of livelihood for the inhabitants. The women go out in family groups into the arid wilderness, often walking for many kilometers, picking gum from the dense, thorny baval bushes. Other times, they spend the nights in the wild and return home after collecting 10 to 15 kilos of gum. When we first met them, the women sold their gum to traders at the rate of 2 to 4 rupees per kilo.

Gum collection is an arduous and painful activity. The bark of the scrubby trees, whose thin and thorny branches form a formidable barrier, is not easily accessible. Little children crawl under the branches and push them aside so that the women can get to the gummy drops clinging on the side of the bark. The thorns of the baval are notoriously tough on skin and clothes; the women's hands are covered with scratches and blood day after day. Infected wounds, heat stroke, and dehydration are common.

The irony, however, is that their arduous activity in this forsaken place is illegal. Under the law, this barren wasteland is part of the national forests and therefore government property. It is forbidden to collect forest produce, big or small, without the permission of the Gujarat State Forest Development Corporation. Knowing nothing of how to acquire licenses, and afraid of the forest officials, the women sold their gum to private traders who took advantage of their illegal status and paid them a pittance for their collection. Traders, however, managed to equip themselves with a license and used the women as cheap labor.

SEWA began to organize the gum collectors in 1991. Ranbai Jemalji Rauma,[1] whose family has lived for generations in Anternesh, was the chief mobilizing force. In order to get a proper license, the women in her village eagerly formed a gum collector's group. SEWA approached the forest officials on their behalf and, after some struggle, secured an identity card and a license for each group member. Within the year, five more villages in the neighborhood had formed groups and procured identity cards and licenses through SEWA.

The gum, however, still legally belonged to the Forest Corporation; the women were obliged to deposit their collection with the corporation, which paid the women 4 rupees per kilo. The Forest Corporation sold the gum in open market for 8 to 10 rupees and kept the profits. The government had a monopoly, and they did not hesitate to take full advantage of it.

Ranbai was quick to point out to the officials that by issuing the licenses to the women, the corporation now had large amounts of gum, whereas earlier they had none. "Just my village alone deposits close to 300 kilos of gum with you every day!" It was time to raise the rate. The corporation reluctantly agreed to raise the rate to 6 rupees, even though the women demanded 8 rupees per kilo.

On the strength of their growing numbers, the District Association, which was comprised of the various producer and service groups, including embroidery, water management, and the gum collectors, took up the

1. Ranbai, the present President of SEWA, has been serving her second term since 2000.

cause of the gum groups with the managing director of the Forest Development Corporation at its head office in Baroda.

Since they were traveling to Baroda to meet a "big sahib" in a "big city," the women dressed in their best colorful skirts and put on their silver jewelry, some of which they had borrowed from other village women. The managing director welcomed us with a big laugh; such quaint-looking visitors were the first of their kind in his office! He began by launching an offensive. "How can I believe you are poor forest women? Look at the pounds of silver on your body!" "I can show you how we collect gum," said Ranbai and tied up her skirt, wound her half-sari around her head, and began a slow, hunched-back crawl, as if negotiating the thorny bushes, toward his chair. Embarrassed, the sahib nervously averted his eyes and quickly reassured us that he was familiar with the region the women all came from; he was sent there on the first posting of his career.

Together, they talked about their jungle with great feeling—the *piloodi* and the *leemdi* trees, the animals, the parched earth, and how the forest changes when the rare rain arrives. Encouraged, the women told him how the gum grows in October and November and how that first white gum is the best, and they showed him their red-latticed arms. The managing director relaxed visibly and eventually said, "So tell me your problem."

As a result of that meeting, not only was the price of gum raised to 8 rupees per kilo, but boots, water bottles, hats, and sunglasses were issued to 300 gum collectors in the region. The advantage of group effort was not lost on the women; more village groups began to form in the area and apply for licenses. A year later, the price went up to 12 rupees a kilo. Again, the number of gum groups rose. Ranbai's leadership generated more leaders—leaders like Paluben and Rudiben.

But then the Forest Corporation's rate started falling from 12 rupees to 10 rupees, and then to 7 rupees per kilo. The Corporation complained of a glut in the market; the Government of India had imported huge quantities of gum from the Sudan. No one seemed to know why the gum had been imported at all; there was more gum in the market than industry could use.

Another reason for the falling prices was pressure from traders. Because the women now had licenses, they no longer needed to sell their gum surreptitiously to the traders. Neither did the traders want to pay the fair prices the Forest Corporation was paying the women. Now the gum traders had to buy gum from the Forest Corporation at regularly held auctions. When the traders learned that the Forest Corporation had agreed to pay the women 10 rupees per kilo, they formed a cartel and came up with a strategy. No trader was willing to buy gum from the government at auction for more than 7 rupees a kilo. With no buyers at their stated price, the government was forced to sell at a loss to the traders. Since they were selling at a loss, the government slashed the prices they had agreed to pay the women. When we protested, the government invited us to come to the auction to see for ourselves the quandary they were in. The government was indeed at the mercy of the traders.

This was a major crisis for the gum collectors, who were in essence bonded to the Forest Department and their rates. The women were paying the price for a system that was blatantly not working. SEWA requested permission from the Forest Corporation to sell the gum in the free market, but received no answer. That year, flouting all regulations, SEWA sold the gum in the open market at 23 rupees per kilo to private traders. It was a conscious act of defiance by SEWA.

The matter went to the chief minister of the state, Keshubhai Patel, and we argued our case. The women were responsible guardians of the state forests; they cared for the trees and in no way harmed them when collecting gum. The women depended on the forests for their survival— they were the poorest of the poor. They deserved fair treatment at the hands of the government. When the national policy of the government was for de-licensing and raising trade restrictions on large business houses, why were the poor restricted from going to the open market?

Despite stiff resistance from the Forest Department, Keshubhai Patel awarded temporary permission to the Banaskantha District Association to sell the gum in the free market. The one-year permission was extended for another five years. In 2004, the market price of top quality gum was 60 rupees per kilo.

The Salt Farmers

In the neighboring Surendranagar district, another group of women was eking out a living from their arid environment. The *agaria* women make salt from subsoil brine. Underground channels of seawater flow deep inland and fill up in cavities, which the salt farmers tap into with small bores. This brine is more concentrated than seawater.

Ranjanben of Kuda producing industrial salt. (Gram Haat)

The third largest producer of salt in the world, India produces 17 million tons of salt a year, 70 percent of which is produced in Gujarat. Surendranagar district in the Little Rann of Kutch produces about 2 million tons of salt annually; the highest production is in neighboring Kutch. Most of the salt made in Gujarat is produced from fresh seawater, but a good deal of salt is produced inland, by the salt farmers of Surendranagar.[2]

The harsh desert climate is tough on the inhabitants. Mornings and evenings are very cold, and the hours in between are scorching hot. The land is parched, its surface fissured. The people live in dwellings called *kooba*—boot-shaped underground spaces with a small opening on which a tarp or a grass covering functions as a roof. The area is sparsely populated; neighbors may live anywhere from half a kilometer to five kilometers away. Because of the distances, farmers often use mirrors to communicate with each other. Small temples of *Shaktimata* dot the landscape like milestones—marking places where there is human activity nearby.

2. Central Salt and Marine Chemicals Research Institute. *Methods of Producing Industrial Salt from Ground Water*. SEWA publication, 2003.

The difficult life of agarias—salt farmers—is expressed in this lament of a young bride:

Desh na joya, pardesh na joya, shiday deedhi maney meethey, ma?
I saw that strange land, and my agaria's pan
And my eyes, welled up with sand.
My mother! Why did you marry me to an agaria?
I burnish those pans with my bare hands, and crush the salt with my
    bare feet,
My tears, they are saltier than salt, my mother!
I rise so early in the morning, and harvest the salt all day, all night
My mother! Why did you give me to the agarias?
I may die young, but don't hurry to my pyre
My flesh will burn, but my bones will wait for you
My mother! Why did you give me to the agarias?

I have often been told that when the bodies of agarias are cremated, they do not burn easily; their bones are dense with salt deposits.

Fifty years ago, when I first visited the agarias of Surendranagar, they used bullocks to draw brine from the ground. During harvest season, the animals were kept busy well into the night. The women walked miles to fetch fodder and kept the bullocks covered with warm blankets, but the animals did not survive more than two seasons. "Neither did the women—they died taking care of those bullocks," said Shantiben, a salt farmer from Kuda village, remembering her own childhood days working in saltpans.

Brine extraction is mechanized now because underground brine levels have sunk to 60 or 70 feet. A small water pump, called a "*dibko*," is used to draw water; they are expensive, though; fuel accounts for 60 percent of their production expenses and the cost keeps going up. In the past ten years, the price of diesel for a 210–liter barrel has increased from 1,680 to 5,305 rupees. "But the price of a ton of salt has gone from 40 to 78 rupees," says Shantiben.

In September, the agaria move out of their villages and go to live in the desert. They look for the flag they left standing by their saltpans the previous year, because in their absence, the desert winds blow all summer and bury their wells, their saltpans, and kooba under layers of sand. Every season, the saltpans must be prepared all over again. Preparing the bottom and sides of the pans requires great skill—the sticky clay must be worked on with the balls of the feet until it is smooth, burnished, hard, and no longer porous—not a drop of water can seep into the ground. It is the women who do this work, and their skill is crucial to their survival.

Equally crucial is the digging of the well. Using shovels, the men dig until they hit water. Then they insert a pipe in the ground and attach a water pump to it. If they are lucky, there will be enough brine to last them the entire season; if they run out of brine, or if the direction of the wind changes and the brine levels recede, they must dig again—they sometimes dig as many as five wells before they have the steady brine flow they need to keep the pans in a constant foot of water. Otherwise, all their efforts are in vain.

Each family operates anywhere from one to five pans; each pan occupies an area of half an acre or so. Brine flows first into a holding tank, where it is kept until it reaches a certain degree of salinity. The brine is then released along channels into the pans, where the wind and the sun cause steady evaporation. The brine must constantly be monitored, not only to keep it clean, but also to maintain a certain degree of salinity. In order to keep the salt from forming on the soil at the bottom, the pans are lined with a desert grass called *shengatra* on which the first fine salt crystals form. This is the highly prized *fleur de sel* salt. Salt is constantly raked and gathered until the crystals are well formed. The salt is then left to cure for a few days, until it is dry enough to handle.

The process begins in late October after the festival of Dussehra, as the winter sets in, and is harvested in March, around the festival of Holi, before the summer winds start blowing. Any delay, and the sand flies into the salt and the crop is ruined. After the harvest, the farmers leave their kooba and return to their villages for a few months.

All through winter, when they are tending the pans, there is steady traffic between the village and the distant koobas where the farmers live. Food, fuel, and supplies must be brought to the families. In the absence of any public transportation, men and women walk twenty to thirty kilometers in the desert with as many jugs of water and fuel as they can carry. On average, they need ten liters of diesel every three days to run their pumps, so trips to town are constant and grueling. Bicycles and motorcycles are therefore highly prized.

Most agarias are too poor to make the initial investment in the year's crop—they need capital to run the pumps and feed their families, so they turn to salt traders for help. The trader lends the farmer money and promises to buy his entire crop at a price that is determined before harvest time. A month or two before harvest, having consulted with other traders and determined the market price, the trader visits the farmer and checks on the crop quality and quantity. He then quotes him the price he has decided to pay for the crop. Of course, the farmer can hardly argue—he is already in debt and has no other buyer for his crop. The price is carefully quoted— it invariably leaves the farmer short, so that the following year he will then have to turn to the same trader again for money. Most of the agarias in Patadi, Halvad, and Dhrangadhara talukas have been indebted in this way for many generations because their income has always been less than what they have borrowed.

The highly organized traders dominate the land, the farming process, the market, the transport service, and even the government offices. Small plot holders cannot hope to compete. For every rupee's worth of salt, the salt farmer gets no more than 5 paise! The bulk of the profit does not settle in the pockets of the traders; the traders in fact sell the salt to large corporate giants like Tata Chemicals and Birla, who make up 90 percent of the salt market and therefore make the lion's share of profits.

SEWA's first contact with the agarias was through their children. The embroidery groups talked about the agarias who took their children to live with them in the desert, where they were left to their own devices for long hours while the parents worked. Because they lived away from the village for many months at a time, the children's education suffered.

We started small. We set up a crèche by the saltpans where children, from nursing newborns to those seven or eight years of age, were supervised by a small team of women. The children were separated according to age. Vasuben, a trained teacher from Ahmedabad, taught a small group of middle-aged women who could no longer work in the pans about childcare and nutrition. The new childcare workers were illiterate, so Vasuben taught the women and the children to read and write at the same time. The mothers took great interest in these new developments and especially appreciated the nutritious midday meals that were prepared for the children. Through this initial contact with the agarias, we gradually began talking, interviewing, observing, and taking survey of the ins and outs of salt farming—especially the income and working conditions of agaria women.

The agaria women needed support in many quarters. First, they needed capital to free themselves from the clutches of the trader. They needed technical expertise to be able to produce both edible- and industrial-grade salt; tools like water pumps and rakes, but also rubber boots and hats and gloves; child care and health care so that their productivity could improve; transportation to carry their salt to market; and most of all, a market to sell to. Just as one need is tied in to the other, our approach too had to be interlinked and integrated.

While SEWA began working with the children and bringing health workers to the area from time to time, SEWA Bank looked into the credit needs of the farmers. As an urban registered bank, SEWA Bank is not permitted to make loans in rural areas or open any branches. Despite years of negotiations, the Bank still cannot play a direct role in providing group credit to SEWA's rural members.

Gram Haat: Links to Market and Technology

DWCRA was interested in providing funds and training to womens' producer groups, but the kinds of women's groups we were forming in Banaskantha were engaged in economic activities based on existing skills. Salt farming and gum collecting were not on any government-prescribed list of suitable occupations worthy of funds and training. Besides, the training that the strong Banaskantha women's groups needed was of a different kind—the women wanted to learn basic management, account keeping, and some technical know-how.

SEWA was interested in access to the DWCRA program for several reasons. The women's groups, which were forming rapidly in rural areas, needed a lot of financial support that stretched SEWA's resources to the extreme. Each group needed capital to start its activities—from buying thread and fabric for embroidery groups, to transportation for the gum and salt that the women produced. Most important, the women needed a market for their products.

Looking to the vitality and strength of our groups, the government agreed to provide the capital of 15,000 rupees per group and also agreed to provide the kind of training and support that the women's groups needed. The collaboration was a success. Hundreds of women's groups in villages were able to form, and more important, survive, even after the DWCRA project was wound down by the government. This would not have been possible had the initial help not been given.

SEWA's rural membership rocketed in the 1990s from 13,000 to 25,000, and by 2000 it reached more than 318,000. I was both elated and concerned—elated because village women were coming together in large numbers and actively participating in bringing change; elated because we had been right in keeping employment as our focus—all other inputs were secondary. But I was concerned because our organizational complexities were compounding and because production, which was growing at such a phenomenal rate, needed marketing to keep pace. How was SEWA to suddenly sprout a marketing arm? Besides, market intervention is a veritable minefield; all manufacturers—whether in the small sector or the mammoth corporate sector—have to tread carefully and nimbly.

The diverse nature of the products and the marketing needs of the different trades within our membership demanded constant monitoring, quick action, and an ability to withstand short-term setbacks. There was no common strategy that could be applied across the board and become a panacea for all our marketing needs.

There were the gum collectors in the forest villages of Santhalpur, the salt farmers in the Little Rann of Kutch, the weavers in Kheda, as well as the small and marginal farmers growing cumin and sesame seeds, who had all formed producers' groups and come together as district-level associations. They had begun the process of stepping out of the contract system of producing for traders and started producing as self-employed entrepreneurs. But they desperately needed to establish their own links to the markets—not an easy task by any means.

I soon realized how urgent the need was for SEWA to build its own capacities to serve each district association in dealing with the market. A single group's individual capacity is very limited; even a district association's capacity is limited. To make their collective enterprise sustainable and profitable, the district associations had to come together to make effective market interventions at several levels. Without a financial cushion, lack of market information, and no direct contact with the market, they had no bargaining power.

In 1998, the answer came from an unexpected source. The Rural Development Commissioner of Gujarat, Dr. K. N. Shelat, approached SEWA regarding expanding our training programs. I told him that the women did not need more training; what they really needed was help in the area of marketing. Was the Gujarat government willing to support a marketing effort on behalf of small-scale women producers? Dr. Shelat, sensitive to the issues of women's producer groups and eager to boost their efforts, took the bold step of offering a support fund for marketing. A three-party partnership between the district associations, SEWA, and the government of Gujarat led to the formation of the SEWA Gram Mahila Haat—the SEWA Rural Women's Marketing Unit. One member from each of the nine district associations is an executive member, which ensures that Gram Haat serves the interests of all districts and does not turn into just a middleman.

I was keen that the creation of Gram Haat should make the poor women stronger. It was important for the women to become owner-managers of their collective enterprise—not just producers. They had to come out of their dependency on middlemen to connect to markets and know everything there is to know about their trade—its production, distribution, and place in the economy—the art, the science, and the economics of their trade. The women needed to come out of poverty with increased buying power. Above all, they needed to produce for themselves and for their own local economy—not just for the urban and international markets. The women needed to realize their own strength—to do it all without receiving charity, without subsidies, and without dependency.

Gram Haat was looking into ways it could give support to the salt farmers when the solution came as the result of a serendipitous meeting with Mr. A. K. Luke, the managing director of the Gujarat Alkaline Corporation Ltd. (GACL). He gave us a good analysis of the salt market and enumerated the advantages of producing industrial salt, which is in great demand. Industrial-grade salt is used for extracting magnesium, calcium chloride, sodium sulfate, iodide, and other minerals and metals, which are used by the chloro-alkali industries. The process is highly specialized, and such chemical plants are entirely owned by big companies. But industrial salt must meet specifications, and so it needs better brine management. Mr. Luke was enthusiastic about helping the poor farmers, and he sent two of his experts to meet with our salt groups. This was a rare chance for the agarias, and the meeting was crowded with both men and women farmers eager to learn about the process of industrial production and its vigilant monitoring.

Looking to the overwhelming interest in producing industrial salt, the district association entered into an agreement with the Central Salt and Marine Research Institute (CSMRI) to receive technical assistance. Gram Haat set up two 5-acre salt farms—one in the village of Kuda and the other in Degam, where the agaria women could receive hands-on training and experience in salt monitoring. It also set up a laboratory in Dhrangadhra, where the women received intense training in chemical testing. Somehow, illiteracy is never a barrier when learning about one's own trade.

With the support of new funds from the government, Gram Haat loaned a revolving fund to the district association of 50,000 rupees per farmer at 6-percent interest. The first year was not easy. Afraid of breaking the age-old relationship with the traders, and still not sure of Gram Haat's capacity to sell their salt, only five farmers came forward. Their hesitation was understandable—it was risky business. Because of close supervision, financial support, and periodic testing, the group's salt quality was high. At the end of the first season, Gram Haat delivered 4,181 metric tons of salt to GACL. The traders were not pleased; day after day, they followed our delivery trucks in the hopes that our supply would be rejected for one reason or another. Fortunately, all our salt was accepted, and the farmers were paid close to the market price.

The success of this effort brought good benefits to the five farmers and generated confidence in others. Having found a source for high-quality industrial salt, GACL was now willing to extend *real* technical assistance to the association, and they signed an agreement to that effect.

The following year, thirty-five farmers joined in the industrial salt production, but this time, the salt was of a relatively lower grade; it did not fetch the maximum price from the market. The agaria women found it very difficult to constantly monitor the brine flow from pan to pan and bring it to the 28-degree crystallization stage necessary for industrial use. Looking to our limitations, the CSMRI in Bhavnagar decided to step in and help the women by directly supervising the technical side of production until they could be self-sustaining.

The training they devised was eminently practical. At the demonstration farms in Kuda and Degam, the women learn about the importance of the gradient of the pans in maintaining a steady flow of brine assisted by the wind direction, about the rate of water release to maintain a constant level of water in the pan, and testing salinity at regular intervals. At the lab, the women learn how to test the chemical composition of salt, so that they can alter and control the various chemical levels and create byproducts of commercial value.

The women can multiply their earnings if they can produce a standard-grade salt for industrial use, but also diversify and produce salt byproducts like gypsum and potassium. By adding soda ash, which is an industrial effluent readily available from the Dhrangadhra Chemical Works, the women can also decrease the calcium in the salt.

Now salt is graded according to its chemical composition: Grade A salt fetches around 100 rupees a ton, Grade B fetches 90 rupees, and Grade C fetches 25 to the salt farmer. The less calcium in the salt, the better the grade.

Around 1,500 men and women have undergone training so far. Gram Haat's revolving fund does not have the capacity to make loans to all the farmers that apply. At present, 106 loans have been made, with a potential of loaning to 250 more, but with limited funds, progress is slow.

Since a lot of the farmer's time and financial resources are spent chasing spare parts for their water pumps, Gram Haat has been working on setting up local tool sheds that would sell pumps, spare parts, salinity meters, and other technical gauges, as well as new technology to the farmers at a low cost.

Fuel cost is close to 60 percent of the agarias' production cost. They need ten liters of diesel every three days. At 27 rupees per liter at today's prices, their fuel expenses are high. The pumps wear out rapidly because salt water is so corrosive; as a result, they need a new pump every two or three years; at 5,000 rupees a pump, it is expensive. No wonder they are perpetually in debt. Gram Haat has been looking into setting up a diesel depot, but the initial investment needed is tremendous. Low-cost diesel tankers now bring fuel to the saltpans.

Since a disproportionate amount of the cost of production goes into fuel, Gram Haat is collaborating with the Renewable Energy Institute to explore energy alternatives like solar and wind-based technology. Transportation, the other major cost for farmers, is also being worked out. A shuttle transportation service has begun that delivers basic necessities from the villages to the saltpans, and the district association contributes toward the cost of transporting salt to market.

Today, the agaria women who have received technical assistance, loans from the revolving fund, and marketing help from Gram Haat have increased their productivity considerably; some agarias now take two crops of salt per year. Their income has increased because the "new" salt fetches a better price. Understanding the market has helped the agarias realize their own contribution to the economic equation. Whereas before, 5 paise out of every rupee went to the farmer, the farmer now gets 20 paise per rupee. This is a step forward, but there is still a long way to go.

Training in grading their product has also helped the gum pickers. The women now grade their gum themselves and receive different prices for each of the three grades. White gum is seasonal, found in October and November. This fetches the highest price at about 25 rupees per kilo. As the sun gets hotter, the gum turns red, and then when the summer sand starts blowing, it turns dark and its quality deteriorates. Red gum fetches 16 rupees per kilo, and black gum fetches the least, around 12 rupees per kilo. These prices fluctuate between the market price and the Forest Corporation's price.

The women need daily cash, so they deposit their gum with the group leader every day. Every week or two, a Gram Haat van goes from village to village collecting gum. The gum is then taken to the district association's godown in Radhanpur. White gum has a short shelf life, so during the white gum season, the van is a great asset in ensuring timely delivery to market.

After Gram Haat's and the District Association's expenses for transportation and marketing are deducted, 7 percent of the after-sales profits go to the district association, and the rest of the money goes back into the hands of the women, who are paid in proportion to their gum collection. There are twenty-one gum collectors' groups within the district association, and approximately 700 women collect gum. Their income over time has increased, but it is a tough way to make a living.

A Vardha-based Village Science Institute talked to us about how one can increase gum output with the help of a chemical injection but without sacrificing the health of the trees. It was worth trying. Some of our women received the necessary training and injected some trees. The first year, it hardly rained, so there was no gum; the next year the yield on the trees was higher, but the women were reluctant to keep up with the experiment. Besides, keeping track of the injected trees in the big jungle was difficult, not to mention that they did not own the trees. Their concern was justified for other reasons as well. Just one company in Bangalore made the chemical, and hanging one's livelihood on one single product was unwise. Furthermore, we knew little about the long-term effects of the product on gum, which is a food product.

The Rural Technology Institute took interest in the needs of the gum pickers, whose hands and feet were shredded by thorns. They designed a tool for gum picking—a long stick with a small scraper at one end to pry the gum off the tree. It was a successful design, because the women all began using it and then slowly adapting it to further suit their needs.

The environmental lobby has been pressuring for the removal of the gando baval from the desert because it has grown prolifically at the expense of the local flora. It is also believed to be the cause of increased salinity in the area. Local men cut the branches to make charcoal to sell in the market. Earlier, charcoal making was illegal; now the men are freely issued licenses to make charcoal because the Forest Department is trying to get rid of the species from the area. No local plants are being planted in its place, so the area is becoming even more barren.

The women are now raising small nurseries of medicinal plants that they sell to the Forest Department. Their knowledge of local plants is considerable, so they choose local species that are hardy and produce byproducts that can be sold.

Gram Haat's operations are not always smooth, and progress is often slow. Responding to the market is not always easy—the orders are often too large, and the women are unable to meet demand or, at times, there is little demand and the gum sits in the storehouse, tying up valuable capital.

Transportation is also a problem that takes a toll on time and profits. The villages are scattered over a vast area, and the roads are in terrible condition. The collection vehicles are not always cost effective, although they do spare the women the long walks to town in the heat, with produce on their heads. When a village producer group does not have a large enough haul, transportation is not cost effective. Attempts are made to set up a gum collection center for every cluster of villages so that pick up is quick.

Over time, the women change too. As they get older, they go to the forest less and less; better incomes also mean they can afford to stay home more. With some financial relief, the families no longer bring the children to the forest for gum collection—the children are encouraged to go to school. Naturally, young women do not want a life spent in gum collection, so over time, as the present generation dwindles, the number of gum collectors will decrease as well.

Training changes the women too. A course in all aspects of gum production and consumption leads them to new areas of awareness. "The gum is the same, but our view of the gum has changed," Paluben said. By understanding how the composition of gum changes, and what environmental factors affect its production and collection, the women understand their role in the process better, so they have more control over it. By learning all aspects of the marketing process—weighing, grading, and storing; the weight advantages of fresh gum over dried gum—and the price tradeoffs between various qualities of gum, the women are learning the business process itself.

Every group member now has a motivation to read and write. Increasingly, the women are able to read the accounts and reports sent by the district association and write a response. Most of them learn to read and write during one of Gram Haat's intensive literacy trainings. Once the utility of reading and writing is apparent in their lives, the women are determined to be literate. At a Gram Haat meeting, Paluben's group asked for a tabletop digital weighing machine to weigh their gum—not only because it was more accurate and more convenient, but also because they could now read the digits in English.

Because climatic conditions affect the gum crop, the uncertainty is of constant concern to the women. Good rains, a cold winter, and a short summer are needed to ensure an abundant crop and provide work for six to eight months of the year. But that is still not year-round income—the women have to turn to road construction or other manual labor to supplement their income. If they had a choice, the women would prefer supplementary home-based work, like pounding spices or processing gum. Gram Haat is therefore exploring the market opportunity for processed gum products. There are small orders for making and supplying glue to a printing press, and for processing white gum for a pharmaceutical firm and a confectionery firm. Value-added sales of gum products would increase the earning capacity of a large number of women, but its full scope is still largely unexplored. "Insha Allah," says Ranbai.

Gram Haat's largest membership is of agricultural workers. Indian agriculture has traditionally been rain-fed, and it continues to be so today. What have changed are the demands on agriculture. With greater population density, increasing urbanization, ecological degradation, soil erosion, and the dominance of larger, wealthier farmers over water and other agricultural resources, the poor farmer is no longer able to subsist on farming.

As early as 1976, when we were still part of TLA, SEWA began working with women agricultural workers in Ahmedabad district. We were active in demanding the minimum wage that the state had recently announced but with little success. The local landholders, long in league with the police, began constant intimidation. But that did not deter us; what made us reconsider our approach was the realization that in an area with surplus labor, merely demanding the minimum wage is futile. No sooner

Newly literate Jadiben, now local manager of a savings group, showing Gauriben her account balance on the computer. (Shreya Shah)

do minimum wages go up, the cost of raw materials and the cost of living go up too. A typical trade union agitation approach in rural areas has limited utility. Without real alternatives, agricultural workers have no true bargaining power; in the drought-prone districts where SEWA members live, the supply of labor far outstrips demand.

Besides, total dependence on the vagaries of monsoon makes it a risky employment option. Add to this the fact that technological progress in agriculture generally translates into joblessness for women who are predominantly engaged in labor-intensive work that calls for mechanization. Women are the victims of mechanization, not the beneficiaries. Unpredictability of yields and the rising cost of input are a major cause of their vulnerability. Year after year, small and marginal farmers bear all the risk while traders and big farmers reap the benefits. The producer gets nothing but a fraction of the market price of commodities. So the poor agricultural worker is in effect subsidizing the nation's economy with her sweat and blood, by taking on mountains of debt and living in dire poverty. She is the backbone of the economy—the beast of burden on which our economy rides.

9

Sukhi

The Sukhi River is absent from most maps. For the tribal or *adivasi* residents of Vadodara District, whose homes and forests lie submerged by its waters, it is a major presence. If the little river is to be found on any maps, it is on those of the Gujarat Government Irrigation Department. A small dam was built on the river in 1983 to strengthen agriculture in the district and to provide more water to the large farms, villages, and towns downstream. The dam was constructed at the cost of 920 million rupees. To the inhabitants of sixteen submerged villages, the dam cost them their land, their livelihood, and their traditional way of life.

There is irony in the river's name. "Sukhi" means "happy," but at its source in the hill ranges to the West, the little river is called "Suki," which means "dry." When Suki meets and marries the river Bharaj at Muthai, it becomes Sukhi. The *Rathwa, Barisa, Koli,* and other adivasis who have lived in the forests along its banks for centuries had plenty of water all year round; the soil was fertile and with relatively little effort they were able to grow paddy, corn, peanuts, vegetables, and other small crops for their own consumption. They kept cattle and poultry and sold milk for cash. They also collected forest produce like medicinal roots and berries; *mahua* flowers, which are used to make local liquor; *tendu* leaves, which are used to roll bidis, or Indian cigarettes; and *khakhara* leaves, which are the large leaves of the teak tree, used in making disposable plates and cups.

Although the Sukhi Reservoir Project was small, it was considered an important water resource management project by the Gujarat government. Its success was crucial, so the government addressed the issue of dam design and human resettlement, both, with extra care. At stake was the success of the Narmada Dam Project, which was huge, involving three states and the resettlement of almost a million people. The inhabitants of the sixteen villages certainly had no choice; they had neither the voice nor the strength to resist the loss of their land and way of living. They could only put their faith in the government's promises to resettle them nearby with cash and five acres of land.

In 1983, eight villages were completely submerged and eight more were partially submerged. Cash and land compensations were handed out to 1,531 displaced families. Some villagers chose to take all their compensation in the form of cash; they took the money and scattered away from the region. Four hundred and sixty-nine families chose to stay together in their village groups; they agreed to resettle in six villages in the far-away tribal region of Sankheda and Bodeli. These "voluntary settlers," by government records, received five acres of agricultural land and a small monetary compensation of 5,000 rupees. In addition, the families were entitled to the cost of salvaging and transporting their building materials, as well as money to buy seeds for planting.

The reality, of course, was nothing like what was promised on paper. The resettlement villages were not only far from their original village sites, they were at some distance from the host villages as well; no effort had been made to integrate them. There was no water, no electricity, no schools, or hospitals; just five acres of Revenue Department wasteland with a surface of stone rather than soil. Tin sheds were hastily put up to function as their new homes until the trucks delivered the salvaged building materials; but the money to rebuild did not come, or if it did, it arrived so late that the old beams were rotten or had been pilfered over time. Money to buy seeds was promised, but it arrived after the monsoon—too late to plant a crop and too little to save one from debt. Clearing the land of stones was backbreaking work; brush had to be cleared and stumps uprooted, all by hand, and by the sweat of one's brow. There was no water for drinking, let alone for irrigation; the promised wells were drilled, but they contained water so high in fluoride, it was harmful to humans and cattle alike. Without adequate fodder and common grazing grounds, most of the cattle did not survive, so milk could no longer provide the cash the villagers needed.

No roads linked the village to the main road, where electricity stopped as well, never making it to their homes.

The forests were gone. The plants and animals they lived with and received both material and spiritual sustenance from no longer surrounded them. Those who had lived with the river at their feet now lived in thirst. Whoever was benefiting from the building of the Sukhi Dam, it certainly weren't the people who had lived by the river for generations.

The resettlement was going poorly; even the government was aware that something needed to be done. They gathered data from the villages in an effort to understand the problems, but they could not think of solutions. In 1991, the State Irrigation Department approached SEWA for help with rehabilitation. They did not understand why their rehabilitation packages did not rehabilitate.

I was surprised and even a little outraged. Why should SEWA help the government in dealing with the consequences of what were essentially its anti-poor policies? How many of the poor were benefiting from the dam's waters? How much of the water was ending up in the taps of Vadodara? Why were the fragile forests easy to submerge while urban sprawl was left untouched? Why is the government's answer to poverty reduction yet another large construction project? After all, whom, besides the construction companies, does it benefit?

Although I had reservations, the matter was for SEWA's Executive Committee to decide. And before we could come to a decision, we needed to visit the villages. Three members from SEWA's rural team—Vishakha, Manju, and Reema—all of whom had considerable experience with village communities, were sent to assess the situation. The district's Assistant Collector—a woman—accompanied them as they talked to the local women about their new lives. On its return, the team reported that they were struck by the homogeneity of the community—its common history, culture, and skill base. The team felt the tribal women's sense of resignation. Despite the presence of the government official, the women neither complained about their loss nor asked why their compensation was delayed. Our team also noted the isolation of their community from the land as well as the local people.

SEWA's Executive Committee included twenty-one elected representatives from various trades in both rural and urban areas and four elected, but nontrade, representatives that included Renana and me. After listening to the report from our rural team, the question before us was whether

SEWA should work with the government. We already knew of some non-governmental organizations that had tried to work with the government on rehabilitation and found it both endless and thankless. Some of us felt that SEWA would be better off focusing on organizing informal-sector workers rather than assisting displaced rural communities.

Chandaben, the leader of the used garment dealers, was not convinced. "Ben, isn't most of our work rehabilitation of one kind or another? What those women need, and what we all need, is the same! Work! If the government is saying we want to do something for the women, why should we say no? Our job is to make sure the women get what they want."

She was right. It was ten years since the dam had been built; the people could never return to the villages. The adivasi community that had so far managed to stay close through all these years of hardship was on the verge of disintegrating. Once the social, cultural, and economic collapse occurs, the displaced just wander away from their settlements to become migrant workers and casual laborers in cities and on construction sites. Their children cannot hope for education or for a better future. We had a chance to make the government accountable for its actions. We had an opportunity to show the women how strong they really were.

The Executive Committee decided that we first needed to conduct a detailed, house-to-house survey of the six villages to learn more about the women, their skills, and their needs before agreeing to anything. The Foundation for Public Interest agreed to conduct the detailed survey;[1] Ramesh has always had a special place in his heart for the tribals of Gujarat. He designed a survey that would allow his team to gather the kind of information we could put to immediate and effective use. At the same time, SEWA began holding talks with the government regarding our approach to rehabilitation. Luckily for us, the government documents revealed high-minded objectives. The stated objective was to "make good the loss" the displaced suffered due to submergence; "bring them out of the poverty trap; and make them self-reliant, viable, and progressive households." The government had a budget to provide for the "Sukhi oustees."

It was important for SEWA to clarify its approach to the government early on. We were keen on the integration of the resettled village with the

---

1. Ramesh Bhatt. "Accelerated Rehabilitation of Resettled Households: A Status Report." Ahmedabad, India: Foundation for Public Interest. Unpublished report, 1991.

Chandaben with her grandchildren. (SEWA Bank)

host village and on working with both communities together. Perpetuating the special status of an "oustee" makes them perpetual outsiders. We wanted to work with the women in both communities because their needs were very similar. This idea was new but acceptable to the government. SEWA also convinced the government that we saw women playing the leading role in the rehabilitation process. SEWA's focus would be on the sustainable, economic recovery of women as part of the local mainstream economy.

It was not always easy. We had arguments with the government officials over several issues, including water. We insisted that the settlers could not be expected to subsist on rain-fed agriculture any more; they were entitled to irrigated cultivation whether it was by well water or canal water. We asserted that the viability of the project depended on the concept of "accelerated development" rather than the concept of "compensation," which at best "makes good the losses" but does not develop the full potential of the people or their resources. On both counts, the government agreed, but only half-heartedly.

In November 1992, the Executive Committee passed a resolution to work with the adivasi women of Sukhi. We also signed an agreement with the government to help with rehabilitation. We began by talking to the women—singly, in groups, and in public meetings. We wanted to know about their old life—about the myriad ways in which they made a living at the edge of the forest; about their knowledge, skills, expectations, disappointments, hopes, and grievances.

Ambaben Bhaisingh Rathwa was resettled in Saniyadri, and she was in mourning. Her young daughter Savita had died soon after giving birth to a little girl named Asha. Ambaben had gone to fetch water to prepare for the delivery, leaving her old mother-in-law to serve as midwife. Her old mother-in-law had plenty of experience delivering babies, so they did not call the midwife. When she returned, her daughter was dead.

When I visited her in her home, Ambaben was thin, her somber eyes lined with darker circles. She was sweeping her long verandah slowly and talking to one of her six goats, asking her to eat well and produce more milk because the little baby was totally dependent on her. I sat down to talk to her, and she poured her heart out.

Ambaben was fifty-seven years old, and she had come to Muthai as a bride. She lived there for fifteen years before it sank under the Sukhi. Ambaben remembered the tension in the hushed voices of the village men discussing the new dam and land, but she found it hard to believe that the Sukhi that flowed so gently could ever wash away village houses and the trees of the forest on account of a government dam. When talk of evacuation became more open and more frequent, she realized that the men had kept the women in the dark. Muthai had already been given official notice to evacuate.

In fact, for two years, the village elders had been traveling across the river to choose land and a new location for the village. They chose with two considerations: the village would move *en bloc* to the new site, and they would select a region where people of their own kind, the Rathwa, lived. They chose Saniyadri. None of the women had been included in the decision making nor had they seen the new land.

On the eve of departure, Ambaben's father-in-law announced that the government truck would arrive the next morning. "I am not going to hell.

Ambaben with her granddaughter and mother-in-law. (Ela Bhatt)

You go!" her mother-in-law screamed; she had to be physically lifted and put in the yellow truck. One by one, the women in the family had to be dragged on to the truck, kicking and screaming. The women were the last to know about the decision to move; they had no say in the timing, the sequence, or the pace of moving out. The men thought it best if it were sudden and inevitable; for the women, it was very traumatic.

It was mid-winter, 1982. The families had very few things to transport; their real wealth was cattle and children. Ambaben carried her ten-month-old son in her arms; her older children, one buffalo, two cows, two bullocks, and ten goats walked by her side. For Ambaben, the journey to Saniyadri was long and exhausting; they traveled in sadness, anger, fear, and trepidation. Every single woman remembers that journey most vividly.

The new land was just a barren expanse under the sky. There was no green in sight. Belongings salvaged from her past—red roof tiles, wooden beams, painted doors, a grinding stone, a shiny tin box from her kitchen, and framed pictures of family elders and gods lay unloaded from the trucks in a heap. She had no place in which to arrange them. No one had thought to allow the families to first build their new homes, prepare their new farms, or acquaint themselves with the new environment before the move.

The government had provided three large tin sheds as shelter for the Muthai villagers. Here, Ambaben and her children lay down. Someone offered her a glass of water, but it tasted salty. Tired and tense, Ambaben rested on the floor, using her arm as pillow.

Later that afternoon, her father-in-law showed the couple the plot for their house and the five-and-a-half acre land they would share between all the brothers in the family. The condition of the farm land! She called it porcupine land—thick with wild bushes and innumerable tree stumps—remnants of a forest of *saadad, dhaavla,* and *saag* trees that had been cut to supply wood for dam construction. Dams are built over a period of years, and the ecological destruction in their wake is huge; if they are built in the name of development and progress, it seems people are not part of that equation.

More importantly, there was no water! For the next five years, the women of Saniyadri would fetch water from the host village. Ambaben typically fetched ten pots of water for the family and her cattle from a farmer, paying 2 rupees per pot. Their predicament caused them such worry that the couple could hardly sleep at night. Her husband Bhaisingh worried about the land, and she worried about feeding the family and her cattle; but now they no longer kept their worries to themselves. Their new home was nothing but four tin sheets for walls and two sheets for a roof. They had been resettled!

According to government records, the family had received their compensation, but neither Ambaben nor her husband had seen it. On paper, her father-in-law, as head of the family, had received the money, but he had no knowledge of it. Either the man indeed did not receive any such compensation money, and his money was pocketed by someone who could read and write and who knew his way around the system, or the father-in-law had taken it and squirreled it away or squandered it on his own. This is typical; but as far as the women are concerned, they wouldn't have seen the money anyway.

For many years, the couple spent long hours clearing the land. One by one, they pulled out the old tree roots from the ground; they cut the dry brush and fired it to produce charcoal, which they sold in Dabhoi market to make some badly needed cash. For two years, the couple labored at a canal construction site, digging and loading sand in trucks, earning

25 rupees per day. Casual labor brings in cash; farming cannot meet a family's daily needs. But casual labor takes time away from labor-intensive farming.

The couple worked day and night on the land. On a partly cleared piece, they grew corn for their own consumption and some cotton as a cash crop for income. The first crop yielded 10 to 12 *mounds* of cotton, earning a net income of 5,000 rupees. Part of the amount was saved for buying seeds, irrigation water, and manure for the next year; the other was spent on buying materials to rebuild their house. The family needed to borrow money for agriculture, but the bank would not lend them money at a subsidized rate. As owners of five acres of land, they did not qualify for a subsidized loan. Ambaben lived in the temporary tin shed earning cash income, bringing up her family, and clearing and cultivating the land.

They made their own bricks from local clay. The materials salvaged from the old house were useful; eventually, they had a house with a tiled roof, three rooms, small storage, a kitchen, a washing place, and a long cattle-shed. Most of her cattle had died because of lack of green fodder and brackish drinking water. She said that as a result of hard mineral salts in the water, her animals developed stones in their stomachs. Without cattle, she did not have enough manure for the farm or fuel for cooking. "Imagine paying money for cow dung!" Ambaben said, still smarting under the blows from the new economy.

As part of the resettlement, two wells were constructed in the village, but both had saline water with very high levels of fluoride. Another tube well was dug in 1993, at great expense, but even that water turned out to be unpotable. A population that once had access to plenty of water was displaced so that others without water would benefit; but in the process, it left the first population both displaced and waterless! Cruel absurdities of this kind riddle the poor's existence.

One evening, the village head—the Sarpanch—asked all the women to come to a meeting after supper. Only women? That was very odd. Bracing herself for some more bad news, Ambaben, like other women in the village, went to the meeting reluctantly. The meeting, had, in fact, been called by SEWA; the Sarpanch was present but was asked not to speak. Ambaben recalled the two SEWA organizers conducting that first meeting. "One was a lady—quite tall, with very long fingers; the other was a simple middle-aged woman." It had been Anjana and Indiraben who had asked the women questions about their living conditions. The women replied in short syllables. But when they were asked about their work, they laughed. "What a question! We work on the land, what else is there to do?" Ambaben snorted. Her outspokenness caught the SEWA team's attention. They asked her if she would be willing to become a SEWA organizer. She would have to keep in close contact with the women of her village, call meetings, and make sure that ideas and information flowed freely with honesty and openness. She would be paid a salary. "Although I was illiterate, I was chosen! Of course, I took the job!" That was the beginning of Ambaben taking responsibility for the Sukhi Rehabilitation Project in her village.

SEWA's first task was to make sure that all available government services should reach the villages. From crèches and midday meals for children, a health care facility, and schools, to water, electricity, and roads, the villagers should have access to them all. Ambaben was selected under a government scheme to cook the "midday meal" for the children in the village school. SEWA would help the women to articulate their needs and show them the process by which they could receive services. The women would have to make the demands; SEWA would not do it for them.

Away from their forests and the riverbank, stranded in a water-starved cash economy, the women had almost no idea of their economic options. SEWA arranged exposure visits for the women so that they could explore new ways of earning their livelihoods. By seeing what other women do to make a living and talking with them about their work, the women would have a better idea of their choices.

Ambaben was responsible for forming the groups in her village. The women were terrified of stepping out of the village; the outside world was "more scary than wild animals," they confessed. But with some persuasion, and taking comfort in the fact that they were not alone, they set off on various visits. One group visited a nursery run by women in Ganeshpura in Mehsana district; another larger group spent time with milk cooperatives run by adivasi women in Valsad district. A series of groups visited government-run demonstration farms to learn about new agricultural equipment, seeds, and ways of farming.

Training was a major component in some of the project activities. One group of women went to the Agriculture University in Chhota Udaipur and learned about mushroom cultivation. It seemed similar to forestry, provided cash income, and had attractive returns. Excited, the women returned and set up a small-scale mushroom cultivation experiment. Under the expert's guidance, the mushrooms did grow, but "our mushrooms changed color before they reached the city market; they did not sell," Ambaben said. The women had no cold storage or transport facilities, so the mushrooms deteriorated quickly. Even though the mushrooms failed, the women blossomed.

Many groups took up nursery raising to make cash income, but saplings withered due to the saline water. Even growing grass was difficult; the grass tasted salty and the cattle would not eat it. That made dairying difficult. After approaching the government for assistance, they received money to dig a well, but there was very little water underground. The women installed a hand pump for common use on one villager's land, but the landowner eventually usurped it for his own use. The women, although angry, did not pursue the issue—there was not enough water to warrant a war.

What succeeded, albeit in a small way, was the construction of a sack dam to harvest rainwater. Sacks of sand are piled up in such a way as to capture and filter rainwater. This water is sweet and potable. When the rains are good, this is the best source of water.

Despite the lack of water for irrigation, most of the women loved to raise bunyan saplings. After their training in nursery plants, they tried their hand at species like bamboo, almond, eucalyptus, and tamarind in their village nursery plot. "In Saniyadri, children grow easily, but not trees," laments Ambaben. Under the direction of K. G. Mehta, the women are experimenting with local species that are hardy. The women have a wide knowledge of roots and plants, which they are now putting to use; they gather seeds from local—and sometimes wild—species of cereals and legumes that have a high tolerance for saline water and plant them in their nursery. They are trying to build a green cover over their rocky ground, plant by plant.

The resettled are in the new Saniyadri; the old host village of Saniyadri is close by and inhabited by people of their own Rathwa community. The women of Saniyadri have played a defining role in building links between their settlement and the host village. They struggled together to build a cooperative dairy, but the lack of green fodder for the cattle has now made it defunct. The new settlement shares its savings groups and nursery units with the host village, and in turn host village shares its kindergarten and primary school. Cordial relations between host villages and the new settlement are not common in government projects. In most cases, they either continue to live a parallel existence or they clash. But when the two face the same problems and arrive at solutions together, rehabilitation becomes a little easier. Like a grafted plant, the cut branch can benefit from the root stem; but such grafting is rarely planned and seldom implemented.

Neither the new nor the old village has a doctor, a nurse, or a chemist; the nearest one is in the small town of Chalamali, more than ten kilometers away. SEWA-trained health care workers attend to the small ailments of women and children, but that is not enough, as Ambaben's experience shows.

Of the six villages, Vadadala, Lunadra, Tandalja, and Saniyadri were the most active in training and organizing. Once again, the women trainers visited poultry farms, a home science college, social forestry centers, milk-refrigeration centers, a veterinary hospital, and a cattle-feed factory. According to the women, the most interesting visit was to the Agriculture Science Centre at Chhota Udaipur, where they learned interesting farming and land development methods like sprinkle irrigation, seed preservation, and pond lining for water harvesting. At the end of the exciting day, they would sing and dance, wishing their men could have come too. Memories of these visits stayed in their minds for a long time. Women from the different villages got to know each other; they spent hours on the bus using the new vocabulary, discussing the ins and outs of raising saplings and the prices they might fetch.

The women that trained in poultry rearing for fifteen days at Baroda and passed the test were gifted twenty-five chicks and a stipend amount of 250 rupees by the government. Some families eventually raised 10,000 birds, while others could not resist the temptation of frequent feasts even when their flock was small.

As the five-year term of the "Accelerated Rehabilitation of Resettled Households of the Sukhi Reservoir Project" approached an end in 1995, we were quite concerned about the future. The training and the economic activities, the project office, night accommodations for women traveling from distant villages, and transport facilities would all be withdrawn. We had made sure that light meters, water tanks, and ration cards had reached all six villages. Links with government organizations like the Tribal Development Corporation, the Revenue Department, and the District Rural Development Agency among others had been established so that the women could avail of their services, but we had no funds of our own.

We had arrived at a juncture. Was it time to withdraw, or to spread, intensify, and consolidate the activities we had started? We hoped that the government would agree to our proposal to set up a revolving fund to continue the ongoing activities, but the government's budget for the purpose had been exhausted. But people are not projects; when a project ends, people cannot cease to matter. It was time to organize women's meetings in each of the six villages to consult them about the future.

At the meeting, which was quite tense and emotional, the women of the six villages were all of one mind, without exception—we would form our own organization and continue the activities. SEWA was willing to help the women set up their organization with the understanding that once on its feet, SEWA would withdraw its support and they would run it on their own. It was decided that each woman would pay 12 rupees every year for membership, and then pay a small fee for each of the activities or services the women wanted. With an initial membership of 200 women, the Sukhi Mahila Mandal was registered on September 27, 1995.

The transition was tough; organizers worked without a salary for four months. The new office in Bodeli had no overnight accommodation for women coming from villages, so members slept in a temple courtyard across from the office. The office could not afford its own telephone line, so they used a neighbor's phone for a fee.

Initially, the Sukhi Mandal worked at providing existing government welfare services to the members: scholarship for school children; fiscal relief for widows, handicapped, and the old; preschool childcare centers and the like. These were activities they had recently become familiar with—how to use existing government programs and resources to strengthen themselves.

At the first general body meeting of the Sukhi Mahila Mandal, Kavitaben asked to sing a song she had composed:

Javani, javani, hun to SEWA-ma jawani
I will go, I will go, I will go to SEWA,
I will go, I will go, I will go to SEWA
Father-in-law tells me *"Bahu, you cannot go!"*
So I said, "Keep quiet and smoke your tobacco!
Because I will go, I will go, I will go to SEWA."
Mother-in-law says, *"Bahu, you should not go!"*
So I said, "Keep quiet and mind my children!

Because I will go, I will go, I will go to SEWA."
Brother-in-law tells me, "*Bhabhi*, you must not go!"
So I said, "Keep quiet, and cut that jungle grass!
Because I will go, I will go, I will go to SEWA."
Sister-in-law says, "*Kavli*, you need not go!"
So I said, "Keep quiet, and finish your studies!
Because I will go, I will go, I will go to SEWA."
My husband says, "Darling, I cannot let you go!"
I smiled and said, "Wait for me at the bus stand!
Because I shall soon be back, but I will go, I will go to SEWA."

Kavitaben Shankerbhai Rathwa of Vadadala was the elected President of the Sukhi Mahila Mandal. She was born in a small village called Vachali Bhit, which means the middle wall, crouched in the forested valley. The river Sukhi flowed by her village, and everyone loved to swim in it. At the age of three, Kavita was already responsible for the care of her six-month-old brother. Their mother worked as a daily wage laborer at canal construction. Her father worked on their land along the river. Kavita's older brother was away in an *Ashramshala*—a residential school for tribal children in that area.

Kavita was restless to go to school. As soon as her little brother could walk on his own, she ran away to her older brother's school without telling anyone. Such desperate hunger for learning is common among so many young women in tribal and other rural areas. The school principal saw Kavita's eagerness and admitted her as a student without hesitation. Her father had no choice but to let her stay. She was allotted a bed, a dress, a slate and chalk, an aluminum plate, a bowl, and a glass. The warden was caring, but strict; the windows of the girls' dormitory were always kept closed to stop girls from looking into the boys' dorms next door. However, if Kavita wanted to meet her brother, she ignored all the rules, fearlessly walked into his dorm, and bore the consequences.

The school building stood on a cremation ground; the children could watch the flames of burning bodies. The warden slept in the same room as the girls and sang them *bhajans* and told them stories of great virtue to put them to sleep. In her absence, the girls told ghosts stories.

Kavita passed the fourth grade and won two prizes in study and swimming. But that was the end of her school education; her father was waiting at the door to take her home. Little Kavita had to take off her school dress and return it. Her father had not brought her any clothes from home to change into, so she walked home naked and crying. It was time to work at home, to help her mother with the chores—fetching water for the buffaloes, taking them out grazing, and cutting grass or weeding fields. Sometimes she would go with her mother to the construction site or to the stone mine. On the way back in the evening, her mother would carry Kavita on her shoulders as she rushed home to feed her hungry family.

Kavita worked hard not forget what she had learned in school; she wrote lists of words and read her brother's books. She wrote letters to imaginary friends and even to gods each year. At fifteen, she married Shankarbhai, who lived in Chaina, a village across the Sukhi. Chaina was bigger and busier than her own village, and she liked living there. Though young, she observed keenly, and she listened "with four ears" to the men's talk, which interested her the most. Talk about earning money, the coming elections, getting government jobs, visiting big towns, riding a scooter, and meeting important people sounded exciting. She heard the men talk about the dam and the evacuation of villages, so unlike most women, she was aware of the construction of the Sukhi Dam and that it would submerge their village.

The government showed the elders of Chaina several lands nearby on which to settle their people. The people of Chaina settled in Vadadala and Lunadra; Kavitaben's family chose Vadadala.

The name "Vadadala" conjured up all sorts of images. She hoped it would have a school and a direct bus to a big town. Her husband too was curious to see the place before they moved there, so the two decided to go on their own. When the couple reached the Vadadala resettlement site, they rested a while and then cut grass from the land and tied it in two big bundles to carry home with them. On the way, they sold one bundle of grass for cash. The couple walked home in a happy mood. Shankarbhai said, "The reason I like the new village is because it is far from your parents' house. Now you won't be able to walk out on me so easily!"

The entire family eventually moved to Vadadala and began life from scratch. When they lived in the temporary tin-shed housing provided by the government, Kavitaben looked for wage labor, while her husband worked on clearing the land to prepare it for agriculture. It was a hard life. Her family had received a cash compensation of more than 60,000 rupees, but again, it went to the head of household; the young couple received no part of it.

One evening, the village Sarpanch made an announcement that the following morning all women in the village were required to attend a meeting at the panchayat office. "Reluctantly, we stayed home from work," Kavitaben recalled. "Three SEWA organizers had come from Ahmedabad to talk with us. They were young; they appeared educated but too modestly dressed. They talked to us about our move and what had changed, and what we wanted to change, but mercifully, they gave no advice. All they did was ask too many questions. They talked about women taking the lead and some such, but I got the gist of it: SEWA was looking for some women to do their village work," Kavitaben said. "There were twenty-five to thirty women present at the meeting; some had tenth-grade education, and a couple were even "college-pass." But the college-educated girls did not want to go to the Bodeli office everyday, and even the school-educated girls said that their husbands would not allow them to leave the village. "Husbands are strange," she said, "They don't mind if we go to work to some far-away road construction site, but if the work is an office, or in a city, they get stubborn."

"But the SEWA women's eyes were on us—the illiterate ones. Some women recommended my name, probably because I am outspoken, but I too refused because my children were little and my husband would have to work all alone in the field. But much to my surprise my mother-in-law stood up at the meeting and announced that if I worked, she could look after my children! She said this in front of so many women, so I thought she must mean it. And then right out in the open, the SEWA women announced that my monthly salary would be 500 rupees! I was so pleased!"

Kavitaben showed up for her job the next morning at the Sukhi Project Office in Bodeli. She had a hectic week. On the second day at work, she was asked to go to Saniyadri to select a local person who could conduct a survey. She selected Kanubhai, who had just returned from the dam site unloading sand from trucks. On the third day, Kavitaben and Kanubhai were sent by the office to select a woman organizer in Lunadra. The women of that village hid themselves in fields when they heard that some strangers were coming to talk to them, but young Ushaben wasn't afraid, so she was selected to be the Lunadra organizer. Local teams are best; no real change can occur without their complete participation. However educated and well meaning the outsiders are, they are effective only up to a point. Even though locals are caught in their own undercurrents of politics and vested interests, they understand the community's dynamics and—given the opportunity—are able to forge a consensus for real change.

Every day, Kavitaben visited women's homes and called meetings to hear the women's complaints. She also visited various government offices to learn about the services they provided. At the end of the day, she sat in the office and wrote a daily diary. She was happy to have the opportunity to write, but she was out of practice. "All day I would go over the words in my mind that I would write in my evening diary," she said. Anjana, the SEWA coordinator, let her write as she liked. Writing took up so much of her time that she consistently reached home quite late after dark. Her family eventually came to a point when they asked her to stop going to work. But she was determined. *"Hun to javani!*—I *will* go," she said defiantly. She was careful not to miss her household duties, particularly fetching water from the well. She would reach the well at four in the morning and collect the fresh water that had sprung up during the night; latecomers often found none left for the day. Despite the long hours of work, Kavitaben persisted. SEWA is made up of thousands of women like Kavita who overcome great odds to change their lives and their environments. They are the ones who keep detailed minutes, maintain faultless accounts, and speak with conviction.

Kavitaben worked hard to bring benefits to each village. Her first act was to arrange for a regular delivery of water tankers to fill the empty well, the pond, and the pots of village women with water. Then, she took on the issues of unpaid compensation, proper housing, and the need for savings groups. Traveling from village to village and commuting to the Bodeli office took a lot of her energy and time, so Kavitaben took matters in her own hand and found a solution that raised eyebrows. She took a loan and bought herself a scooter. The sight of an adivasi woman driving between village and town, working with men and women, speaking for both the literate and the illiterate, and trying to link the past with the future was thrilling and inspiring for everyone around her. Her spirit was probably a bigger catalyst for change than anything else.

At this time, another government scheme to build Jeevandhara wells, with full government subsidy, was proposed. Tandalja already had three wells with brackish water; Saniyadri had eleven wells out of which only seven struck mostly nonpotable water; Vadadala had two wells and three hand pumps, but the water was not potable. Most women fetched water from neighboring settlements. The government had dug a tube well, but that too failed to bring up water. However, with luck on our side, nine of the Jeevandhara wells dug during the period that SEWA worked on the project struck sweet water. Vadadala could even afford to have piped water in homes.

Water changed the village scene; the women now could multiply their economic activities. They raised dairy cattle and sent milk to the nearby village dairy cooperative; the farmers grew a better quality of cotton whose seeds were in great demand among the big farmers of the host village; Vadadala and Tandalja grew abundant tomatoes—a crop they cultivated for the very first time. The women even learned how to make tomato ketchup although they could not find a suitable way to enter the market. Lives were changing, the community was changing, and occupations were changing—Kavitaben and her team made it happen. Perhaps with more resources, better changes could have taken place; with more care, the changes could have been more effective, but because the adivasi women themselves were leading these changes, the impact would be long-term.

There were plenty of failures; Kavitaben and her colleague Somabhai organized stone-mining cooperatives in Vadadala and Lunadra. The first one went into liquidation because of mismanagement and in Lunadra, the application papers to lease the land carried the wrong survey number, so it was three long years before the government records could be corrected. But despite the pitfalls, the women discovered that stone mining could be an income-generating occupation, and it is an enterprise they could set up without any outside intervention.

The women also set up a leaf-plate making unit; but although demand for leaf-plates was ample, it is seasonal. During the season, orders have to be fulfilled without delay. Because the supply of electricity during production was irregular, the unit missed delivery dates and eventually it disbanded. It can certainly be revived, but who would help the women do it? If a government-run bank or industrial unit fails, the government comes to the rescue and finds ways to revive it; but if a small village unit fails, there are no second chances. At times, it seems that only large losses deserve public support!

All the houses in the village had, by now, installed electricity meters and received power. But the villagers found the supply of electricity erratic and expensive. Unused to paying monthly bills, they were often late in paying. Consequently, they constantly faced high fines and disconnection notices. The families now all possess ration cards to buy basic necessities from government-run fair-price-shops; but the shops are situated in distant villages, so the villagers must either walk great distances for everyday necessities or pay higher prices to local traders.

The community in Vadadala was in good spirits, particularly the women. The panchayat had successfully merged with the host village. With some encouragement from the women, and without any party affiliation, Kavitaben decided to run for election for a seat on the panchayat. She won the election and served for one term, from 1991 to 1996. "My husband remained quiet, but my parents-in-law always denied me permission for any such activities. All they wanted was that I should labor in the fields."

Kavitaben's colleague Somabhai also won a seat in the Panchayat and was elected Sarpanch. This was a rare case where the hosts and the "settlers" came together without joining hands with any political party. The cooperation, which had begun well, soured by the end of the term; the members of the host village brought a no-confidence motion against the Sarpanch for certain management lapses and Kavitaben had to help him win the confidence vote.

Kavitaben spent her term in the Panchayat productively. She took special pains to get land for a Tadvi family, the poorest and in the lowest social strata amongst the tribals; at her initiative, the District Development Office awarded a housing scheme to her Panchayat, and six of the poorest families of the host village got new houses. In the resettled Vadadala, every family had both land and house; she brought street lighting in the lanes of the host village. Because she was well trusted by both the host villagers and the resettled population, she played a major role in settling internal disputes. She was the guest of honor when the first marriage between a girl from the resettled village and a boy from the host village took place. That was the beginning of a real integration between the two villages.

In the meantime, her husband Shankerbhai fell seriously ill. He was taken to a hospital in Baroda despite his reluctance to leave the village; he cursed his wife for bringing him to this death hole in the city, but she was firm. A tumor weighing 240 grams was removed from his stomach, and his health improved considerably. Shankarbhai could never thank his wife enough for his recovery. Since then, "he never contradicts me. He has faith in whatever I say or do," Kavitaben said.

Other Panchayat members respected her for her clean and efficient execution of government programs. "All these years, they called me, Kavli, Kavli. Now they call me Kavitaben and sometimes just 'Ben'!" Kavitaben

said. The 'Ben' of Vadadala, after two years, got elected to the SEWA
Executive Committee, representing not only the tribal women, but also
all the rural women members of SEWA in Sankheda Taluka.

As promised, in 1997, SEWA withdrew Anjana and her colleagues
from the Bodeli office. The Sukhi Mahila Mandal became a local, self-
administered, independent organization with good, local leadership and
a strong sense of direction. It also continued to maintain strong links with
SEWA.

SEWA's assistance was sought in preparing an action plan for two
activities: women's banking and nursery raising. SEWA also provided
intensive practical training and capacity building of the unit managers in
charge of those areas. Local members formed spearhead teams in banking and nursery raising and organized field activities. The Sukhi Mandal's
days of exposure and experimentation were over, as was the period of trial
and training; now they had to face the mainstream economy on their own
strength and the power of their savings and credit.

The forced entry of the adivasis into a cash economy was not easy. To
begin with, it was important for the women to understand and learn the
workings of a new economic system. For economic self-sufficiency, the
women needed capital; access to savings and credit was only possible if
the women could save on a regular basis. Considering their meager incomes, saving anything is not easy, but it is a skill that can be learned.
Progress is slow but steady. The group determines the sum of money that
every member can afford to save every month—say 10 or 20 rupees. Every
month, the women meet to deposit their money.

An organizer from SEWA Bank is always present at the meetings to
make sure that the group understands each and every part of the savings
process. New deposits are recorded, and the previous month's balances
are read out. The process takes place in the presence of the entire group
so that it is comprehensible to everyone. Interest is paid yearly. When the
group has a substantial amount of savings, they make loans to the members at interest rates they determine themselves. Some groups charge as
little as 12 percent, others who want their capital to grow faster charge 18
to 24 percent; in the event of an emergency, they even extend a second
loan for as little as 2 percent. Money as a productive asset becomes real
and within reach.

Ambaben of Saniyadri took the leadership in her village and formed
a savings and credit group. Every Wednesday, fifty-one women met on

her verandah and conducted their banking business; they deposited their savings, repaid loan installments, and decided on new loans. Some women were wary of taking any loans; they feared debt in any form. Others preferred to take a loan and leave their savings untouched.

The small loans from the women's groups are used for the redemption of old debts, for jewelry, or for wedding celebrations. Because their saving capacity is limited, the groups cannot accumulate capital soon enough. Ambaben's savings group wanted money to develop their village nursery, but local banks would not lend to them. Because the village men were neck-deep in debt to the commercial banks, the entire village was blacklisted. Because of the defaulting men, even the Sukhi Mandal found it difficult to link its women's savings groups with these banks. The Sukhi Mandal then turned to SEWA Bank, who charged them at the bank rate. This allowed the women to develop the nursery as a commercial activity.

The savings groups suffer setbacks of all kinds. When Ambaben's daughter Savita died, Ambaben stopped holding the group meetings. She also stopped saving, and as a result, other members also stopped their transactions. The default rate began rising every month, and the group almost became defunct.

Ambaben, once the recipient of an award for the best performance of a savings group, was listless and depressed. The death of her daughter, the care of her granddaughter, and the fact that in two years, her son had changed four wives, leaving another child in her care, was proving too much. Ambaben's niece, Gita, eventually came to the rescue. She began spending her time recovering loans and resuming savings activities; this put the group back on track and out of distress within a few months.

Despite the ups and downs of individual groups, the entire savings and credit unit of the Sukhi Mahila Mandal attained operational self-sufficiency within two years. The next issue was to revise their business plan. Pressure on the Sukhi Mandal from the women of other villages to extend their financial services to them too had increased. They too were part of the local extended family. Once that was agreed on, the Sukhi Mandal grew from the 6 to 177 groups in Sankheda taluka.

A common feature of the savings and credit groups has been that the women are keen to save but do not want to spend their savings. When they need money, the women would rather borrow 2,000 rupees at a 24 percent interest rate from the group rather than touch their savings of 2,500 rupees earning 6-percent interest. Surviving mainly on rain-fed agriculture, the repayment of loans tends to be seasonal. Also, it is a challenge for the groups to stay self-sufficient when the broader community around them is lapsing toward more government subsidies.

At SEWA's General Body meetings, which are unusual and colorful by any standards, and where annual reports are often sung or danced or performed, the Sukhi Mandal women presented theirs with a *timili* dance.

> O mara baap sarikha jhaad.
> The Tree is my father,
> Little saplings my children,
> O Father, spread your roof over us.
> The *Limdo* is my doctor, the *Jamboodo* my nurse,
> O Hill, you are my doctor-in-chief.

The dormant wish of the adivasis to reclaim their life in the forests is evident in everything they do; raising saplings is one way they have brought the forests into their new homes. The women are visibly happier when working on the land. Their knowledge of the utility of different species of trees is much higher than of other farmers; although they are forced to cultivate food grains and cash crops for survival, their real interest is in growing a tree-cover over their village.

The plant nursery as an economic activity was first started in Tandalja under the Social Forestry Scheme of the Forest Department. There were problems from the beginning. First, funding was delayed; then the rules were impractical—the government-specified prices were lower than in the market. And no sooner had the program started to meet with some success, the Forest Department discontinued collaboration with the Sukhi Mandal, saying, "We have to give other NGOs a chance too"—as if they were distributing sweets to schoolchildren! Such an ad hoc policy does not allow people to really benefit from the program; their training becomes redundant if not used, and inadequate funding does not allow any success to grow in a sustained way. The Forest Department's Nursery Scheme is riddled with problems because the policy itself needs to change. Why in the world does the Government of India's mammoth Forest Department have to get into the business of running village nurseries? Nursery and plantation activities should be "liberalized" and left to the local women. It is time to feminize our forests.

The Sukhi Mandal had no option but to develop the nursery program, independently and without outside assistance. Gangaben of Tandalja took the lead. Gangaben planted five Ambla trees on her land, of which two died. The next year, she planted thirty-five eucalyptus trees, and this time they all survived. She planned to use the wood as pillars for her new house, hoping the trees would be grown by the time she had saved enough money for construction. She hoped to sell the surplus wood of fifteen trees. Thin as a string, Gangaben was confident in her ability to make things grow. She borrowed 10,000 rupees in December from Sukhi Mandal to grow saplings. She worked as a wage laborer, but spent two hours everyday on tending her plant nursery. By May, 6,000 saplings were ready for the market. She sold grafted saplings at 10 rupees and ungrafted saplings at 3 rupees in the local market. These prices were far higher than those the government paid for their contracted saplings. After subtracting her expenses on seeds, manure, pesticide, water, and loan repayment, Gangaben earned a net income of 8,000 rupees that year. The news spread like wildfire among the women. Other women began flocking to her farm to see for themselves the key to her success; the wiry woman had proved that developing plant nurseries can be a viable economic activity. This is social forestry in action, through self-employment and micro-enterprise. Today, more than half of the nurseries in the area are private backyard businesses started on bank loans.

Of course, the nursery program does not work in all the villages in this area. In a village like Saniyadri, where there is little water and arable land is being eroded or washed away, the farmers have gone to work for rich farmers, selling their labor for one-fourth of the yield. The Patel farmers prefer to hire adivasi couples who work as a highly dependable and productive team.

In 2000, with financial support from the World Food Programme to promote plant nurseries and water management, the Sukhi Mandal trained a group of three teenage girls—Suraj, Champa, and Foodi—to repair water hand pumps. In an agreement between the government and the Sukhi Mandal, this team of young technicians was responsible for the maintenance and repair of all communal hand pumps in the entire Sankheda taluka. The ever-cheerful team that has repaired more than 700 defunct pumps is in great demand. Initially, the men of the village would gather around and watch them work and make jokes about them, but the girls' efficiency and capability soon earned them respect. But as with all government projects, when the agreement ends, any interest in this trained team will also end; there is no effort to build on a success or to learn from a failure with a view to modify. In the end, the only efforts that work are those where the people stand up with support from each other.

It is now twenty-two years since the resettlement. Far too much has changed; lives and landscape have been altered. The people have experienced great trauma, and they have found renewed strength. Old knowledge is sadly being forgotten; new knowledge is rapidly crowding their minds. Changes occur far too rapidly for some, and not fast enough for others.

Stony Saniyadri is still without adequate water—it is officially listed as a "no-source village." Almost all families now live in brick houses; new houses to accommodate growing families are being built with loan money. There are elementary schools for the children, and a middle school is being considered. The greater demand is for vocational training schools.

The link with the past is not completely broken; many families still go back to their old fields in the months when the Sukhi river basin is dry to cultivate groundnut and other crops. Some even go to nearby forests, now off limits to them, to collect fuel wood and fodder. Their relationships with individual traders in the town of Jetpur Pavi are still alive; farmers still sell them their crops of grain and buy seeds, fertilizers, clothes, and jewelry on credit. Whatever they need, and whenever they need it, the traders remain their main providers. Accounts are settled in spring, around the festival of Holi; any unpaid debts are carried forward to the next year. In sum, the relationship is so old that the villagers hardly know the extent of their indebtedness. The new link with the mainstream market is now in Bodeli, where they sell cotton and vegetables. Their relationship with traders is still relatively debt-free—the poor-quality land is not easy to mortgage.

The adivasi women have begun to abandon traditional dress in favor of the urban sari; and their jewelry is increasingly of gold rather than silver. The *mahuda* forests that were their lifeblood are gone, forever changing their diet, their culture, and their identity. They provided flowers for food, berries for oil, timber for housing, and medicine for the sick. The mild alcohol made from the flower is gone; a potent brew made from jaggery is taking its place. *Doli* oil, which they extracted from the berries, is now replaced by commercial edible oils. Locally grown corn and legumes have now replaced their meal of *kodara*, a dark millet-like local grain, and wild leafy greens from the forest. Their festivals have changed, their rituals have changed, and even the gods they worship have changed. Giving up their past with its rich culture has been the price they have paid for assimilation.

Men and women view these changes differently. The women are glad for the greater sense of community they have felt in pursuing new economic opportunities. They are also glad they have greater mobility. Because they visit offices to pay the electricity bill or water tax or the revenue tax and come into frequent contact with government officials, traders, village leaders, and city folk, they are no longer shy or afraid. In fact, they are comfortable enough to pick a good quarrel with anyone if they need to.

The men see it differently. They are always aware of how they compare with others in society. Those from the six villages where the old and new communities have forged alliances feel the jealousy of those that chose a cash compensation over stony land. They were disqualified from the government's rehabilitation programs and have not done as well over time. Compared to the amount of cash and the quality of land the Narmada Dam settlers received, the men feel they have been shortchanged.

Somabhai felt that those who once had more than twenty-five acres of land in their old villages had become poorer than before, but those who had only one or two acres have done better. But all the families were impatient with the government as well as their own village elders. "How could our elders agree to settle on such wretched land and give up the forests!" wonders Ambaben.

The first ten years were very hard for everyone, but over time life has improved. Kavitaben just wished to forget the past; she was sad that their simple way of life had ended. "If you were the Chief Minister, would you build a big dam?" I asked. Kavitaben said, "If I were the Chief Minister, I wouldn't decide on my own. It is good for some—I have seen the benefit of canal irrigation in some areas, but for us, losing our forests and native land has been very difficult. It depends on who benefits and who doesn't. Any way, I don't like to think about the past. Our women are doing new things. With time, the Sukhi Mahila Mandal may make us all Sukhi."

The Sukhi Mandal has now reached out to 18,000 adivasi women in Sankheda. Recently, it has decided to enroll nontribal members as well. There is new blood in the tribal community. Ranjan Bhamore, a young adivasi from the Panchmahal region with a Masters degree in business administration, is a new coordinator. The Sukhi community is growing.

10

Reforms

The world of work has changed over the past three decades. Economists assumed that developing countries would grow along the lines of the developed countries where, sooner or later, all jobs would belong to the formal sector. But with globalization, the opposite has happened; the private sector has begun to "de-formalize" and the public sector has begun to shrink. Contract labor, casual labor, and outsourcing have increased in the so-called formal sector. The textile industry of Ahmedabad, for example, has moved from large mills to power looms and small processing houses—all jobs performed through a contract and subcontract system. Where no direct employer-employee relationship can be established, labor laws do not apply. Sixty percent of the workers in Ahmedabad, for example, work in streets, homes, or makeshift sheds in deserted compounds of closed factories.[1] So in many ways, the world of work has changed, but labor laws have not kept abreast and are losing relevance.

Globalization is all encroaching. Corporate power is rapidly increasing; the tiny businesses of the poor cannot compete. Rapid technological changes constantly demand new skills, leaving the poor feeling hopeless, inadequate, and lost. The power of the middle class has increased; the

1. Jeemol Unni and Uma Rani. *Urban Informal Sector: Size and Income Generation Processes in Gujarat. Part II.* New Delhi: National Council of Applied Economic Research, 2000.

Puriben urging the village Panchayat to support
the water project. (Amit Dave)

state's role of intervening in support of the poor has declined. In any case, the state itself has been bypassed by the fast increase in international trade and huge investments by transnationals. Decision making is at such a global level that local trade unions or the people's organizations have no reach.

International unionizing had become a necessity. For the poor to survive in a global economy, they need to join hands across all sorts of borders. Women in particular, a great many of whom are home-based workers in various occupations, need to come together so that they are not exploited. But opening trade unions to the informal-sector workers means more women would enter the mainstream of the labor movement. That is bound to change the work style and the culture of trade union movements; women's priorities are not always the same as that of men.

SEWA has taken the initiative in establishing workers' networks across national borders. HomeNet, one of our first international networks, grew out of our long campaigns for the rights of home-based workers at the International Labor Organisation (ILO) in Geneva. We were able to mobilize unions and nongovernmental organizations of home-based women workers in many countries in Asia, Latin America, and Europe. We aimed our efforts at establishing codes of conduct to improve the working conditions of women workers in poor countries and worked for the ratification of the ILO Convention on Homework to strengthen the links between workers in the North and the South. But again, formalizing HomeNet's status as an organization is not easy—again, that age-old problem of conceptual blocks stands in our way.

SEWU, the Self-Employed Women's Union in South Africa, is a sister SEWA. The amazing Pat Horn, founder of SEWU, also came from the formal labor movement, having had first-hand experience in organizing and an acute awareness of the limitations of formal-sector trade unions. After her visit to SEWA, Pat was struck by how similar the working conditions were of self-employed women in the two countries, and she formed SEWU to claim the right of street vendors to the marketplace. Apart from the grassroots work of organizing hawkers and street vendors, SEWU has also been successful in collaborating with researchers and urban authorities to frame the Informal Sector Policy of Durban City.

SEWU is the head office of StreetNet International, an alliance of street vendors. At its inauguration in Durban in 2002, I was struck by the curious connection between the two cities of Durban and Ahmedabad. About a century earlier, Gandhiji was here in Durban, as an "apprentice," still formulating and testing his ideas on work, freedom, and human dignity. The birth of the TLA in Ahmedabad in 1920 was in no small way a result of his experiences in South Africa. The women of SEWA and SEWU were just coming full circle, seeking *doosari azadi,* a second freedom—freedom from poverty.

After the first debate on the Convention on Homework at the ILO, I found that we needed to lobby more rigorously with the governments of the member countries if we wanted to win their votes. But one of our major difficulties was that we needed reliable statistics on the number of home-based workers in the world. We found a sincere sympathizer with our cause in Dr. Martha Chen of the Harvard Institute of International Development, an old friend of SEWA. Marty mustered up the considerable resources of facts, figures, research, and researchers at her command and produced a document that carried considerable weight in scholarship and authenticity. Our collaboration was so dynamic we formed WIEGO (Women in Informal Economy, Globalizing, Organizing) in 1996 to demonstrate by way of data and statistics the contribution of women microentrepreneurs in the global economy. SEWA also sought support from UNIFEM, the United Nations' statistical body, as well as from academics in the fields of labor and economics. We were right in assuming that facts and figures would speak to governments far louder than the pleas of common people.

At SEWA, we have come up with a set of questions to measure the effectiveness of a program. The answers give us a good idea of whether or not we are headed in the right direction. We ask ourselves, Will our action . . .

Increase employment opportunities?

Increase women's income?

Increase women's assets?

Improve access to food and good nutrition?

Increase access to health services?

Improve access to child care?

Improve housing, water, and sanitation?

Strengthen the organization?

Encourage more poor women to take leadership?

Increase self-reliance individually and collectively?

These simple questions supply simple and straightforward answers; in the end, one needs to know the bottom line.

It is often tempting to take on large-scale projects and implement them quickly by hiring professionals. Instead, SEWA's policy has been to go through the long and difficult process of empowering grassroots-level

Sabiben, a landless agricultural worker, runs the cooperative's power tiller. The cooperative also loans her services to local farmers. (SEWA Academy)

people to run them. It is not easy; progress is slow, sometimes frustrating, not always efficient, and full of seemingly avoidable setbacks. Yet it is in this process where groundbreaking change occurs. When women learn at their own pace through self-help and feel comfortable in their knowledge and actions, they change their lives and their environment for the better and for the long term.

Change, to be real, has to come from the people; it cannot be trickled down, imported, or imposed. As a country, we can create a climate for change if we can put our trust in the people. For that, everyone must have a voice. The poor, because they are in the majority, especially need to be heard—even their silent voices must be heard. But India's democracy, although strong, has feet of clay.

During the 300 years of British rule, India witnessed its traditional social, political, and economic structures weaken, wither, or die at a steady pace. What replaced them were new structures that facilitated colonial rule—centralized governance, policy and bureaucracy, industrialization, urbanization, to name but a few. They were never people friendly, and they didn't need to be. But even after Independence, these structures have remained intact. Gandhiji's effort to break them through khadi, panchayat, trusteeship, was a way of focusing our attention once again on building new structures that met the needs and faced the realities of our own people. He felt that India could be built on institutions that were small, local, democratic, and dynamic.

Today, our political structure is democratic but so riddled with vested interests that it increasingly marginalizes the poor masses. There is little accountability. Local self-government structures are weak and getting weaker. The arms of the government—the legislative, the judicial and the executive—when they reach the poor, are feeble and fumbling. Partly, it is the legacy of colonial rule, but perpetuating outdated structures and policies has been convenient because so much power now resides in the hands of our educated urban elite.

The urban world dominates the economic front. Our cities consume enormous amounts of the state's energy and resources. The middle class demands and therefore lays claim to education, transportation, media, health, and government services. The job of providing these services goes to the rural and the newly urban underclass that are all part of the informal economy. More than 92 percent of the country's workforce is in the informal economy, and they contribute 63 percent of the country's gross domestic product, 50 percent of savings, and 40 percent of exports to the national economy. Yet the infrastructure to support the needs of these workers is minimal or nonexistent.

India has made remarkable economic progress in the past decades. Yet it can neither maintain nor accelerate its economic gains if it continues to marginalize the poor. On the contrary, by investing in people and their economic potential, India can accelerate its economic growth more actively and more effectively.

Gauging from our experience at SEWA, I would say that poor women are the key. We need to put poor women at the center of economic reform and planning. We need to recognize work as key to removing poverty. We need to build cooperative economic structures built around work. We need to invest in initiatives taken by poor women and provide sustained access to resources so that women can enter the mainstream economy and create a countervailing impact. We need to create a network of social security, so that health care, child care, housing, and insurance are universal.

We need to build the capacity of poor self-employed women to enter global markets by strengthening their skill and knowledge base, individually as well as institutionally. Only a truly democratic process—of the people, by the people, and for the people—will give birth to a democratic nation.

Focusing on employment will boost our economy at every level. Self-employment, because it is entrepreneurship and initiative taken by the poor, has even greater potential. It develops all aspects of the person—the social, the economic, and the political. There is room for all kinds of development, and it is crucial to nurture the entrepreneurship the poor show in their fight to survive. By focusing their efforts on the dire need for credit among the working poor, the banking industry can potentially revolutionize our economy. How can one afford to ignore such a large, untapped, economically active client base? The SEWA Cooperative Bank pumps 15 million rupees into the smallest levels of the city's economy each day through its women account-holders. It helps poor women build ownership of productive assets to fight life's vulnerabilities. This way, our economy grows, woman by woman.

By focusing on women, there is potential for a different kind of change—a more integrated growth—and this occurs at the family level. Women are resilient, hard-working, used to sharing and pooling and creating mutual support systems. They nurture and sustain the family unit under all circumstances. They need access to home-based work so they can care for their families as well; they need markets for their products, both locally and globally; they need credit and banking services; they need health care and child care; they need education, learning, and skill development; and they need a voice in the society in which they live. Investing in people and their living and working environments is true nation-building.

When the poor come together on the basis of their work and build organizations that decentralize production and distribution and promote asset formation and ownership, build people's capacities, provide social security, and allow for active participation and a voice, they are dynamic and healthy and need our full support to grow. We need policies that encourage self-help, support local cooperative economic initiatives, and emphasize sharing and pooling of resources at every level. This strengthens the community and stops migration; it prevents alienation and exploitation, and it stems the spiral freefall into poverty.

Although it is accepted as general wisdom that politically decentralized bodies are essential to an active democracy, the economic decentralization of power and resources is largely ignored. It is unfortunate that centralized production, skills, technology, and ownership of resources are seen as the most efficient way to progress in India, today. Decentralized political power with centralized economic power can be a dangerous mix. The working poor must be brought into the fold of the macro environment and given full support; they must not be controlled or removed from the economic scene as is being done with street vendors, cart pullers, marginal farmers, and their kind.

Vendors' markets exist in every neighborhood of our cities—make these markets pedestrian; provide the vendors with access to water, cold storage, and garbage disposal; and watch entire city neighborhoods change for the better. The public transport system, if geared to the commuting needs of the poor, has a huge potential for further growth.

On the one hand, employment opportunities are shrinking: construction workers are losing employment due to mechanization and because contracts are going to large national and international construction conglomerates; handloom weavers have difficulty getting raw materials such as cotton and yarn because they are exported; many of the traditional economic activities of poor self-employed women are becoming redundant because of changing times and demand. On the other hand, we see that the lifting of trade barriers presents opportunities to women in crafts, textiles, and perhaps even agricultural produce in the future. If organized, the poor can gain from these opportunities.

When I was appointed to the Second National Commission on Labour in 2000, one of our terms of reference was to suggest umbrella legislation for the unorganized sector labor. Here was our chance to take an integrated approach to labor, where every person who contributes to the national income, regardless of the type of industry or workplace or form of employment, would be recognized as a worker. This would mean an opening up of the definition of work. The introduction of identity cards to validate each worker's place in the economy would also be considered. But when the government fell, any chance we had of making the state think differently was lost.

Work has many dimensions. Work has many meanings. Work takes many forms. Meaningful work enables a worker to earn and live a balanced life. However, the world over, there is a tendency to promote only certain types of work—work that fits into the global market economy. Any work that falls outside of that narrow definition is either eliminated because it is "unproductive" or it is downgraded by reducing the price of its worth. This way of viewing work, backed by economic theories and adopted by our policy makers, manages to disenfranchise millions of workers around the globe every day. In India, where a majority of our workers fall outside of this current definition of work, perhaps it is time we asked, what is *Karma*?

Glossary

aagewan	group leader
adivasi	native inhabitants, indigenous people
agarbatti	incense stick
agaria	salt farmer
angreji	Western, British
apheen	opium
arogya sevikas	health workers
ashramshala	residential school
baba	father
bahu	bride
banksathis	SEWA Bank field workers
baval	mesquite plant
Bay topla-ni jagah	space for two baskets
ben	sister
bhai	brother
bhajans	devotional songs
bhangi	street sweeper, member of the lowest caste
bidi	Indian cigarette

burkha	Muslim woman's veil
chalam	smoking pipe
chamar	leather worker
chania choli	Indian skirt and blouse
chhapra	roofs
chindi	strips of fabric
cholaphali	chickpea snack
cholis	short Indian blouse
crêche	childcare center
crore	10 million
daghi chindi	used, dirty chindi
dai	midwife
dal	lentils
dalit	the oppressed
dharana	a form of protest by strikers
dibko	small water pump used by salt farmers
doli	name of a fruit
doosari azadi	second freedom, economic freedom
fleur de sel	high-quality salt
foto	photograph
gajia	satin-weave fabric
gando baval	gum tree
ghaghra	Indian skirt
gram sabha	village meeting
gujari	flea market
gutka	chewing tobacco
heer	silk yarn
indhoni	doughnut-shaped cloth base to balance water pots on
Insha Allah	It is God's will
jamboodo	Indian fruit tree

kamakho	open-backed Indian blouse
khadi	handwoven, handspun cloth
khichdi	dish of rice and lentils
khol	quilt cover
kodara	dark milletlike local grain
koli	caste of agriculturers
kooba	traditional desert dwelling
kuchha	make-shift
kurta	Indian tunic
lakh	one hundred thousand
leemdi	neem tree
lengah	loose Indian trousers, skirt
limdo	neem tree
mandali	cooperative
mahuda	flame of the forest tree
mashroo	cotton cloth
mehta	billing clerk
mohallas	neighborhoods
nagar	city
namaz	Muslim prayer
odhni	head scarf
officewalla	office worker
olakh	identity
paisa	money, coin money
Panchayat	village council
Parivartan	name of program, meaning "change"
piloodi	name of local tree
pitha	godown
pole	city lane, city neighborhood
powershakti	power and strength
pucca	solidly built, permanent

purdah	Muslim veil
roti	bread
rotlo	large bread, usually made with coarse grains
saab	boss
sadu bharat	plain embroidery
sahib	boss
salwar kameez	Indian dress of long tunic and loose trousers
Sarpanch	village head
saundarya	beauty
shakti	power, strength
shengatra	desert grass used to line salt-collecting pans
talukas	blocks of a district
thela	large cloth bag
theli	small cloth pouch, bag
theliphone	cell phones
timili	name of a dance
topi	hat
vaghari	name of a community
vankar	weaver
vijay	victory
wallahs	common suffix for worker, doer
zari	metallic thread embroidery

Index